The
Intentional
Christian Community
Handbook

The
Intentional
Christian Community
Handbook

**For Idealists, Hypocrites, and
Wannabe Disciples of Jesus**

DAVID JANZEN
AND A COMMUNITY OF FRIENDS

PARACLETE PRESS
BREWSTER, MASSACHUSETTS

The Intentional Christian Community Handbook: For Idealists, Hypocrites, and Wannabe Disciples of Jesus

Copyright © 2013 by David Janzen

ISBN 978-1-61261-237-9

Unless otherwise noted, all Scriptural references are taken from the HOLY BIBLE, NEW INTERNATIONAL VERSION®, NIV®. Copyright © 1973, 1978, 1984, 2011 by Biblica. Used by permission of Zondervan. All rights reserved.

Scriptures marked NRSV are taken from the New Revised Standard Version Bible, copyright © 1989 National Council of the Churches of Christ in the United States of America. Used by permission. All rights reserved.

Library of Congress Cataloging-in-Publication Data
Janzen, David.
  The intentional christian community handbook : for idealists, hypocrites, and wannabe disciples of Jesus / David Janzen and a Community of Friends.
    p. cm.
  Includes bibliographical references (p.   ).
  ISBN 978-1-61261-237-9 (trade pbk.)
  1. Communities—Religious aspects—Christianity. 2. Spiritual formation. I. Title.
  BV4517.5.J36 2012
  253—dc23   2012022552

10 9 8 7 6 5 4 3 2 1

Published by Paraclete Press
Brewster, Massachusetts
www.paracletepress.com
Printed in the United States of America

To Joanne,
who first caught the vision of church as community,
which made her even more attractive to this
young adventurer half a century ago.

While David Janzen wrote most of this book, others made vital contributions. In a few cases, chapters were written by others or cowritten by the author with others. These contributors are noted here in the order of their appearance:

Brandon Rhodes

(Springwater Community, Portland, Oregon)

Sally Schreiner Youngquist

(Reba Place Fellowship, Evanston, Illinois)

Andy Ross

(Reba Place Church, Evanston, Illinois)

CONTENTS

SHANE CLAIBORNE AND JONATHAN WILSON-HARTGROVE

This is a book that we've needed for a long, long time. Over the past fifteen years, we've sat in living rooms and around kitchen tables with people who have asked the same question: "How can we follow Jesus with our whole life?" At The Simple Way and at Rutba House, the communities that respectively we call home, we've wrestled with this question in the company of friends and neighbors. We've talked about it late into the night, and we've invested all we have into ongoing experiments in the truth of the gospel.

In our communities, we've read and reread the Sermon on the Mount. We've been inspired by ancient monastics and twentieth-century community movements. We've passed around books by Dorothy Day and Jean Vanier, John Perkins and Dietrich Bonhoeffer. We've tried to learn from those who've gone before us, and we've tried to listen to the distinct new challenges of our day. We've seen some miracles. We've failed miserably. We've learned to forgive and be forgiven. Community has been a classroom for our conversion.

As we've shared the good news that we've seen and heard through these little experiments in the truth of the gospel, we've met thousands of other people who are asking the same question, hearing the same call— the call to follow Jesus into a life of discipleship in community. Seeing in their eyes a look that we recognize from those small circles of friends, we have recognized our common cause in a movement of the Holy Spirit.

God is up to something. Hope is springing up, not in one mighty trunk, but in thousands of shoots. Those shoots are rooted in the Song that gave birth to creation, the Love that moves the sun and other stars. God is stirring something new in our time.

But these shoots of new life in community are fragile, and they need tender care to grow into maturity. We've learned this the hard way—by seeing firsthand the pain of community-gone-bad. And we've seen so many new communities spring up and die, as Jesus speaks of the seeds that are beautiful but short-lived if they don't grow roots. But in the midst of that pain, we've also seen incredible grace. Most often, grace has come in the form of older mentors who've come to gently share their wisdom.

For both of us, David Janzen has been one of those wise voices. The book that you're holding in your hands is the fruit of his efforts to listen closely to what is happening in dozens of communities today, all the while reflecting back on what he's learned from his own experience in community over the past five decades.

Because David has been formed by community for so long, though, he can't simply tell you what he thinks. He has to tell you what those he's listened to think as well. So this book is also the fruit of conversation and the best kind of conspiracy—friends working together to speak the truth that they know and live. It's a book that truly speaks in a "we" voice, passing the collective wisdom of generations on to the next.

This is a book for people who long for community and for people who've found it; for young seekers and for old radicals. Like a farmer's almanac or a good cookbook, it's a guide that doesn't tell you what to do but rather gives you the resources you need to find your way together with friends in the place where you are.

We couldn't be more grateful to have a book like this.

And we couldn't be happier to share it with you.

The
Intentional
Christian Community
Handbook

With some books you can skip the introductory stuff where the author tells you what he or she is going to say again later on. However, in this preface I tell stories you'll find nowhere else in the book—about the title, about how I grew up in such a way that nurturing communities has become my passion, and about a group of friends from many different communities who have collaborated to bring together the stories and insights for growing communities that are found in this book. Thank you for coming along.

We live in exciting times, when many new intentional Christian communities are springing up, where young people (and older folks, too) are making a courageous experiment with their lives, moving into "abandoned places of empire," trying to live by the words and example of Jesus to "love one another as I have loved you." Along the way they are discovering what monastic communities and lay communities have discovered in every generation: to be capable of authentic community we need to undergo a major conversion of life. This is especially true if we have grown up in the soil of a society like ours that has become toxic to community; worships self, money, and power; and scorns the poor. We may know what is wrong with the old world, but we seldom realize how much of that world we still bring along with us as we plant seeds of a new society in the manure of the old. (Hey, I get to say that word because I grew up on a farm.) Although we may be idealists and hypocrites, there is hope for us and for the world if we stick with Jesus—who will surely stick with us.

Concerning idealists, many of us long for community because of our critique about all that is wrong with society, the church, and the people we have lived with so far. Our vision of an ideal world and a model community may bring us to the door, but it will not show us how to live in the house of community itself. As Dietrich Bonhoeffer wrote in 1933, "The man who fashions a visionary ideal of community demands that it be realized by God, by others, and by himself." Unless we let go of our ideal community, we will end up hating the sisters and brothers who, inevitably, do not live up to our expectations, and so, Bonhoeffer warns, we become the destroyer of that very real community God is already growing up around us. We need honest people to help us channel our idealism into practical work and who love us anyway.

Now about hypocrites, the distance between ignorance and knowledge can be a moment (or the latest book), but the gap between knowing and faithfully doing with others what we already know can be more than a lifetime. We love to judge others by their worst behavior and ourselves by our highest ideals. As alcoholics learn in AA, there will always be a hypocrite lurking within us, ready to take over our lives in a moment of self-confidence. We might practice introducing ourselves in community meetings with the confession, "Hello, my name is David, and I'm a hypocrite." Hypocrites were some of Jesus's favorite people not to be like. We believe that Christian intentional community is a support group for recovering hypocrites who discover by living together the great chasm between what we know and how we live—and find out that we are loved anyway.

So where does this impossible love come from that makes community possible? As you might have learned if you went to Sunday school, the answer to every question is "Jesus." Alas, with Jesus the right words don't get us to first base. "Not everyone who says to me 'Lord, Lord' will enter the kingdom of heaven." We come close to the love of Jesus as we join a particular band of his disciples, learning from him the "one another" skills of community. "Therefore everyone who hears these words of mine and puts them into practice is like a wise man who built his house on the rock" (Matt. 7:21–24).

"The whole point of what Jesus was up to," according to N. T. Wright, "was that he was doing close up, in the present, what he was promising long-term in the future. And what he was promising for that future and doing in the present was not saving souls for a disembodied eternity, but rescuing people from the corruption and decay of the way the world presently is so that they could enjoy, already in the present, that renewal of creation which is God's ultimate purpose—and so they could thus become colleagues and partners in that large project."

"That large project" is what this book is about: Spirit-led movements that are giving birth to new communities and new vocations for community in our day. These communities are called to be living demonstrations now of the future that God has for the whole world. "Behold, the kingdom is among you."

This book was created by a "we," a team of young folks of all ages who have banded together to learn from and to nurture this most recent crop of intentional communities. But before I tell you about how the book came to be, I think it would be fair for you to know some of the life experiences that gave me this passion to nurture Christian intentional communities.

As you have already been warned, I grew up on a farm, in a Kansas Mennonite family, learning how to milk cows, drive tractors, and sneak away whenever possible with my sister and two brothers to play basketball on a goal hanging from the south side of the barn. Church was a regular part of our week, as were devotions at the breakfast table and bedtime prayers. More formative, perhaps, was our parents' insistence that, whenever there were fights during the day, we confessed our faults and were reconciled with each other before going to bed, because the Bible said, "Do not let the sun go down while you are still angry" (Eph. 4:26). Once I remember my father waking me in the night and asking my forgiveness for losing his temper and chewing me out before my friends. I grew up learning about a radical peacemaking Jesus in the Gospels, but I also encountered enough rigid and authoritarian church leadership that I had a hard time seeing this Jesus embodied in the church.

At Bethel College, a Kansas Mennonite liberal arts college in North Newton, Kansas, I felt the freedom to figure out who I was apart from the pressure to conform. I tried on whatever philosophy I was reading at the time and decided I could not honestly call myself a Christian. In my senior year (1961), during Kennedy's presidency, I found myself in a delegation of peace-movement activists, fasting and picketing in front of the White House in Washington in opposition to atmospheric nuclear testing. In a mysterious and wonderful way, I felt God entering my life and calling me to be a peacemaker in a world preparing for total war. I was a young radical angry about injustice, but God promised me companionship on this journey—not just an inner personal relationship but also a community of fellow seekers who would experience something of that reconciliation we would proclaim to the world.

Back on campus I sought out Joanne Zerger, a peace club coworker who was willing to hear about my calling to some kind of prophetic mission. Joanne herself belonged to a renewal movement on campus led by Al Meyer (John Howard Yoder's brother-in-law) and other mentors. They were not content to read about the recovery of the Anabaptist vision and the communalism of the early church, but they formed small groups of students to *be* the church with each other in community, with Jesus's teachings at the center of their life.

Let's fast-forward through two years of divinity school, where I discovered I was not becoming a pastor, marriage to Joanne, history study at the University of Kansas, and then high school teaching in the newly independent Democratic Republic of the Congo under the Mennonite Central Committee—my alternative to military service during the Vietnam War. Wherever we went we found ourselves gathering with like-minded friends into base Christian communities to read Scripture—often Jesus's Sermon on the Mount—and asking how to live together in response to this call of radical discipleship.

Back in the States in the early 1970s we plunged into "the movement," resisting the Vietnam War and seeking more of that intentional community life that we had tasted while in the Congo. We were idealists with visions of the model community that would change the world and hypocrites filled with prophetic rhetoric of all the great things we were going to do in contrast to the rest of the church, which slept while the world was burning.

God was merciful to us and allowed our first attempt at community to fail for many reasons, but mostly because we pursued too many good causes without clear priorities, and with people who were not sure about Jesus as the center of our life. After some floundering first steps, a new community, New Creation Fellowship, was born in 1973 with some essential coaching from Reba Place Fellowship (RPF) in Evanston, Illinois, and from other communal groups who soon banded together into the Shalom Association of Communities.

We were half a dozen families and some single people intentionally living within a block of each other, sharing in a common treasury, tending community gardens with energetic children running in a tribe from one house to another. We experienced the Holy Spirit baptism and launched a charismatic, communal, peace-and-justice Anabaptist church that met in the basement of our largest house. I led a construction crew that gave us an economic base from which to organize other revolutionary projects.

From the outside, for a while, it looked like we had it together. But we would come home from antiwar rallies and fight about the right way to clean, or not clean, the kitchen. Peace for the world, but not for each other. We offered hospitality to a few troubled souls and were quickly overwhelmed. Mental breakdowns and marriage crises caused us to urgently look for help from therapists and wiser mentors in other communities. The traumas of our lives were catching up with us, and we realized we needed to get wise about resources for personal healing if we wanted to continue living together and not devour one another. We joked about how God was gracious to us, allowing us to take turns with our breakdowns. "No shoving in line. Your crisis has to wait 'cause I'm not finished yet with mine."

We learned what Jesus meant by the first beatitude, "Blessed are the poor in spirit, for they shall see God." We learned to pray for love and forgiveness with sincere desperation, with empty hearts that God was eager to fill. We learned to let go of our community ideal—achieving something we could be proud of—and just accept who we were with each other, broken people in whose presence Jesus dwells. Through many struggles we received the gift of a tender love that began to nurture us and other people as well, where we and our children were bonded together in ways that still run deep. The Scriptures came alive for us when we heard Jesus say, "Today salvation has come to this house" (Lk. 19:9).

At New Creation Fellowship we soon wore ourselves out trying to make all our decisions by consensus. By God's grace, the weariness set in about the time we learned to trust the pastoral gifts of those who could conduct our meetings in peaceful and orderly ways. We began to function more like a body where each one had gifts to exercise for the good of all. Community proved more educational than a college campus. We were learning basic community-nurturing lessons and skills, usually finding a good path after trying all the others.

I discovered that others experienced me as a judgmental, principle-driven idealist who had a lot to learn about listening and extending grace in relationships. Fortunately, these folks—mostly sisters—put up with, corrected, forgave, and hugged me anyway because we were all trying to learn the courageous and humble way of Jesus.

I tell this story so that you can get acquainted with me a bit, know what experiences and biases I bring to this project, and also to illustrate that newly forming intentional Christian communities go through similar discoveries and developments if we wait for God to change us while persisting in forgiveness.

Others felt the love of Jesus in our life together and came closer in hopes of finding healing, too. We organized vigils at a local missile silo aiming destruction at the people of the Soviet Union, and we had a part in launching the Newton Area Peace Center.

However, by the mid-1980s, some of the original communal members had moved on and the common purse was abandoned in a time of harassment by the Internal Revenue Service. The community morphed into a Mennonite congregation, which has grown over the years, retaining some of the community character from its birth. At the time of these changes, Joanne and I, with our two middle-school-age children, were taking a sabbatical year at Reba Place Fellowship. With New Creation's blessing, we chose to stay on at Reba, where we had found good work, healing, and community that more closely fit our sense of calling.

Now that I look back on this demise of the communal life in Newton, Kansas, with the eyes of someone called to "nurture communities" and be a guide to their sustainable development, I ask, what happened? Well, actually, the life of community still goes on in many ways with intimate small groups that retain a knack for deep relationships, traditions of common work, ministry, and celebration from communal times. I see now that the challenge of growing community brought together some insecure young people who had more leadership gifts than they could figure out what to do with on one pile. We were peers without older mentors who might have nurtured a vision of working together using all our gifts. Our leaving was actually a sending, a healthy development for the church that continued on with a generation of younger leaders eventually finding their places.

Our family came to Reba, where I found elders I missed out on in our community of peers. Here I was supported to run a nationwide network of churches and communities resisting the U.S.–sponsored war in Central America and assisting refugees in "el Norte" to find asylum. Julius Belser basically gave me his job, coached me enough to not let me fail, but also trusted me to carry the responsibility and grow with it. What an incredible gift that Julius and I have been meeting now every Monday morning for more than twenty-five years, baring our souls, talking about work, dreaming up new visions, praying about relationships, and keeping on track with the Lord. When in a crisis, I now know what Julius or my other Reba mentors would do, which is a lot like knowing what Jesus would do, because that's who they look to for guidance.

In 1995 Reba gave me half a year of support to visit twenty-some communities and write the book *Fire, Salt, and Peace: Intentional Christian Communities Alive in North America*. Since then I have divided my time between directing an affordable housing ministry, serving on the RPF leadership team, launching an apprentice program for young people to learn about community, and coordinating the Shalom Mission Communities—an association of communities to which Reba belongs. During this time I was in the thick of many community issues, both at Reba and in other communities, participating in consultations, mediations, and community reviews.

In 2004 Rutba House, in Durham, North Carolina, hosted what turned out to be a landmark event, bringing together new community activists, veterans of longer-term communities, and scholars of the intentional community movement. Word leaked out about this "by invitation only" meeting, and a swarm of young people showed up eager to tell about the new community movement. The energy and excitement of the young communitarians reminded me of the '70s and caused me to wonder if this community movement would flash up and burn out quickly as did so many groups a generation ago. But contrary to the youth movement of the '70s, whose mantra was "Don't trust anyone over thirty," these activists clearly wanted the old monasticism and lay communities like Reba, Church of the Sojourners, and Church of the Servant King to walk with them. There was also a familiarity with Anabaptist theology that gave coherence to following Jesus in prophetic communities that give witness to the possibility of justice and peace in this age as it will be in the age to come.

We came together at Rutba House's invitation, with a goal to name the basic commitments of this "New Monasticism" movement. I was skeptical at first. The Shalom Mission Communities (of which Reba was a part) had worked a whole year to agree on a list of shared commitments. How could this be done in one weekend by people who hardly knew each other?

Well, the Holy Spirit had something else in mind. Jonathan Wilson-Hartgrove wrote while others talked, and we ended up affirming a manifesto named "12 Marks of a New Monasticism." Following the conference, twelve persons were asked to write chapters on each of the marks, which came together under the title *School(s) for Conversion: 12 Marks of a*

New Monasticism. I was asked to write the chapter titled "Intentional Formation in the Way of Christ and the Rule of the Community along the Lines of the Old Novitiate." Not many communities actually imported these "12 Marks" as their covenant, but they inspired many groups to study them as they drew up their own rule of life.

Since that time Shane Claiborne wrote *The Irresistible Revolution* and has taken the message to countless college campuses and youth conventions. Jonathan Wilson-Hartgrove launched Schools for Conversion—retreats hosted by more-established communities around the country, offering seekers a weekend of immersion in the life and teachings of one local Christian community. Here visitors explored starting new communities or becoming interns at the communities that already embodied the life.

In 2010 Reba set me free from most local responsibilities to visit about thirty intentional communities, often accompanied by younger "apprentices," in a program that Jonathan dubbed the Nurturing Communities Project. Support for this project has come from Shane and The Simple Way, Jonathan and Schools for Conversion, Shalom Mission Communities, and various other intentional Christian groups. As we visited communities, immersing ourselves in their stories and issues, we kept hearing suggestions for chapter headings in case we would ever write a manual for nurturing intentional Christian communities. That is how this book began to hatch and grow wings.

In the summer of 2010, Jonathan was approached by a publisher asking if the time might be ripe to write an instruction manual for the new intentional communities appearing across the map. He said he had too many commitments but knew someone who ought to write that book, and he called me. So, in a way, the tables are turned. The younger generation is mentoring the elders, but things like that keep happening in the kingdom of God. A team of younger community leaders has joined in the planning, writing, and review phase of this book project. A mark of the Spirit's work is to reconcile the generations to prepare the way of the Lord (Lk. 1:17 and Acts 2:17–18). This is a time of rare opportunity.

A longing for deeper community is growing in our land. Many observant Christians have lamented that, despite the hype of worship and glitz of church buildings and programs, the lives of most American church members look very much like the rest of the world. Statistically speaking, those who identify themselves as Christians are characterized by rootless pursuit of wealth, consumerism, divorce and broken relationships, hedonistic entertainment, moving often while living in neighborhoods that no one loves, segregated by class and race—pretty much like everyone else. A church that expects Christians, on their own, to live a life that resembles Jesus is fooling itself. We live with the myth of a Christian nation and the tattered remnants of what was once called Christendom. But there never was a time when the surrounding world would socialize us into a Christlike way of life.

Our church scene is so different from the first centuries of the Jesus movement, which was notorious for its familial affection and sharing across class and ethnic lines, with a reputation for feeding the urban poor and supporting widows to serve the church, its nonviolent response to persecution, and its refusal to bear arms or join in imperial wars. The joy with which members faced martyrdom subverted the empire particularly because they had no overt power. What is the difference?

One Greek New Testament word for this difference is *koinonia*, which we often translate as "sharing" but could be translated more concretely by "intentional community."

Our working definition of intentional Christian community is a group of people deliberately sharing life in order to follow more closely the teachings and practices of Jesus with his disciples. The more essential dimensions of life that are shared—such as daily prayer and worship, possessions, life decisions, living in proximity, friendships, common work or ministry, meals, care for children and elderly—the more intentional is the community.

Communities come in many flavors. There are accidental communities like the people who happen to live on the same city block. There are traditional communities like a third-world peasant village where shared land and history of relationships bind people in expectations of solidarity—where people basically inherit their roles. There are communities thick and thin depending on how much is shared. I belong to a thin community of those who enjoy playing basketball twice a week at the local senior center. I also belong to a thicker community in Reba Place Fellowship, where we share the love of Jesus, possessions, proximity, some common work and ministry, and many informal ways of serving one another that have grown up over the years. Our experience is that these commitments of koinonia give Jesus more power over our lives than the world around us, which does not count him as Lord.

Whatever we share becomes a matter of group discernment as we seek together how the kingdom of God can find expression in these areas of life as well. By contrast, those areas of life that are not lived intentionally tend to resemble the world. Where a community agrees to share possession because of Jesus, there is a Mammon-free zone. Where a group agrees to forgive one another as Jesus taught, there is a condemnation-free zone. Not only are individuals changed, but the world can see how it could change as well. Every group that hopes to be good news for the world must have an intentional life together that will be different from the world. Or, posed the other way around, a group that is like the dominant society has no good news to offer it.

Renewal movements in the church have again and again discovered the power of intentional community to transform lives and demonstrate to the world what the way of Jesus looks like in visible social and economic relationships. Clarence Jordan, founder of Koinonia Partners in Americus, Georgia, farmer, and Greek scholar, loved to talk about these communities as "demonstration plots of the kingdom" not because they get everything right but because they are local experiments the world can see of what the Sermon on the Mount looks like among a group of people sold out for Jesus.

So, now you have an idea of the winding road that has led to the creation of this book. What remains is to explain the developmental approach of the book itself.

As we visited communities young and old, we could not help but notice that they pass through stages of development just like individual human beings. We have certain character-developmental tasks for each stage of life, from infancy to maturity and wisdom. Likewise, for Christian communities these tasks change as they grow from seed to plant to fruitful harvest.

I've been a farmer and a carpenter—as was Jesus, apparently. His preference for organic rather than construction metaphors is important when it comes to communities. Community pioneers do not build community; they do not even plant the seeds of community; but they are called to nurture a garden that God has planted in the unique persons and context of shared life. Our outline moves along in the following developmental sequence:

Part One: The Yearning for Community in Context

Part Two: Is Intentional Community Your Calling?

Part Three: Before You Move In Together

Part Four: The First Year of Community

Part Five: Growing Tasks for a Young Community

Part Six: A Mature Community Becomes Soil for God's New Seeds

If you, too, are on this road, or preparing for this journey into intentional community, you will see yourself in the chapters of these sections. The good news is that communities, like people, need not complete a life cycle and die but that God is active to prune and restore so that we can be born again and again.

ACKNOWLEDGMENTS AND THANKSGIVINGS

Since this book is the overflow of a lifelong passion and calling, my list of debts to acknowledge is beyond all remembering. But I must begin with thanks to God for my parents, Hilda and Louis Janzen, for raising our family on a farm where we learned to serve one another in the way of Jesus and become proficient at whatever needed to be done. They taught by example how to build up community by making friends, extending hospitality, and seeking the common good at all scales from farm neighbors, to local church, to the ends of the earth. They would take pride in this book (as in everything their children wrote) and would understand it from the inside out.

Thanks to my mentors over the years—C. J. Dyck, Al Meyer, Jake Pauls, Virgil Vogt, Julius Belser, John Lehman, Allan Howe, Sally Youngquist, Hilda Carper, and a host of other encouraging fellow travelers.

Collaborators on this book have welcomed me into their homes, dreams, and communities, and in the process of nurturing other communities we have become a remarkable and extensive network of friends. I want to especially express my gratitude to Jonathan Wilson-Hartgrove, Shane Claiborne, Natalie Potts, Luke Healy, Jolyn Rodman, Bren Dubay, Leroy Barber, Brandon Rhodes, Karima Walker, Amanda Moore, Celina Varela, Marijke Stob, Kara Clearman, Mark Van Steenwyck, Anton Flores, Jason and Vonetta Storbakken, Chris and Lara Lahr, Sarah Jobe, Sally Youngquist, Andy Ross, Karl Lehman, Bliss and Jonathan Benson, Jodi and Eric Garbisson, Tricia Partlow, Brian Gorman, Patrick Murphy, Tim Otto, Katie Rivers, Daniel Burt, Louise and Mark Zwick, Bobby Wright, Tom Roddy, Tim and Sharon Doran Moriarty, Josh McCallister, Charles Moore, Allan Howe, Celina Varela, Anali Gatlin, Sarah Belser Tucker, and to others whom I may have forgotten to mention.

My gratitude goes out to Reba Place Fellowship, the Shalom Mission Communities, The Simple Way, Schools for Conversion, the Louisville Foundation, and others too numerous to mention, for their financial support of the Nurturing Communities Project that is behind this book.

Thanks to my buddies on the Levy Center Senior Olympic basketball team, who keep my body young as my hair turns gray.

Thanks to friends around the world, especially mission partners Das and Doris Maddimadugu in India, who kept me in loving and faithful prayer.

Thank you to a decade of Reba apprentices, who educated me about their world and fascinated me with their spiritual journeys shared in trust.

I want to return some love to the students of North Park University in the fall 2011 Intentional Christian Community class who read and discussed early chapters of this book, thus collaborating to make it better.

Thanks be to God for Jim Stringham, now twenty years deceased, who taught me to journal while "listening to the Lord."

Glory be to the Holy Spirit, who wakes me in the night with one more good insight to write down that would never have occurred to David Janzen.

Blessings on Jon M. Sweeney, Robert Edmonson, and others at Paraclete Press who believed in this book project and expertly guided it to completion.

Love to Joanne, who has patiently taught me how to listen, who found the right place for many wayward commas, and has walked in loving forgiveness with me for forty-eight years.

Halleluiah for our vast and amazing genealogy of grace including all who have prayed before us, "Your kingdom come on earth as it is in heaven."

And finally, thanks for your attention, dear reader, with whom we are pleased to share these stories and insights on the way to a thicker Christian community life. No matter what our place on this journey, may we have the humble courage to accept that we are slow-learning idealists often in love with our own visions, and relapsing hypocrites who are, nevertheless, invited by Jesus to become disciples in his beloved community.

PART ONE

THE YEARNING FOR COMMUNITY
IN CONTEXT

CHAPTER 1

Five Stories of Longing and a Call

The following stories tell of five quite different spiritual journeys to Christian intentional community. They are all accounts of what Jesus would call "repentance" as in "Repent and believe that the kingdom of God is at hand." Repentance here is not an emotion, like feeling shame over sin in one's life—worthy as that may be—but it is rather a moment of turning, taking on a new life path because one has found that "treasure hidden in a field" worth selling off everything he or she has to buy it (Matt. 13:44).

These stories, begun here, continue in later chapters of this book. After you have walked a mile with these five people, we'll meet again and reflect on the differences and the common themes that emerge in these stories of longing and a call.

A YOUTH PASTOR AND HIS FLOCK EXPLORE A THIRD WAY
Natalie Potts's Story

The summer before my senior year of high school, I did an internship at Woodland Hills Church in St. Paul, Minnesota. At that time I was not so passionate about following Jesus but more concerned with leadership development. One day our youth pastor, Seth McCoy, asked another intern and me, "What if Jesus didn't know he was God?" It sparked my interest again by imagining Jesus as human, more like us, and thinking that we might be more like him. That was my first interest in understanding the kingdom of God. As part of my internship I did a lot of reading, including Shane Claiborne's *Irresistible Revolution*. It's almost all stories, so readable. We talked with Seth about what we were reading.

After that I read a book called *Manna and Mercy*, a Bible story book that gave me more accessible language to talk about issues like communities of resistance to "the empire," which the book called "the Big Deal System." That sparked my interest in intentional community, church as shared life—something more than just going to youth group and trying to love everyone.

The Prophetic Imagination, by Walter Brueggemann, helped us talk about the prophetic community and its task. Not only were we called to live together sharing everything but also to be a prophetic witness to the world around us, a witness to the way of life that God has for human beings.

The Inner Voice of Love, by Henri Nouwen, contains journal entries from a time he spent in retreat from his community, and he reflects on his need for healing from a codependent relationship. This gave me a vision of community as a place of healing, too. Nouwen stressed the importance of spiritual guides and mentors.

Seth became acquainted with Anabaptist theology from a friend, a framework that made sense of all these ideas together, which he began to teach to our youth group. At that time I was thinking about becoming a doctor and going to Africa, but when Seth told me about his vision for intentional community, I dropped those other plans. I knew right away I wanted to do this. I saw it as my task to start a shared household. For nine months I talked to all my friends—anyone who would listen—about starting a community.

In April of my senior year, some friends and I went to a conference at Willow Creek Association where Brian McLaren, Shane Claiborne, and Mark Yaconelli were speaking. There we heard a lot of the ideas that are behind intentional community living. From there it was a process of finding others who would want to do this with us. Friends from church, Danni and Ricky, caught the excitement with me early on. I asked Sara, one of my close friends, to come and check out a house for the community. She got excited and said, "I think I'm supposed to do this." That was an apartment above a pizza place on Hamline Avenue. In June 2008, we moved into "the Hamline House" in the Midway neighborhood, between downtown St. Paul and Minneapolis. I was barely eighteen.

At that time Seth and his wife, Jenn, had started a small group with one other couple who had been volunteers in the youth ministry. They read *Jesus for President* together and then decided to move into the neighborhood in November 2008. The next year other singles started a second intentional household, and in May 2009 we started to worship together and called ourselves "Thirdway." This refers to Jesus's nonviolence, which neither flees conflict nor retaliates. But instead we are learning from Jesus a third way of suffering love. About that time Seth spoke at Woodland Hills Church about his decision to devote himself to the care of this new intentional Christian community. Some other families heard that and also wanted to join. . . .

OUR GROUP CAME TOGETHER FROM A CAMPUS MINISTRY
Luke Healy's Story

Our community's story begins with each of us becoming inspired by our contact with other communities. My first communal experience was at a one-year Bible college that stressed community as essential to the Christian life. I thrived in this environment, so different from my religious upbringing that stressed personal knowledge and individualized responsibility for faith. It was a safe place to open up and pursue healing for difficult issues from my past. In short, it "ruined me" for normal life.

Then, at Kansas State University, a further experience of community unfolded when Ichthus, our campus ministry, changed from Bible studies to what we called "lifegroups"; instead of just learning together we desired to let others know our struggles and joys, building small communities to intentionally share our lives.

After a season of leading my own lifegroup, I was made leader of all the lifegroups—first as a student and later as a full-time staff member of Ichthus. We tried hard, and people's hearts were in the right place, but always the same tensions arose—how can we be a Christian community while full-time students, often with part-time jobs? And how can we grow deeper in community when everyone moves on in a few years? Every semester our schedules changed, and people often had to change groups. The Lord was able to do a lot with us, but a thirst for deeper relationships in community grew in me and in others as well.

Now and then a few drops of more holistic community experience would fall into that thirsty soil, which only increased our longing: a visit to the Taizé community in France, a story of folks living differently in the inner city of Chicago, Shane Claiborne's book *The Irresistible Revolution*, about The Simple Way community in Philadelphia. Most of us got to know a community in Oklahoma City called The Refuge—a loose, large, and often changing group of people living in an old hotel, formerly a crack house, in an area with a sizeable homeless population. Their approach and vision seemed to change each time we visited, but their willingness to live differently in the face of the dangers and challenges of their neighborhood inspired us to talk about becoming a community of our own.

Kansas State University is located in Manhattan, Kansas, just a two-hour drive from Kansas City, where many of us in the campus ministry came from. We were inspired to form a community that challenged our typical American lifestyle of affluence and (often isolating) independence in the suburbs. Our community began with seven or eight people gathering once a week for prayer, often after a meal together.

Then an article came out in the *Kansas City Star* titled "The Murder Factory: 64130." Research showed that a majority of the murderers incarcerated in Kansas City listed their home address in this zip code. This area was "on the other side of the line," so to speak, which is Troost Avenue, the racial divide in Kansas City. The way this article moved us was more than just a coincidence—it was a call. . . .

I WANTED DEEPER RELATIONSHIPS
Jolyn Rodman's Story

When I was younger, in junior high and high school, I thought I couldn't be a Christian because I was so broken. I heard people talk about spirituality, but it never fit who I was. In college I chose to be a Christian, but I had no idea where to apply myself. After college I was doing education work with kids in various camps, and I discovered I had gifts, crazy ways of giving joy to children. I realized that God had been moving me into something like this all along, and now the gifts were coming out. I was amazed and joyful looking back over those "lost years" to realize that God had been shaping me to connect with others who felt lost too.

After a while, it wasn't enough to spend an intensive week with youths who would move on, followed by another group. I wanted deeper relationships. I wanted to spend months and years getting to know people better. That led me to join Mennonite Voluntary Service (MVS) doing elder care and housing ministry in Hutchinson, Kansas. God had given me a heart of compassion for people who were struggling. I found that their lives were very important to me. Service is my love language. It didn't become "I give and you receive," but when I gave I got back tenfold. Nevertheless, in MVS, with a new set of volunteers and housemates every year, I usually felt like I was always starting over on relationships. After four years of this, I felt isolated.

That's when I got serious about asking God what was next for me. I was meeting with a person in the church for discernment and gradually realized it wasn't a job I was searching for, but a vocation. I was advised to keep listening to the Lord. I learned a lot about prayer during those eight months. I learned about intentional Christian community and realized this is what I had been trying to do everywhere I'd lived. Others wanted a year or two of service and adventure, but for me it was a lifestyle. I wanted to live with hands open rather than clenched, to let go of control and trust God to provide. My spiritual guide mentioned that Reba Place Fellowship might be the kind of place I was looking for.

The day I showed up here, in Ronn and Nina Frantz's back yard, I knew instantly that I was supposed to live with them, that God had brought me to this community, to the job I was offered, to the Reba apprentice program, and the Rogers Park neighborhood. . . .

EVERYTHING I KNOW ABOUT CHRISTIAN COMMUNITY
Leroy Barber's Story

I sometimes say that everything I know about Christian community I learned growing up in the inner city of Philadelphia. Common purse, simple living, talking things out—these were community-type things that we African American folks did just to survive. White people get there by stepping down economically, by stepping out of society as they know it. But this is what we lived. As I became an adult I saw some hard things happening, and, as a believer, I wanted to respond.

It's so weird. I'll be forty-seven this year. Donna and I have been on this journey to more intentional community since our marriage at the age of twenty. We felt a call to hospitality. We asked, "How can we set up our home so we can be hospitable to strangers and people who may need a place to stay?" We started living intentionally with other couples, with single moms, inviting them to live in the home with us, functioning with a common purse at some points. We shared life with a mom who was struggling financially, so we did a rent/savings plan. The rent she paid we set aside into a savings fund to get her back on her feet. This is where we cut our teeth on these ideas in a pretty practical way—helping families reestablish themselves in the inner city of Philly.

I began working in a missional internship program started by Tony Campolo, called Cornerstone Ministries. I found that what I was experiencing at a grassroots level fit what others (white folks) were trying to do in intentional Christian community. Now, looking back, what matched up was my experience with struggling people in the city. Those concepts started coming together as I directed this program. . . .

I'VE ALWAYS HAD AN ATTRACTION TO COMMUNITY, BUT...

Bren Dubay's Story

I've always had an attraction to community, but that was not the way my life developed. At seventeen, I discovered my roots in the Catholic Church. I studied church history and was attracted to the monastic stories, to Saint Teresa of Ávila, who founded so many monasteries. The seeds of community were there way back then. Later, the work I did in theater resulted in intensely communal relationships that I thought would last, but when the set was torn down, people went their own way. When I became a mother, my children went to a Montessori school, which is very communal. The school has weekly community meetings, and everyone works in deep reverence and respect for one another. It is very holistic. But it somehow wasn't enough.

I did not come to Americus, Georgia, with the idea of community. I came from Houston to the Habitat for Humanity headquarters in Americus, to their Global Village exhibit on a field trip with a group of kids. The guest coordinator insisted that we see Koinonia Partners, birthplace of Habitat, before we went back to Houston. Being a polite Texan, I said, "Yes, Ma'am."

What happened to me at Koinonia has been hard to explain. The moment I stepped out of the car I sensed a spirit of love, a holiness, something about the land and the community's history. I was only there for forty-five minutes, but later I went online and ordered all sorts of books and CDs, not thinking I'd ever come back.

Then I got a little devious. I said to another group of city kids, "I know this farm we could visit . . ." and, surprisingly, they thought it was a great idea. We visited in November 2003, and by January 2004 I had agreed to move to Koinonia! At that time the Koinonia board was conducting a search for a new executive director. They pursued me, I filled out an application, and I was hired.

I have to say, it was not in any of my plans to do something like this. I'd been a playwright in residence at Rice University and hoped to return to that. But I really felt God at work. I said yes. It was out of obedience that I uprooted my life and went.

An important factor in saying yes to coming here was my husband, who has been supportive of everything I've done. I was still in the "this is crazy" stage, but Jim said, "I think we should do it." Life would have been so much easier, staying in Houston where our three sons still live. But Jim was drawn here, too, and found ways to plug in and serve the community as well.

Then Jim was diagnosed with cancer, and our medical insurance would not cover his therapy in Georgia. So he stayed on in Houston, where he could continue teaching and get treatment. Our routine has been this: every month either I go to Houston or Jim comes here for a few days. We talk on the phone several times a day. We know this will not be forever, but it works for now. We hope that by next summer he should be here, after the medical things are cared for and our house is fixed up to sell. . . .

REFLECTIONS ON FIVE STORIES OF LONGING AND A CALL

The journey of individuals to community often begins with an ache that has no name, a longing for God, it turns out. These stories include a series of "conversions," experiences that awaken the spiritual travelers to a call to follow Jesus with other disciples on a more radical path than they ever could have managed by themselves. This experience of calling happens in the context of social and spiritual movements that the Holy Spirit uses, like the local geography of a hiking path, to inspire the personal journey of individuals seeking the community where God is calling them. We will review and reflect on the wider context of these movements in subsequent chapters.

I am intrigued by the different ways these people tell essentially similar stories of life change, of a vocational discovery. Natalie Potts marks her journey of transformation by the books she read, by conversations with her youth pastor who discovered Anabaptist theology, and by conferences attended. At an early age she poured her enthusiasm into a miniyouth movement among her peers. In the background we see the astute mentorship of Seth McCoy, who offered spiritual and intellectual nourishment while making space for Natalie's precocious gifts to unfold as an organizer and servant of community.

Luke Healy discovered God's calling as a visionary pastor and coordinator for an emerging group of college students who themselves were called to more and more intentional community life. With prayerful steps, Luke and his fledgling group were moved to pioneer community "across the line" in Kansas City from the suburbs where they had grown up, to partner with an African American congregation where the deeper dimensions of racial reconciliation are still to be explored. Although the community has moved to an abandoned place of the empire, God has not abandoned them, the church, or the neighbors they meet.

Jolyn Rodman's journey to community was a more solitary path, beginning with the painful conviction that she was a broken person incapable of relationships, with nothing valuable to offer. But then she discovered a gift of goofy joy with children and blossomed as a soul alive to God and compassionately energized for service. Her longing for relationships of depth and fidelity led her to a spiritual guide, a life of prayer, and only then did she discover that her vocation matched up with others called to intentional Christian community.

Leroy Barber and his wife began their married life with a call to hospitality the way many African American families have practiced it, usually as a means of survival for an extended family and for those refugees of urban poverty whom God brought their way. Theirs was a practical and experimental way of putting faith into action. Only later did they discover that this ancient communal wisdom from African village life matched up with what Christian intentional communities have been doing for two thousand years, supporting the downward mobility of privileged Christians who hear the gospel call to leave all and follow Jesus.

For Bren Dubay, this turning point in her life was drastic, a decision to move from a comfortable and productive life in Houston to Koinonia Partners in rural Georgia. There her appointment as executive director was, in fact, an open-eyed acceptance of a vow of poverty. She knew she was called to lead a failing nonprofit service agency back to its gospel roots as an intentional Christian community. As miraculous as her conversion of life and work is, equally amazing is her husband Jim's affirmation and faithfulness to the Spirit's call despite the painful seasons of separation it has meant for them both.

Despite the different ways these stories unfold, a common and powerful theme is striking. From a sociological perspective we could describe all these stories as discoveries of a common vocation to sacrificial service in the context of community. Historically we could show how these persons joined a minority movement of radical discipleship communities, one option that has always been present in the life of the church. From a spiritual perspective, we can note how these individuals have all come alive in their relationship with God, tuned into a deeper dimension of and purpose for life.

All these perspectives, though true, are but slices of something unified, alive, and God-empowered. It is the movement from a "me" to a "we," which, according to Jesus, participates in the kingdom of heaven coming to earth, a life here and now that is already eternal, something that is good news for the whole world. However we try to describe it, our words are less than the whole. But we are fascinated, heart-tugged, invited to enter the story.

CHAPTER 2

The Landscape of Disintegrating Community and Our Longing for It

BRANDON RHODES

The yearning to decisively share life as followers of Jesus has been more or less constant for two thousand years now. From the earliest house churches to the Desert Fathers and Mothers to the medieval monastic orders to the early Anabaptists, from William Penn's Philadelphia and American frontier utopian sects to today's thriving organic/simple church and new monastic movements, it seems that in every generation Jesus issues a summons to radical community. A remnant persistently refuses the status of civil religion or the navel-gazing piety of self-enlightenment spirituality—seeking after a grounded Christianity with the grandeur of a mustard seed and the piety of fools. Jesus's call to share life as a reflection of the Triune God (Jn. 17) has not changed, for the Lord has crafted us in the image of a *social* God. Deep down, we're meant for this stuff.

This timeless call's contemporary reception is rooted in both attraction to the call itself and in repulsion from the world's alternatives to it. Individualism, consumerism, and careerism just aren't cutting it. We're more than isolated selves, more than the stuff we own, more than our résumé. We know there's more, and we hear Jesus's call to community clearly answering it.

More positively, fresh insights from philosophy, theology, sociology, and neuroscience point to the connectedness of all things and awaken us to the beauty of community. This isn't a wishy-washy New Age "all-is-one" attitude: it's a humble rediscovery of the ancient truth that God's plan from the beginning was, as Paul wrote, to unite all things in Christ

(Eph. 1:10). We've been awakened by the beauty of this truth in myriad ways—that we are called to the mending of all relationships through Jesus Christ. Ecological, spiritual, social: you name it, Jesus is healing it! Salvation is the establishing, then, of community on earth as it is in heaven. Many of us are increasingly aware that to resist community is to deny a basic truth about our humanity. Jesus doesn't want to bring shalom only to you and me, but to everything *between* you and me, to vivify our relationships with the life of heaven. This is the big timeless call to community that God is waking us up to.

And God's timeless call is also always uniquely timely. Hence Benedict's monasteries look different from the early house churches and the Amish look different from The Simple Way. Like the incarnation of Christ, God's restorative call to community works within the context and capacities of the culture where it is planted. This is what some call the missional impulse to incarnation.

Today, to be sure, the call to community feels hugely different. Western culture has experienced tremendous upheaval in the past two hundred years. This means that while there is nothing *new* under the sun concerning Christian community, there is ever the need to freshly incarnate it in a given context. The summons for community-seekers to start something fresh is both very old and very new. And it requires us to see our neighborhoods with missionary eyes, discerning critically how to answer the call most faithfully there.

We don't know your neighborhood, though: that's up to you. But for the remainder of this chapter, we'll look at the big picture of our historical context, exploring those big upheavals in Western culture that make our times so distinct. In particular we'll consider how two big trends behind that upheaval have awakened many to Jesus's call to community. Knowing our times in these ways can help us better discern our calling, our context, and ourselves.

AUTOMOBILITY AND ITS CULTURE OF CONSUMERISM

The twentieth century will be remembered as an age of wondrous creativity, when Americans voluntarily shattered their lives into distant and dissonant fragments. America's industries learned how to assemble atomic bombs, airplanes, iPads, and the genetic codes of life itself in the same era that American society disassembled the ancient overlap of family, food, faith, and field of work. Americans reached for the stars as they withered their roots, inhabited space but lost any sense of place. What created this rootless, dis-placed society? The answer is not far from us: that great agent of identity and opportunity, the automobile.

This American life is a life dispersed: we work ten miles away with people who live twenty miles beyond that, buy food grown a thousand miles away from grocery clerks who live in a different subdivision, date people from the other side of town, and worship with people who live an hour's drive from one another. We may want to be "seven-day-a-week" Christians, but we struggle in our dispersion to do that as more than individuals. Christians don't break bread with those who make their bread, still less with those who grew the wheat! We serve soup to the poor folks on the other side of the tracks, but we don't know the person on the other side of our fence. There is little sense of consonance, commitment, spontaneity, or stability in this paved new world.

Because there is so little overlap in our different spheres of life, there is little chance for our socializing, creativity, or service to be spontaneous. The nearest thing to spontaneous occasions in the fragmented lifestyle of suburbia is the persistent stream of texts, tweets, and status updates on our cell phones, which we can just as easily ignore. Instead of bumping into one other and receiving those surprise encounters as gifts, these electronic notes invade as distraction from what is truly before us. The spontaneity we *do* enjoy is intrusive.

Instead of spontaneity, much of our socializing, creativity, and service is rooted in sheer choice. Don't like this store? Don't worry: the products at the store a couple miles east will be more to your liking. Too many loud kids at that Starbucks? Fear not: the one inside Barnes &

Noble has a chiller crowd. Life is not a *gift received* but a *choice made*.

This is as true of where we shop and dine and play as where we worship and minister. If a church is too charismatic, or not charismatic enough, too conservative, or too progressive, too big, or not big enough, too single, or not single enough, we can drive past it to a church that's more to our liking. There's a reason, after all, why we call it "church shopping." And it is a spiritual novelty enabled singularly by the automobile.

Contrast this way of being human, and this way of being God's new humanity, with how Western civilization has operated for thousands of years. When you can only worship as far as you're willing to walk, your options are limited. For the vast majority of people who worked in agriculture, their church was the folk in the nearest village. And for the few living in urban areas, their choices were likewise limited by a pedestrian's geography. Trade, art, recreation, and education were all scaled to how far anyone could walk. This is who you were stuck with, for good or ill. You can accept them as gift, nuisance, or mission field, but this is who you're in Christ with.

This isn't to say that most of church history lived in anything like intentional Christian community. Far from it! Rather, the integration of all aspects of life at the scale of small places, neighborhoods, and parish churches made such a notion seem less obviously needed. The necessity of traditional Christian wisdom concerning holiness, reconciliation, steadfastness, and patience were much more apparent in an era of tangled, not tweeted, relationships.

To be sure, the parish church still had much to learn from historical and contemporary intentional Christian communities; common purses, shared commitments and daily prayers, vowed stability, and so on are always likely to be life-giving, countercultural acts. But the *need* for a shared life that is so present in our fragmented society would have felt quite peculiar in those days.

The truth is, though, that our car-scaled societies have made a shared life—a shared anything, really—of utmost novelty and attraction. Consider the following sketch, and see if it doesn't resonate with your experience.

```
home                                              coworker
                              church
                              building


                  work
                              friend           grocery
                                                         café
              barista
        soup  kitchen



        church
        friend                                 pastor
```

This imagined map visualizes how scattered our lives have become. Just consider the locations we commonly associate with church, how far they are from one another—church building, pastor, church friend, and soup kitchen are miles apart! We have no chance of bumping into each other except in controlled settings like the church building. No wonder suburban congregations built megachurch buildings in the 1980s with cafés and gymnasiums, and in the twenty-first century many pastors have settled for an online "Share" button instead of any way to embody a shared faithfulness among the laity.

Our lives are fragmented and we crave connection. Intentional Christian community offers this connection as it relocalizes and reintegrates our lives. Suddenly, church building, church leadership, friendship, fellowship, and service contexts all begin to tightly overlap. Contrast the map below with what's above. Isn't this a much more humanly scaled way of living? Intentional Christian community brings back together, under Jesus Christ, what the automobile has torn asunder.

coworker

soup kitchen   church
friend

pastor   church
building   friend

home

work   grocery

barista   café

Automobility, meanwhile, has been producing a crisis in the wider church. As church attendance became a consumer choice, church tactics shifted accordingly. Entertainment-driven worship, seeker-sensitivity, hit-and-run evangelism, competing for members as a scarce commodity, roadside reader boards, and affinity-based small group ministry are all symptoms of the deeper suburban captivity of the church. In adapting to automobilized American life, the church also moved in these directions in an attempt to provide meaning, identity, and value to potential attendees.

These tactics and accommodations worked for some, and for a time. Churches of an independent, free-church, and Pentecostal persuasion were particularly effective at adapting to automobility's upheavals. Meanwhile the mainline traditions, in an attempt to not make church a choice, overwhelmingly failed to adapt; they were easily outcompeted by evangelical churches in suburbia. Now, most megachurches are independent franchises that specialize in a flavor of the faith especially suited to suburban culture.

But the megachurch has not ultimately satisfied that culture, nor has it always grown a faithful church or pointed to the kingdom in lasting ways. The church of automobility is increasingly recognized as irrelevant to the wider culture, displaying neither an alternative to it nor salving its deepest pains. No wonder the contemporary move toward intentional Christian community has drawn so heavily from suburbia's expats. It uniquely embodies an ancient alternative, out of which it offers balm to suburbia's pains.

END OF CHRISTENDOM AND POSTMODERNISM

Talk to most Christian communitarians and you'll hear a sassy remark about Constantine's captivity of the church. It's something Anabaptists have long focused on and has only recently come into view of the wider church as a real problem to be addressed. Constantine's captivity is what we now call *Christendom*, the historical monolith that assumes church/ Christianity and Western culture are basically one entity, that church membership and citizenship constitute the same circle. This could be as idolatrously proud as presuming that one's nation is supremely Christian and blessedly chosen by God for divine purposes, to as innocuous as assuming biblical literacy and Christian affection among one's fellow nationals. For centuries, this spectrum of the Christendom presumption was the norm for Europe and America. Critiques against it were stones slung at a Goliath that didn't seem likely to fall any time soon.

In the latter half of the twentieth century, however, that changed. Euro-American Christendom's promise of Christianizing the world and healing its wounds with progress, reason, and democracy were found wanting. Our legacy of ecclesial complicity with genocide, colonialism, racism, and nuclear armament was an affront to Christendom's beatific assurances. *If religion cannot escape responsibility for these evils,* many wondered, *then what good is it?*

Consequently in postwar Europe the faith has been on a rapid decline. Many Europeans born after Auschwitz have a deeply ingrained skepticism against Europe's legacy, namely, the Christian faith and the Enlightenment's smug certainty that reason and democracy can melt any obstacle to human flourishing. Constantine's church has in less than a century been cast from the center of power to the uttermost margins.

American churches, it turns out, are only a few decades behind the European church in their decline. With each passing year, fewer and fewer Americans identify as Christians or regularly participate in a local church. Ten churches close their doors every day in America, and among teens growing up in the church, 88 percent leave their faith by their second year in college. It is no longer fair to assume that Americans have any biblical literacy or belief in one God, in heaven, or in the notion of sin. Our context is rapidly becoming *post-Christian.*

Consequently Christians have shifted from slinging stones at Christendom to writing its eulogy and sorting out its will. American churches are experimenting, writing, blogging, and tweeting like crazy to try out different ways of faithfulness that can actually survive in this post-Christian world. Christendom's demise has forced an *identity crisis* on the churches, which has, in turn, ignited a furnace of ecclesial imagination and wit. The missional, emergent, organic, and New Monastic movements are all streams of creative response to post-Christendom.

Christians everywhere are developing new ecclesial imaginations, waking up to the need for something that will connect people in meaningful ways to Christ but that do not necessarily look like church used to look. Many of these are along the lines of intentional Christian community. These post-Christendom ecclesiologies make most sense when rooted in place, in community, and in humble service. If Christendom assumed that the church served the body politic, post-Christendom ecclesiologies are stumbling into what Anabaptist-leaning Christians have been insisting on all along: that, like the early church, we are to be pockets of an alternative politics, an alternative society within a crumbling empire. Note the poetry of what God is up to here. Intentional Christian communities have long fortified their identity as anti-Christendom, to the rest of the church's confusion and chagrin. Now, in a post-Christendom culture, the wider church is waking up to her need to reimagine her ecclesiology and, not surprisingly, is arriving at similar conclusions as the intentional Christian communities. A post-Christendom church and an anti-Christendom church sound remarkably alike. It may not call itself intentional Christian community, but to linger on labels is to miss the point: there is a broad undertow toward holistic discipleship within the context of shared life.

These emerging contexts of post-Christendom and fragmented life are moving many in the church toward more expressions of intentional Christian community. We may not recognize these forces with the vividness outlined here, but they have been pressing in on us all the same. The church's imagination is relentlessly challenged by these crises, and it seems God is using them to craft much of tomorrow's church in the vein of intentional Christian community. If that is the push toward community, what is the pull?

THE PULL TOWARD COMMUNITY

The call to community has been a normal component of the faith's fringe since Constantine and was normative in much of the church for three centuries before that. And for good reason: there are many, many biblical inspirations for entering intentional Christian community, which will be explored later on in this book. It is an ancient mode of faithfulness that flows out of the biblical narrative and so will always be with us.

But a walk through most American downtowns reminds us Christians that we are not alone in our impulse toward communal life. Urban gang culture, hipster enclaves, MeetUp groups, and religious ghettos reveal that many of us are looking for a tribe to belong to. This common yearning points to something that we instinctively know "in our bones," as if our very humanness is fulfilled through community. Where might this come from? Maybe we are even hardwired for community.

The earliest Christians talked about salvation as Jesus restoring in us the ability to bear God's image, which as early as Jesus and Paul meant a sharing in God's very life. This marital union between humanity and God through Jesus is remembered in church tradition as _theosis—Christ_ becoming one with us that we might become one with God. Over time, this sense of salvation was cauterized from Western tradition but lived on in the Eastern Orthodox churches as an increasingly mystical, personal, interior truth. Our image-bearing union with the Lord, amid Christendom's highfalutin hallowings, was flattened into contemplative mystery.

Paradoxically, ancient church fathers and mothers were hashing out just what kind of God it is whose image we are saved into reflecting. They came to this vision of God's life that we now call the Trinity, and they used the word-picture for a joyous circle-dance, perichoresis, to summarize it. God's life, then, is a perfect and active community of delighting in and glory-reflecting toward one another.

One another: a suspiciously New Testament phrase for church life! We can sense anticipations of these themes throughout Paul's writings, though as through a glass dimly. There, the vital element of salvation which the theosis tradition muffled with mysticism was that Jesus makes us able to bear the life of the circle-dancing God. Which means we're not saved only for heaven but also for one another. We're saved *into* one another, because theosis and perichoresis go together.

But not everyone seems ready to join the circle-dance. I've enjoyed friendships with many people who do not believe God would ever call them to intentional Christian community. *If God had*, they have stiffly assured me, *then they'd be there.*

I'll be up front about this: I do not believe communal life is the only way of faithfulness, nor is there a best way for any of it. But, while humanity may be crafted for community, some of us are just more ready than others to dance. What gives? My suspicion is that few choose to join or stick with intentional Christian community because it is so radically different from our hypermobile, consumerist, individualistic culture. The change is simply too radical to be joined into at once. Our fragmented lifestyles agitate and activate our impulse to circle-dance, but they have also deeply formed us *not* to be able to circle-dance. Exposed to radical forms of community as one more consumer choice, many of us count the cost and depart alone.

I have no interest in saying these things to frown upon those who hesitate about community. The circle-dance is, as I have said, massively countercultural. It would be supremely arrogant of me to equate intentional Christian community with the circle-dance, no matter how useful I find it to be in becoming better spiritual dancers. What matters, I suggest, is that we be journeying deeper toward a perichoretic way of life, and that is happening in a great variety of ways.

DIVERSITY IN THE MOVE TOWARD COMMUNITY

If our communities of circle-dancing are to genuinely live into that metaphor, we should expect a rich diversity of dances to be happening all over the place. And indeed, that's what we find! Although we are variously responding to the same historical trends and inner longings, we should also happily note the sheer diversity in the contemporary move toward intentional Christian community. Having reviewed the bigger historical trends that are pushing us toward community, and having reflected on the link between theosis and perichoresis that is pulling us into community, we can celebrate the many movements that are embodying a relocalized, shared, and rooted faith. What is presented in the table below is a list of groups that have been practicing intentional Christian community, some far longer than others. We have here a multigenerational roll of radical witness to Christ, a common trajectory of a localized, shared, and small shape.

I name these groups not as a comprehensive catalog of thoroughly distinct community types. There is much overlap and redundancy, which should encourage us to have a charitable ear when we talk about these topics. Some will identify themselves as type X, be labeled as Y by their critics, and written about as Z by others (like me!). And each could be *sort of* right. Rather than "rank" these kinds of communities according to height of commitment or depth of radicalness or width of popularity, I have simply made my own standard of "degree of obscurity relative to mainstream commuter evangelical churches and missions." After all, let's face it: if you're used to conventional expressions of Christianity, this trek toward intentional Christian community can seem like a journey into a foreign land.

Type	ID as church?	Summary	Distinctives and Charism	Examples
Multisite	Yes	Megachurches teleconference sermons to satellite campuses	Financial girth and organizational prowess	ubiquitous
Small Groups	Part of	Where many churches say church "really happens"; may simply be affinity groups	Many folks' first step toward a lower-to-the-ground Christianity	ubiquitous
"Third Place" Churches	Yes	Missional church plants that gather, outreach, organize through enterprises like bars, art galleries, cafés	Shared work, tentmaking, local entrepreneurial activity	ubiquitous
Campus Ministries	No	InterVarsity, CCC, Chi Alpha, realized emerging Christianity is deeply communal, and so experiment in cohousing for students	Where many people have first deep experience of intentional Christian community	ubiquitous
Missional Communities	Varies	Neighborhood tribes of creative discipleship connected to central-hub church office/organization	Discipleship-centered, honest engagement with post-Christian culture	Adullam (Fort Collins, CO), Soma (Tacoma, WA)
Church-affiliated "Community House"	Part of	Churches experimenting in cohousing. The bounded set of those houses become wells of living water for the rest of the congregation	Done in partnership with traditional church, not "off the grid"	Rosewood Manor at Church of the Beloved (Edmonds, WA)
Church-unaffiliated "Community House"	No	Thousands of young people experimenting "living in community"—cohousing, Bible study, naming their house, parties where no one gets drunk	Many young, unmarried Christians try this out after college.	ubiquitous
House Churches	Yes	Gather in living rooms, often live in proximity, often practice cohousing, often stress commitment	Focus on every member as a minister, know how to live in reconciliation	Church of the Servant King (Portland and Eugene, OR)
Parish/ Neighborhood Churches	Yes	These churches are of/for a neighborhood. Membership and creativity of mission and worship happen in this place.	Expertise in theology of place, presence	Springwater (Portland, OR), Zoe Livable Church (Tacoma, WA)

Type	ID as church?	Summary	Distinctives and Charism	Examples
New Monastic Communities	Not often	Includes other community types, but with focus on shared devotional rhythms	Overcoming individualism in spiritual disciplines	Rutba House (Durham, NC)
New Radical Churches	Yes	Anabaptist churches with assertive peace and justice witness through activism, simplicity, cohousing	Creative missional witness, deep critique of American culture	Missio Dei (Minneapolis, MN)
Farms	Not often	Some are eco-villages for Jesus. Others focus on racial reconciliation through shared farmwork	Emphasis on shared work habits, sustainability. Food often sold to urban communities	Plow Creek Fellowship (Tiskilwa, IL), Tierra Nueva (Skagit Valley, WA), Koinonia Farm (Americus, GA)
Catholic Workers	Part of	Diverse crowd of Catholic sisters, Protestants, nontheists, and other volunteers cohousing and pursuing justice among the poor	Organizing for peace and justice, friendship with the homeless, radical hospitality	ubiquitous
New Radical Communities	No	Like New Radical Churches, but members often attend a local church	Prophetic witness in relationship with traditional church	The Simple Way (Philadelphia, PA)
New Friar Communities	No	Live in solidarity and proximity with the poor and other marginalized peoples	Radical hospitality, relationships of mutuality with the poor	Servants Vancouver (Vancouver, BC)
Anabaptist Community Churches	Yes	Churches that take communal life as normative, have deep ideas of membership. Some involved with in peace and justice	Often hold a common purse; rooted together for the long haul	Reba Place Fellowship (Evanston, IL)

COMMON NEEDS FOR A COMMON JOURNEY

What I love seeing in this list is the unique assets and strengths that each group brings. Some focus on devotion, others on hospitality; some excel in reconciliation, others in announcing Jubilee and shalom. We've got so much to learn from and be thankful for in one another! Each community has its own charism, something unique the Lord has done in them that blesses the rest. We each do a slightly different, if especially dazzling, part of the circle-dance. In our diversity we are, like parts of the body, able to bless one another.

Rooted, localized, shared faithfulness is, it turns out, a surprisingly wide space. And in that wide space on the journey into intentional Christian community, I believe we are called to begin playing, working, and worshiping together. The struggle of community life, of choosing rootedness together, is too hard to do alone. As will be explored in a later chapter, this diverse move toward the circle-dance in our day cries out for mutually life-giving relationships between intentional Christian communities. The New Radicals and the campus ministries, the parish churches and the small groups *need* one another. Unity in friendship and partnership under the Spirit of the living God will bring us forward and help us see the kingdom of heaven on earth.

CHAPTER 3

Contours of Resistance to Community
BRANDON RHODES

Chapter 2 was pretty optimistic about intentional Christian community within today's context, as if all of history and human nature were combining to bring us into the vortex of its loving, plush embrace. The truth is far from that. North Americans and particularly today's generation of young adults—for whom I venture to speak in this chapter—are in many ways deeply ill-prepared for community life. Some of these "contours of resistance," such as how many of us come from divorced families, both attract us toward community while also inoculating us with a deep fear of it.

You probably already know most of the contours of resistance that are listed in this chapter. But in the experience of many people who have lived in intentional community for years, we either take them for granted, or don't explore them sufficiently, or dismiss them as wishy-washy signs of weakness and moral flaccidity. Jointly we rarely tease out the implications of these contours for deepening discipleship within our communities.

Please note that this list represents broad strokes only, but ones that have been found to be true, borne out by personal experience.

Contour 1: We come from many different family situations. Most of humanity grew up among an extended family of grandparents, aunts, uncles, cousins, and neighbors. That changed after World War II, when suburbia's emphasis on single-family houses shoehorned us into the nuclear family (dad, mom, and two or three kids), and for a while—for most—that *was* what home life looked like.

But that's not how it has been for most of the past two American generations. Some of us were latchkey kids, raised by a single parent or by two working parents. We were welcomed home from school not by parents but by television. Others had several fathers or mothers while growing up, as parents divorced, dated, or remarried several times.

In community this translates into a variety of unmet expectations, where we carry forward our experiences of growing up into community life. My first experience of this was when I began to annoy my housemate Tommy every time I came home. Before I had even dropped off my backpack, I was leaning on the doorframe of Tommy's room asking him about his day and telling all the interesting details of mine. Likewise when he got home, I'd follow him to his room and assume my usual spot against the doorframe. Not surprisingly, this drove Tommy crazy. He finally burst, leaving me feeling rejected, unheard, and unwelcomed.

It didn't take long to sort out what was behind each of our needs. Growing up, I was welcomed home with good questions and a listening ear from my mother every day. Afternoon check-in was an informal relational ritual embedded deep within me. Tommy, however, grew up with two working parents. This daily check-in wasn't in him. We had vastly different childhoods and brought vastly different expectations with us into community. With time and listening, we learned to honor our various needs for daily check-ins and personal space.

Consideration: We carry our family-of-origin rhythms, strengths, and weaknesses into community undeclared. We come from different contexts. Therefore all shared life can feel like a cross-cultural experience.

Contour 2: We come from divorce-torn homes and communities. It's a commonly repeated belief that half of all marriages end in divorce. Although the most recent US Census shows that the marriage and divorce rates in fact vary considerably by state, the statistics won't matter to you if you're one of those people whose parents divorced during your childhood. So never mind the statistics—if you came from a family that was splintered by divorce, then you have some issues in common with other kids of those marriages. We tend to have a fear of commitment, a slowness to trust, and a skepticism about vows of any sort. The nagging question in many of us is, "How can I be sure this is where I'm supposed to be, and who I am supposed to be with?"

Unsurprisingly we apply these anxieties to intentional Christian community. Why take vows, why commit, why give ourselves to the body of Christ, when our memories of divorce and separation remind us just how little power any vows actually hold. They didn't work for our parents and in some cases kept our parents trapped in abusive relationships. How can we be sure others won't hurt us too?

This fear and distrust can wreak havoc in intentional Christian communities because we haven't experienced genuine trust or fidelity. We have seen marriages collapse with little effort toward restoring the relationship. We will tend to be only half-invested in a community. This inability to practice the Christian virtues of loyalty and fidelity makes us prone to scatter easily. We carry our broken homes into our communities.

Consideration: Divorce is a massively destructive force; we need emotional and relational healing from its wounds if we are ever to join in community for long.

Contour 3: We're used to planned obsolescence. Every year Apple updates all of their products. This means that in three to five years their products are rendered incapable of running the newest programs. At one level we can attribute this to the brisk pace of technological innovation. Yet for Apple and other companies, this obsolescence of products isn't just a consequence of progress but is actually planned through delaying the deployment of certain features. For example, while new iPads have cameras, Apple geeks have discovered that the first generation (camera-free) iPad actually has a camera mount inside the chassis! It looks like the company intentionally withheld that feature to make future versions more appealing.

Planned obsolescence is what younger folks expect, and it is how we often treat churches and communities. Why put down roots here when over there will be a savvier group in a couple years? Thus we hold out on moving into the community, pursuing membership, or trying common-purse finances because we're used to something better soon coming along. Our eyes are always looking for greener grass on the other side. We struggle to embrace the mediocrity and the beauty of the community we're in. Like the eminently functional phone in our hands, we blithely gaze forward to what's next instead of receiving with gratitude what we already have.

Consideration: Communities must retrain hearts out of the narrative of planned obsolescence and disappointment and into a narrative of gratitude and satisfaction.

Contour 4: We're growing up, and marrying, later. Historic rites of maturity such as catechism, a bar mitzvah, or marriage gave form to what it meant to be an adult. Adulthood used to mean becoming responsible for others in the context of marriage and parenthood; that was when one moved out from the parental home.

Today, we have no agreed-on markers for adulthood. Is it at puberty? Sexual maturity? When you can drive farming equipment at fourteen? Drive with an adult at fifteen? Drive alone at sixteen? View R-rated movies at seventeen? Vote, smoke, and pack heat at eighteen? Or when we can drink alcohol at twenty-one? Or perhaps we're adults when our car insurance lowers at age twenty-four, or when we cannot remain on our parent's health insurance any longer. Or is it when we have graduated from college? Chosen a career? Gotten married?

In losing our ability to narrate adulthood, we have lost the purpose of adulthood. What's the point of living independently, or choosing a career, or marrying? Social commentators have arrived at the phrase *delayed adulthood* to describe this phenomenon. In making adulthood a *choice*, many have opted to gladly postpone it.

Don't misunderstand this delay as irresponsibility. Many who are delaying traditional moments of adulthood such as marriage are simply being *a*responsible: neither taking on the weightier things of family and commitment nor living in outright waste. It is, as I have observed it, a doe-eyed come-what-may nihilism with little hope or aim for the future.

Delayed adulthood is underdiscussed among enthusiasts of intentional Christian community, but it is in part behind the contemporary move toward intentional community. Many of us had a great time in dorms or a campus ministry or the Greek system. So we choose to extend that college experience by cohousing with other Christians and then call it "living in community." I know how curmudgeonly this sounds, but it must be stated: this situation has led to a cheapening and a relativizing of the word *community* to mean cohousing among Christians with little sharing of life, work, worship, or service. It sometimes means Christianized bachelorhood and little else.

Community in these cases enables delayed adulthood by making responsible, relational rootedness a *personal choice* instead of a vital context for following Jesus for singles and families alike. Many of the communities I have met and been part of disintegrate when too many members get married in one year and leave the life of the community entirely. Marriage, rather than a new beginning, can be a death knell to young communities.

Yet delayed adulthood is not *all* bad. Look carefully at why some people are delaying adulthood: *they recognize that living alone and "independently" is an unsatisfying myth!* They opt to live at home by intuiting that we are tribal creatures, not independent beings. Delayed adulthood in the form of the return to our families of origin and of living in shallower modes of intentional Christian community, although easy to scorn, also presents exciting opportunities for the gospel of Jesus's invitation into a circle-dance way of life together.

Consideration: A community's vision should be broad enough to include families or older mentors. Otherwise, intentional Christian community becomes a niche form of delayed adulthood instead of a durable way for all stages of life.

Contour 5: We want a tribe but don't know how to live tribally.

Sharing life either as a close-knit, extended biological family or as an intentional Christian community requires a relational toolbox of habits, wisdom, rhythms, and values to hammer out challenges and construct durable friendships. But suburbia, as we have learned, corroded these tools for tribal life. Compound that with the context of collapsed parental marriages and our own moral immaturity, and you've got a slew of folks who never learned how to live in durable relationships. Habits such as learning to listen to one another well, how to initiate confession and forgiveness, how to defer and submit our preferences, doing others' dishes cheerfully, sharing discernment over major life decisions, and sundry other tools for living in unity with others must often be instilled from the ground up.

The irony in this is particularly acute for those of us who grew up in the church. While I was living in an intentional Christian community in Eugene for the first time, my heart sank when I realized that eighteen years of growing up in God-fearing, Bible-believing, Spirit-filled, zealous, orthodoxy-rooted churches had taught me nothing about how to live in reconciled relationships. I knew quite thoroughly about how God was reconciled to me through Jesus on the cross. But I didn't experientially know how to forgive or be forgiven. My home life was healthy, and I suppose I learned a bit there. But isn't it odd that, for all those Sunday school classes, youth retreats, prayer summits, and Bible studies, I received *zero* lessons on how to live into our vocation as "ministers of reconciliation" (2 Cor. 5:18)?

That doesn't mean we're all complete jackasses. Still, there's no getting around the truth that community life regularly brings out the worst in us. It puts us in relationships with people who drive us crazy. Yet what better place can there be for our weakest parts and crankiest moments to happen than among those who love us deeply? Living in community is inevitably a choice to lie down on God's operating table and open our hearts to the Holy Spirit's healing through one another. It is an invitation to spiritual surgery, made all the messier by our inexperience in using and submitting to the "surgical tools" of gracious truth-telling and patient listening. It surprises me how the Spirit shows up again and again to help us through these messy surgeries. God's strength is made perfect in our weakness.

Consideration: There can be a steep learning curve for some in their first experiences of community. Therefore, they should enter with the fourfold expectation that they will sin, they will forgive, they will be sinned against, they will be forgiven.

Contour 6: We fear "legalism" and cherish the "authentic." Activities that are programmed, or inflexible, or that don't feel genuine and organic will agitate us. For a variety of reasons, mostly to do with a resurgence of what smarter folks call *romanticism* and *existentialism*, we only favor activities that emerge spontaneously and low to the ground.

For a great survey of what's behind this and how biblical ethics can help us escape its orbit, I recommend N. T. Wright's *After You Believe.* But the gist of how this works for many of us pursuing intentional Christian community is a distrust of scheduled, organized activities and an idealization of activities that bubble up outside of our stated plans. *We're sick of religion, man, and just want spirituality.* We push the biblical vision of church as "people, not programs" and "relationship, not religion" into a needless contention between schedule, faithfulness, and shared practices on the one hand and spontaneity, relationship, and freedom on the other.

Of course, this couldn't be more ironic. We want *intentional* community but expect it to be *spontaneous* and *un*intentional. The truth is, you're going to find a good deal of each of these in every community, and probably a good deal in yourself. Many of us have seen extensively detailed shared practices produce busyness but no fruit of the Spirit. And many of us have lived in a culture of "spontaneous" intentional Christian community that never gets the dishes done, the dirty laundry aired, or the kingdom sought. What is the way forward?

I have only learned to laugh at this tension. Or rather, laugh *in* this tension, for it is one that I do not expect to leave anytime soon. Both ends of this tug-of-war have great values and hopes that I regularly sympathize with. And I have found that the Spirit often steers communities from both ends.

For as much as I sympathize with both, each tends in my experience to act more out of fears than hopes. Out of fear of never getting anything done, or of being let down, we find security in schedule and structure. And out of fear of never spiritually growing, of being told what to do, of being reminded of the religiosity we grew up with, or of forsaking our own freedom, a large number of us find security in never pledging toward much of anything.

The way forward must be grounded in our common hopes instead of our divisive fears. In Springwater, for example, we have drafted our common hopes into a common vocation by way of a mission statement:

To be the family of God, following the way of Jesus,
living simply and sacrificially loving our neighborhood.

These common hopes provide orientation and calibration, freeing us to discern our way through both structure and spontaneity. This helps us to be up front about our fears and make space for people to air them going forward. This is done, though, to build trust and safety, *not* to let those fears torque us from our common hopes.

Consideration: As my friend Jim says, the delightful paradox of building organic community is that "organic" doesn't happen spontaneously. Organic farming takes years of intentional soil preparation, careful observation of nutrient levels, and patiently disciplined nurture of each particular field.

Contour 7: We are postpartisan. Fewer and fewer of us fit into conventional left-versus-right categories. To be sure, there are many Christians who fit the bill of one political party or another. But a fresh breed of Christian is emerging, one who will be pro-life, but also pro–circle-of-life, also pro-peace. We'll practice chastity and eat a vegan diet. We could boycott Wal-Mart and homeschool our kids. We'll oppose prostitution but do so by befriending women caught in the sex trade behind it. The polarized Christianity that we grew up in and the media wars that provoke an older generation are fading fast. We've left it behind.

More than a move from right to left, I have noticed generationally a shift from politics-through-voting to politics-through-living. We're increasingly postpartisan, fed up with what we feel is the pompous poppycock of elections that lay claim to God's authority for human power struggles. We're more into an embodied politic, one where opposing war (for example) is about how we vote and more—it also means driving less, teaching and practicing nonviolence, mentoring teenagers tempted to enlist in the military, and so on. It's no wonder so many of us are interested in community life.

Many people in my generation have built friendships with gay and lesbian folks and found them to be far less morally menacing than we were taught in church. That doesn't mean we know what to do with the relevant biblical passages. I've met scores of Christians in their twenties and thirties who have unresolved doubts about traditional biblical interpretations in these matters and who want further conversations with LGBTQ persons (their preferred acronym for "lesbian, gay, bisexual, transgender, and queer") in the context of church before making up their minds.

As this generation moves toward intentional Christian community and out of right-wing political captivity, the question of including LGBTQ persons and families *will* surface at one point or another. I'm not soliciting a right way forward on this, but it will come up and our communities may have a unique role in hosting the conversation.

Consideration: Intentional Christian community provides a compelling context for reimagining how we talk about all of politics and can help us escape pigeonholing ourselves by polarizing buzzwords. Community lets us respond to persons and places instead of ideological positions on issues.

Contour 8: We're afraid of exclusivism. The journey of my generation concerning LGBTQ persons is in part an outworking of our anxiety regarding social exclusivism. Nothing makes us as nervous as a delineated "in-crowd" and "out-crowd."

Clear membership structures, for example, worry many of us because of the potential power dynamics that can come with them. That is, membership to us invokes a "who has power, and who doesn't" paradigm that we find repulsive elsewhere in Christianity. *That's why Jesus stood up against the Pharisees, so we damned well don't want that!*

Some well-known and brilliant authors have legitimized this apprehension with a framework that favors "centered set" visions of membership over "bounded set" alternatives. That is, making proximity to Jesus (the center) as our guide for membership is, to many, a healthier way to describe belonging in community than, say, a written charter of membership that sets up fences.

Responding to these fears, membership models of intentional Christian community *can* distinguish important dimensions of belonging, such as depth or duration of commitment. In short, membership can help formalize not power but shared expectations and responsibilities.

In Springwater, we are still learning to converse healthily about membership. We began with one form—"trial membership"—where we all took the same plunge for the first year, followed by mutual discernment about what happens next. Eventually we settled on three modes of membership: novice, practicing, and vowed. These correspond roughly to "exploratory," "called here for now," and "no longer actively looking elsewhere." During that transition, however, some members carried the tone that "if you've not discerned that you're to be here for a long time, then what are you doing here?" or "vowed membership is the goal of all membership." Not surprisingly, most everyone under thirty (and some over) were offended by that tone. It sounded so impatiently exclusive and in-crowd!

Nowadays, we've got what feels like a healthier culture about the whole thing. Preferring to side with those who have a healthy allergy to exclusivism, I'd like to think of it as the vowed members learning how to talk more cordially and sensitively about membership. But that's not the whole story. Truthfully, as we grew in trust of one another (with the help of a few thoughtful ambassadors who helped interpret one side to the other), we younger folks learned *at the heart level* how to hear one another, and how to give each other the benefit of the doubt. We are learning to face one another beyond the mediating effects of membership structures while also appreciating their purpose. Now, I'm still not entirely persuaded by our membership model, but I think it's at least okay. For as many emotional bruises as we dealt out, the important thing about the whole process is that the Spirit used it to bring us closer in trust, cooperation, and mission.

Consideration: Most of us are roundly allergic to membership: to be otherwise, we'll need good arguments for its positive role and have our fears of it invoking power relations taken seriously.

Contour 9: We inherited individualism but also desire unity. Many of us, at some vague level, are convinced that everything is connected, that unity is the intended bent of all things. Nevertheless, we function as community-resisting individuals. With so few experiences or examples of how to live in the radiance of God's vision of unity, we settle for that all-American virtue of tolerance. Proverbs such as "live and let live" and "don't impose your values on others" teach us its virtue. However, rather than letting diversity be an opportunity for shared creativity, tolerance offers us a lukewarm cordiality. It offers cacophony for harmony, stalemate instead of shalom. Tolerance is not a transcendence of individualism but its most natural extension.

In this case, is tolerance what we really need? Let's return to the metaphor of the circle-dance. Dancing involves *harmony* among dancers—something tolerance cannot deliver. Tolerance on the dance floor is a swath of disharmonious individuals doing their own thing. Tolerance would claim that because we're all dancing, we've achieved unity. But the point of community, and of unity in the Bible, is that we are dancing *together*. Tolerance is, after all, a civic virtue in a democracy, not a Christian virtue of the kingdom.

The apostle Paul writes of unity as shorthand for the kingdom of God or the new creation. And like those images, unity is something the universe is bent toward, which has been decisively launched by Jesus Christ but is not yet present in its fullness. The Christian disciplines of reconciliation, service, sacrificial love, and mutual submission make that hoped-for unity real in the present.

That last discipline, loving submission, characterizes Christ's accomplishment on the cross. It is the gate through which Christian unity emerges into the present. Like dancers taking cues from one another and the music, so also in community we move toward unity through mutual submission to one another out of reverence for Christ. We transcend individualism and tolerance by giving ourselves to the bigger story of harmonizing with Christ together.

Consideration: Tolerance and mutual submission both promise unity. Yet the difference between them is that of peace-loving versus peacemaking. Tolerance believes conflict can be overcome without sacrifice. Mutual submission offers the making of genuine peace—defined as the presence of harmony and reconciliation. In this way we escape individualism's orbit.

Contour 10: We are online. As far as I have observed, intentional Christian communities tend to attract persons ill-disposed toward technology. Between enthusiasm for the writings of Wendell Berry, values of simplicity and creativity, and frustration over Facebook-addicted peers, we seem to prefer the real to the virtual. Some of us therefore nurse a healthy skepticism, if not outright grudge, against digital technology.

But that's the minority report of a generation wholly engrossed by their ubiquitous connection to the digital world. Smartphones, social networking, and cloud computing are revolutionizing how humans relate to one another, and the scale of that revolution becomes more evident the younger the person to whom you're talking. It's uncharted social terrain with clear advantages and possibilities, and some real concerns as well. The revolution underway can help humanity flourish—and entrap it.

Most concerning can be the church's lack of shared discernment about technology's limits. And what discernment it has seems strangely polarized, demonstrating depth but not much subtlety. Some techno-entrepreneurs promise this brave new world of ubiquitous virtuosity as the way forward for the church and a thrilling tool for advancing the gospel. Others eschew technology as a symptom of sin and deem it an everlasting kryptonite to authentic Christian community.

A healthier way of exploring this generational contour is practicing *local* discernment concerning the technology we use within and beyond our communities. Discernment can begin with conversations at the household level about how our digital existence may distract us from or assist in our shared lives. You may find, as Springwater has, that tools like Google Calendar are much handier than Twitter or Skype. Or perhaps a household will assign certain rooms to be Internet-free spaces or agree that one week per month will find the Internet unplugged entirely. Some communities, after discussing how easily text-messaging can withdraw people from the present, may begin a tradition of courtesy wherein a verbal conversation trumps any phone call or texting impulse. Still others will balance the consumptive tendencies of our gizmos with creative disciplines of music and cooking.

The point is that discernment will be particular to each community and neighborhood. Communities flush with kids will discern differently from a community of empty-nesters. Some will prioritize restricting how technology intrudes on conversations and household relationships, while others will let minimalism and austerity guide their discernment. We can expect to find communities with both canning equipment *and* iPhones. And when our discernment may be out of whack, it is our friendships of vulnerability and accountability with other communities that can keep us in good health.

Consideration: Technology can have a tight grip on our understanding of human relatedness when we don't patiently question it together. Questioning technology according to its effect on community will be a startling countercultural idea for some intentional Christian communities.

Contour 11: We build our passports, not our résumés. Whenever I arrive at a coffee shop or restaurant, I log into the Gowalla app on my iPhone and "check in" to that business. This lets me keep up on what bars, parks, and cafés my friends are frequenting, check out what others have suggested about wherever I'm at, and sometimes I even get deals if I check in enough to become a "regular." It's a silly thing, to be sure, but I'm kind of hooked on it. (Maybe my community needs to help me do some discernment on this technology!)

Gowalla's passport parallels a disposition I find among many young Christians these days. As we tumble into delayed adulthood, we wind up defining our life so far based on our experiences instead of our accomplishments. Spend a few months volunteering in Africa, immerse yourself in graphic design for a couple of years, try living alone, try living in community, go on a road trip to different churches, be passionate about nonviolence for a while, then move on to protest gender oppression.

Now, I don't mean to belittle any of those things. But this persistent wanderlust and dabbling is an extension of our prolonged adolescence, continuing that season in life where we try to figure out who we are.

More concerning is the possibility that this is really just another version of consumerism. If consumerism is a cultural force of identity formation rooted in personal choice, then we are living in an entire stage of life—the Gowalla years—of choice after choice after choice. People try out intentional community, they've got their passport stamp, feel traveler's itch, and move on.

St. Benedict coined the term *gyrovague* ("circle wanderer") to refer to monks who travel from monastery to monastery, never satisfied with what they find. He said it's a personality to avoid and instructed not to give them the time of day. Now, I won't be quite that harsh with them, but he's got an immensely wise point: this culture of Gowalla years gyrovaguery is toxic to intentional Christian community and needs to be treated with compassionate, but straightforward, honesty and an invitation to healing. The temptation to always be "looking elsewhere" will need to be lovingly addressed.

Consideration: The ordinariness of community life will bother some explorers. The temptation will be to find more thrilling experiences elsewhere or decide that God is calling them to something else. While the latter may be true, the Gowalla itch needs to be publicly discussed.

WHEW, THAT WAS ROUGH!

Confession disciplines us to speak honestly and publicly about our weaknesses. And that is what I have tried to do concerning the current major hurdles in living healthily in intentional Christian community.

Although my own experiences in intentional Christian community give me pause for concern, they have consistently given me even more cause for rejoicing at how wondrously the Holy Spirit has made God's power manifest in those weaknesses. God is good!

PART TWO

IS INTENTIONAL COMMUNITY
YOUR CALLING?

CHAPTER 4
Seeking the Community Where I Am Called

As seekers of community we may look in many places, but the call is to a particular group of persons, local and few, where we will stick and learn the deepest lessons of life on a common journey. We begin with the story of an articulate young college student seeking community where she can let her aching soul be known and grow in capacity for trusting and fruitful relationships. A second type of community seeker is illustrated by a story from the author's youth in which, as an adventurer, he seeks a challenge worthy of his life's devotion. He finds this in Jesus's call to peacemaking and discipleship in community. Sooner or later, both of these two impulses—the need for love and a challenge to serve—emerge and merge in most persons called to community.

I CAME IN SEARCH OF FAMILY AND HEALING
Karima Walker's Story

In high school I made a commitment to Jesus. Though my relationship with Jesus was private, I joined a youth group that reached out to me in many ways and gave me a first taste of community. In my first two years of college I questioned a lot of that. I encountered the shortcomings of trying to find God all by myself, but I didn't have a way to understand my story as God's revelation through other people. In many ways I felt lost.

As a junior at North Park University in Chicago, I took Greg Clark's Intentional Christian Community class. We participated in the Reba Place Fellowship Monday night potluck, followed by small group time and a seminar. This was my first experience in an intergenerational small group. I was able to talk about many of my painful family experiences and share my doubts in matters of faith. Community opened to me in this refreshing model of church that allowed me to be vulnerable and honest about the struggles of my life. I wrote a paper for that class trying to integrate my small group experience with the theology of community and church that went with it. I see now that I came to community in search of family and healing.

Once the class ended, I kept coming back to the potlucks. In fact, I drove the van that brought other North Park students, too. I formed relationships that were powerful for me. At the same time, the theological challenges of Reba also intimidated me. Coming from a more conventional church, I was shaken by this expression of faith where people took Jesus so seriously. It was like culture shock. But I wanted to be with these people who had been so gracious with me, and I wanted to pursue those relationships. I remember a conversation with Greg Clark where I asked in the most timid way if the Clark family might possibly want to maybe invite me to live with them. They did, and after college I moved in.

I was really shy around them for a long time. But they invited me into their family in ways that have been powerfully healing. Watching how Greg and his wife, Heather, communicate with each other and the way Heather interacts with their boys has touched me deeply and helped me see how things are supposed to be in a healthy family. In January 2008, I joined the Reba apprentice program for six months. At the end, in June, I was brainstorming with a friend how we might live in an apartment next to the Clark family. That experiment blew up and my roommate needed to leave. But perhaps because of it, the practical skills of nonviolent (nonthreatening, yet direct) communication began to take root in me. Oddly enough, this isolating and negative experience brought me closer to the Clarks and the community in some important ways. So I became a practicing member at Reba—the first step toward full membership.

I've also done some healing prayer work with a counselor, Charlotte Lehman, that has helped me process other painful and difficult relationships with my peers. It's amazing how these current conflicts and frustrations have churned up old family issues and forced me to deal with them too. But I've been given tools and a safer place to open up without running away, as I had to with my family of origin.

Now that I've found some relational and emotional freedom, I can ask, "What do I want to do with my life?" I probably have some unrealistic expectations to sort through about calling and work. But that is where I feel the tension.

To really grow you need to be rooted in something, somewhere, with a people. I don't have to read Wendell Berry to know that—the message seeps through the walls around here. At the same time, I feel an urgency to try out certain areas of creativity and interest. I've been taking guitar and banjo lessons and dabbling in folk singing. Sometimes I see I might grow here, and at other times I'm attracted to how it might happen in other places. Is this itch just my generation's hypermobility bug, or is something else happening?

I talk about this stuff with my small group and with Greg and Heather, my mentors. I'm facing some deadlines if I want to apply for academic programs or an internship that attracts me. I hope in the next month to ask a few people to be a discernment group, to hear me out and pray with me about all this.

In the past year things have happened in my family that I never would have anticipated, people coming back who relate to me with more maturity and acceptance. I'm so grateful that I've been here while that has happened, to process it with others. It is so exciting and also scary to be going back into the family circle for a visit in the next few days.

Karima shows great courage in sharing her powerfully revealing story. She embodies the rare combination of a wounded soul determined to find healing and a mind able to reflect on that painful journey with integrity and insight.

Karima has taken some very adult steps in accepting responsibility for her own emotional and spiritual condition, asking for the help and healing she needed. Being in community for her has been like going back to school and finishing an "incomplete" that she missed in her family of origin.

Jesus said, "Blessed are those who mourn, for they shall be comforted." The wisdom of this beatitude is apparent when we consider the other options that people often take who have suffered abuse or loss—perceived victimhood, prickly defensiveness, depression, addictions, a series of disastrous relationships, neglect, or abuse passed on to another generation. But when we grieve the ways we have been hurt, the losses we have suffered, we allow others and God to comfort us, to love us and fill in what the Destroyer has taken away. And we are healed—not all at once, but our healing path gives us the tools we need to care for ourselves and, as "wounded healers," to care for others on the painful journey of life. (In chapter 24, "Healing the Hurts That Prevent Community," we look more deeply at the resources of communities that become places of healing for its members and those God sends.)

What Karima's story does not tell, however, are all the ways she has given herself to the Clark family, offered friendship to others in and beyond the community, cared for children, made music, supported various task teams, and served a stint on the Reba Place Fellowship Leadership Team. A few years of community have given her the confidence to emancipate herself, if need be, from her second family. This is a stage of life to celebrate. And having "grown up" in community, she now feels a need to try something on her own—whether this is a break from which she will return or another community that will become her home.

In our age of hypermobility and frenzied distraction, it takes longer for young people to make commitments of marriage and community, to become life-givers to others rather than consumers seeking their own fortune. That is a sickness of modernity. But it has always been a struggle of humans to grow into adulthood, to become soil in which the seeds of new life can sprout, on whom others can depend because of their sustaining connection with God and community.

WORTHY OF A LIFE'S DEVOTION
David Janzen's Own Story

I remember a scene from my childhood where our family was in a huge tent with a big-voiced preacher up front making vivid the torments of hell for those of us who were afraid we might be headed there and offering Jesus as the way of escape. At an early age I did not trust to put my soul in the hands of someone who was scaring the hell out of me. Even though my parents took us to this evangelistic event, I believe I had already gained from them a certain confidence of character that would not allow me to be bulldozed by fear.

I grew up in a solid Mennonite farming family, a generally healthy context for learning basic skills, surrounded by people of integrity who gave me assurance that my gifts were of value. I thought this was everyone's inheritance, and only in my twenties did I discover how broken were my peers and, later on, how broken I was too.

Although raised as a Christian, I had enough experience of rigid authority in local church settings that I felt compelled in college to explore other paths. I could not escape the existential question, "Why are we here?" Many answers beckoned.

To gain scientific knowledge? That's not a bad thing. But science has absolutely no answer to that "why" question. A thousand observations of what *is* will not tell us what we *ought* to be, as I read from the philosopher David Hume. Some scientists, the ones who have made a religion of their craft, say the purpose of life is to expand knowledge— which is as smart as doubling your speed without checking your direction.

The question kept stalking me, "What is worthy of a life's devotion?" How about working really hard to buy a big house and other neat stuff, with enough insurance to take care of whatever might happen, and hope to have a life once I could afford retirement. That direction didn't appeal to me either. Long before my cousin Doris Janzen Longacre wrote *Living More with Less* I was on a path of downward mobility.

We live in a pluralistic age. Many religions and ideologies offer answers to "Why this gift of life?" In my junior year in college I awoke to the realization that I had to major in something besides girls and chose philosophy. I could see that a lifetime of studying ideas would not be long enough to know all the options, much less to decide which one was right and to follow it.

So, what if nothing matters? The prophet Isaiah, 2,500 years ago, already had caricatured that mood with the sarcastic adage, "Let us eat and drink, for tomorrow we die" (Isa. 22:13).

Then, when I was twenty, God found me. In 1961 I was with a group of college students fasting and picketing in front of the White House in protest of atmospheric nuclear testing. If I could translate my wordless experience into English, God was saying something like this: "David, I have prepared you for this kind of work, to be a witness for peace in a world preparing for total war. You are not alone; we can always talk like this. And I will lead you to community with others in that same calling."

At this crucial point in my journey I also happened to read Gandhi's autobiography, titled *The Story of My Experiments with Truth*. His search modeled a very practical path. Each of us must begin with what we know in our own particular tradition and experience of God. The important thing is to make of your life a series of experiments: "Do the truth you already know, and it will lead you to more truth." I had never heard of truth as something you do. For Gandhi, the best of Hindu scriptures and the teachings of Jesus in the Sermon on the Mount led to a profound understanding of the usefulness and truthfulness of the way of nonviolence. Gandhi, the Hindu, understood Jesus better than an imperial Christianity bent on colonizing the lesser nations. "The whole world," he wrote, "knows that Jesus is a pacifist, except for the Christians."

So, on Gandhi's advice, I reread the Sermon on the Mount (Matt. 5–7) and discovered Jesus as if for the first time. And then I started looking for others interested in becoming a community that looked like Jesus. The gift of faith is always a mysterious thing. It is like a hypothesis for life in which one experiment leads to another with more insight and cause for wonder as you go.

Back on campus I sought out Joanne Zerger, who felt a similar calling to peacemaking, having been formed by an Anabaptist Christian community cell group on campus. By God's grace our courtship and marriage made us a community of two. After graduate school and two years teaching in the Democratic Republic of the Congo, we started a family and found others in the antiwar movement seeking a more radical way to live for peace in community. We gathered with other community seekers in Newton, Kansas, to study Jesus, ready to make an experiment of our lives.

As you can see, I lived a lot in the realm of ideas. I wanted a challenge of service as large as the world made new. But what God gave us at New Creation Fellowship was a humble community where we had to let go of some of our visions of peace movement organizing in order to first learn how to live at peace with one another. These sisters and brothers loved me enough to feed back their image of David as hard-edged and judgmental, in need of much grace and forgiveness. My family was breaking down, and I needed to come home from newsworthy projects elsewhere, to learn how to let other people's needs define my life, seek my own healing, become an adult.

So in a surprising way, my journey to community ends up where Karima's story began—searching for love and healing, liberated for service in the family of God. From that humble soil new seeds can grow. But that is a story for another chapter.

My hope is that these two stories might call you to also make an experiment of your life. Perhaps you too are searching for more than religion with a fire-insurance policy. Perhaps you are intrigued by the possibility of journeying with Jesus and his followers, to see if deeper community is a foretaste of the kingdom of God coming "on earth as it is in heaven."

CHAPTER 5

The Gospel Call to Discipleship in Community

One way to observe how the Good News has been straitjacketed by the individualism of our culture is to pick up any collection of contemporary Christian music and count how many songs are about "me" rather than about "us" as the objects of God's love. "Mine, mine, mine; Jesus is mine." You will find the vast majority are actually anticommunal in character, reducing the gospel to a private understanding of God's work in the world, unaware that being a Christian is a team sport. As a sometimes unpoetic experiment, notice how most of these songs would be more powerful, encouraging, and biblical if the pronouns were changed to "we," "us," and "ours." "Spirit of the Living God, fall afresh on *us*." "*We* have decided to follow Jesus." Contemporary worship in the first-person mode, too, is reduced to the experiences of separate individuals who happen to be in the same place rather than a shared experience of the body of Christ united in a common life to care about the things Jesus cared about—the kingdom of God coming on earth as it is in heaven.

The same could be said of most books on "Christian Living" or "Christian Spirituality" in your local bookstore. They, too, are full of personal advice as if the Christian life is all about Jesus helping you to have a better life in the context of the same old world.

This reduction of the gospel to the personal and private is what we might expect in a post-Enlightenment society where individuals claim the "self-evident" rights of life, liberty, and the pursuit of happiness. We have been herded by postindustrial capitalism into a consumer mentality, plugged in and instantly responsive to media-driven needs. What do I want? What will meet my needs? We live in an aggressively anticommunity society, and the church has mostly gone along for the ride. How did we get here?

Two hundred years ago in America (and the rest of the world) most persons still were rooted in extended family systems of support and sharing for survival—living close to the land that provided for most of their needs in common work and shared goods. Those days weren't all good, and what has happened since isn't all bad. But let's try to see where this train is headed and how it compares to the call of Jesus.

By the 1950s the nuclear family had become the norm, with its own house, car, and freedom to move wherever the economy provided a better job. "Automobility," Brandon Rhodes calls it. Now, in the twenty-first century, two-parent nuclear families are increasingly rare, while the majority of housing units are occupied by single persons or a single parent with children. And even where the whole family lives under one roof, each person must have his or her own media center, cell phone, vehicle, and stash of stuff so that no one has to share. Everyone is on a separate schedule so that it is rare for a family to eat together at a common table.

We have become acculturated to an anticommunity society, for which humans were never designed. We suffer increasing stress and social and emotional ills that we hope to heal by more individual therapy and self-help advice. In the history of the human race, the attempt to build a society of accelerating material consumption and disintegrating community is a recent development with many indications that it is unsustainable and will fail.

In such a society it is inevitable that we will look at the New Testament with "me-prescription lenses" and find much of what Jesus teaches strangely out of focus. When we read, for example, "Those of you who do not give up everything you have cannot be my disciples" (Lk. 14:33), we already "know" Jesus did not mean for us to actually do this. This was just another of his typical hyperbolic expressions to shock the disciples into greater dedication. Or, perhaps this message is for peasant societies but not for twenty-first-century urban professionals. Or, he meant for us to have an attitude of detachment about our possessions and give more to charity. Or more likely, we don't even know this verse is part of the Good News because our pastor never had the courage to preach on that text.

Let's take a new look at the social context of the gospel Jesus proclaimed and of those people he recruited as his disciples. First of all, we need to understand that the basic unit of production, consumption, and survival in ancient times was the extended family, the household, which in Greek was called *oikos*. The Greek term for household management was *oikonomia*, from which we derive our word *economy*.

In ancient times (and in most poorer societies today) the extended family household, the *oikos*, had an obligation to take in, feed, and offer a livelihood to any kinfolk who might be in need. Everyone in the *oikos* owed one another solidarity—familial loyalty and basic support. And sons, like their fathers, had an obligation to shoulder the extended family's burdens, as we see immigrants still doing as they faithfully send remittances back home. Ideally, everyone belonged to an *oikos* because apart from it your life expectancy was very short. This was the normal social net, which we see stretched to the limit in the story of the Prodigal Son (Lk. 15:11–32).

However, the Roman military occupation of Palestine put the squeeze on this *oikos* support system. The empire not only demanded the usual taxes for administration of its colonies, but the Romans also demanded tribute—a humiliating extra burden the Jews owed to cover the cost of their own conquest. Add to this the annual temple head tax and the load was crushing to the lower classes. All this money left on a one-way trip to Jerusalem and Rome, centers of power and wealth for which the system was designed. Meanwhile, more and more families fell deeper into debt, forfeiting their land, dignity, and means of survival to creditors (often regional tax collectors) who increased their holdings as the poor increased in number. Under these pressures, the *oikos* system of family solidarity was breaking down. The best hope for the landless poor was to find a patron, like the Prodigal Son, who begged to be taken on as a servant without any rights, rather than starve.

Furthermore, in Jesus's time the Pharisees, in their zeal for holiness, pressured the faithful to shun "sinners" in the fervent hope that God would see a righteous people and deliver them. This destitute underclass, which could neither afford temple sacrifices nor manage all of the requirements of an observant Jewish life, was considered a source of defilement; no decent person would befriend members of this group or offer table fellowship to them.

A desperate multitude of outcasts without communal support roamed the land; these were usually unattached widows and orphans, the chronically ill, daylaborers, beggars, prostitutes, thieves, and would-be revolutionaries whose lives were miserable and short. It was to these people that Jesus directed his disciples first of all. "Go rather to the lost sheep of Israel." That the house (*oikos*) of Israel was not an extended family of care, that the poor were excluded from the common good, was a scandal to Jesus. "As you go, proclaim the message, 'The kingdom of heaven has come near'" (Matt. 10:6–7).

Jesus's movement manifesto spoke clearly to the desperate condition of those on the margins: "The Spirit of the Lord is on me, because he has anointed me to proclaim good news to the poor. He has sent me to proclaim freedom for the prisoners and recovery of sight for the blind, to set the oppressed free, to proclaim the year of the Lord's favor" (Lk. 4:18–19).

"The year of the Lord's favor"?! In the ears of the destitute this could only mean the Year of Jubilee promised in Leviticus (25:10), a year of trumpet blasts and jubilation, when debts would be canceled, prisoners released, and land restored to the original families. None of Jesus's followers could imagine how he might accomplish this without an army to overthrow the Romans and the temple establishment. Nor could his enemies!

His was a stealth operation begun in Galilee, away from the centers of power. Jesus came healing the sick, casting out demons, calling disciples to leave their homes and form a new society on the move, raising hopes by announcing that the kingdom of God was at hand. The vehicle of his revolutionary movement was not an army but a new kind of *oikos*, not one united by bloodlines but by discipleship training in community. Let's look at a familiar story to see how this drama plays out.

> While Jesus was still talking to the crowd, his mother and brothers stood outside, wanting to speak to him. Someone told him, "Your mother and brothers are standing outside, wanting to speak to you." He replied to him, "Who is my mother, and who are my brothers?" Pointing to his disciples, he said, "Here are my mother and my brothers. For whoever does the will of my Father in heaven is my brother and sister and mother" (Matt. 12:46–50).

Jesus called into being a new society within the shell of the old by creating a new family system. "Whoever does the will of my Father in heaven is my brother, sister, mother." The obligation to care for one another that used to belong to the blood family was taken up by communities of disciples that would love and share with whoever wanted to follow Jesus. This was good news to the poor, the "sinners," to the "lost sheep of the house of Israel" who now had a family network where they could belong, share, and find their purpose in the work of God.

To this family, this new *oikos*, Jesus gave instructions for life together such as we see in the Sermon on the Mount (Matt. 5–7). It is an ethic that makes no sense to people who assume the church is a collection of individuals saved for heaven while individually also trying to get ahead in the world. It is a strenuous ethic but livable for those who have been transformed into a "we" that belongs to Jesus.

Notice the pronouns of the prayer Jesus taught his disciples. It begins with "*Our* Father" and refers to "*our* daily bread," which assumes that food is shared. By praying, "forgive *us our* debts as *we* also have forgiven *our* debtors," he makes cancellation of debts and forgiveness of sins a communal practice. "And lead *us* not into temptation, but deliver *us* from the evil one" (Matt. 6:9–13) conveys how much our spiritual battles are won or lost together. Jesus has given us a common prayer for a community of followers that loses much of its content when prayed by isolated individuals.

So, how could this high communal ethic of Jesus, which surpasses the righteousness of the scribes and the Pharisees, include the "lost sheep of the house of Israel"? Jesus instituted two practices that maintained the standard and yet allowed the weakest and poorest to belong in community: first, intensive discipleship training; and second, forgiveness up to "seventy times seven" for those who, after failure, were restored to try again. Jesus insisted that the disciples' *koinonia* ("fellowship, sharing") be extended to the poor and outcast as a matter of salvation. "Truly I tell you, whatever you did for one of the least of these brothers and sisters of mine, you did for me" (Matt. 25:40).

Jesus's discipleship community included both women and men who shared and cared for each other on the road.

After this, Jesus traveled about from one town and village to another, proclaiming the good news of the kingdom of God. The Twelve were with him, and also some women who had been cured of evil spirits and diseases: Mary (called Magdalene) from whom seven demons had come out; Joanna the wife of Chuza, the manager of Herod's household; Susanna; and many others. These women were helping to support them out of their own means. (Lk. 8:1–3)

To his inner circle of twelve apostles, who would soon instruct and form another generation of disciples, Jesus summed up his ethic: "A new command I give you: Love one another. As I have loved you, so you must love one another" (Jn. 13:34). In his teaching, practice, and impending life sacrifice, Jesus himself becomes the definition of love for his ongoing community. And after God vindicated his Son's ministry of nonviolent suffering love by resurrection from the dead, Jesus returned to forgive and restore his band of disciples in disarray, promising the Holy Spirit and commissioning them to "make disciples of all nations," as he had done with them.

The early church in Jerusalem, in the power of the Holy Spirit, embodied the life of Jesus in an emergency *oikos* of five thousand people holding all things in common. They did this by means of many smaller households of shared food and communion, and by a common purse in the hands of the apostles to fund daily distributions of food so that those with larger resources could share with the most destitute (Acts 2:44–47). The *oikos* motto of the Jerusalem community still fit the church as it was scattered all around the Mediterranean: "No one said that anything they had was their own," and "there was not a needy person among them." A generation later, the missionary apostle Paul expected the same of his disciples and of their house churches: "Therefore, as we have opportunity, let us do good to all people, especially to who belong to the family of believers [*oikos*]" (Gal. 6:10).

This, then, is how the early church understood and lived Jesus's saying, "Everyone who wants to be my disciple must give up all their possessions," not as something heroic performed by individuals, but as a way of sharing with the poor, as an extension of the solidarity already experienced in the *oikos* of Jesus with his disciples. This community of "all things in common" is both the means and the goal, the context for training new disciples and a shared way of life that is good news to the poor.

HOW DID WE LOSE THIS "HOUSEHOLD OF FAITH"?

Somewhere along the way, Christianity lost this vocation of "discipleship in community" that was the norm (both as guideline and normal way of life) for early Christians. The space of half a chapter is not sufficient to track twenty centuries of transitions in the twin concepts of "calling" and "vocation." Instead, we will note a few high points of change with some concluding observations.

The story begins with God's calling prophetic figures like Moses and Samuel to be spokespersons and actors directed by God, to save and guide the children of Israel. God's calling becomes their vocation. Jesus is similarly called at his baptism and proceeds to call other disciples, apprentices to a new vocation, announcing and demonstrating the kingdom of God coming on earth as it already is in heaven.

Following Jesus's death and resurrection, the apostles are called to make other disciples to the ends of the earth, disciples in communities who together will do the things that Jesus did, and more. In the early church Jesus's Sermon on the Mount (Matt. 5–7) and similar teachings (Lk. 6:20–49) were the core curriculum, the catechesis of discipleship for new recruits to The Way. Some common New Testament expressions of this calling include "saints" (Rom. 12:13), "in Christ" (Phil. 2:1), "a new creation" (2 Cor. 5:17), and "one new humanity" (Eph. 2:15). Such metaphorical identity markers were at the same time personal and communal, expressing the solidarity "in Christ" of shared economics and salvation.

Three centuries later, Anthony of Egypt left behind a lax urban Christianity and moved into the desert in response to the call of Jesus in the Gospel to the rich young man to "sell all and follow me." During Anthony's lifetime the emperor Constantine made Christianity the imperially favored and fashionable religion, and multitudes of citizens became nominal Christians. A minimal version of Christianity emerged, focused on personal salvation, assured by participation in the sacraments and belief in officially sanctioned doctrines. At the same time thousands of aspiring spiritual athletes flocked to the desert in imitation of Anthony to recapture a more disciplined way of following Jesus. From this time forward we will see the impulse to live a more faithful life of discipleship in community emerge as a persistent minority critique of that alliance of state, dominant culture, and church called Christendom.

Benedict of Nursia, in the sixth century, pulled together some of the best practices of the emerging monastic movement and organized them into a Rule focused on work and prayer that has guided the Benedictines and inspired other monastic traditions to our day. By the Middle Ages celibate priests and monastic orders (both men and women) had church-sanctioned "vocations" to live the life of Jesus with community support, whereas, for the rest of Christendom, Jesus's "counsels of perfection" were considered optional or impossible.

In the sixteenth century, Martin Luther urged the abolishment of convents and monasteries with their "religious vocations," and in their place he taught that everyone had a calling, a vocation from God to "love your neighbor" by performing well the job they happened to fill in society. These vocations, now accessible to everyone, were not based upon discipleship of Jesus but upon whatever the world had become in the way of professions and trades—"butcher, baker, candlestick maker." And because the state needed soldiers, judges, and executioners, Luther "baptized" their roles (despite what Jesus said) by labeling their work a "strange love."

In the eighteenth and nineteenth centuries, fueled by the rise of modern capitalism and the Industrial Revolution, a mobile working class emerged, "freed" from the solidarity of clan and church. They could go as alienated individuals wherever a job awaited them in the economy.

Nowadays, in the hands of vocational counselors and university programs, most young people are steered toward roles in the Mammon economy whence supposedly come all jobs worth having. So the answers to the two questions most frequently asked when meeting someone new—"Who are you?" or "What do you do?"—depend on your niche in the marketplace. That is where you are supposed to find your identity, validation, and the meaning of your life. But in today's global economy, where economic growth and extraction of wealth for those with capital has transcendent value, the system is careless about sustaining vocations for the people in them. The promises of post-college careers often go unfulfilled. Few people actually have careers anymore where they can work long-term in the profession of their training.

After a disheartening week of work, more and more young adults are asking, "Is this all? Is this really what I was created for—to generate wealth for those at the top of the ladder, to earn and consume as if status in this society really mattered?" In our day, Wendell Berry, the new agrarianism, and many communitarian experiments are helping us imagine how local community-scale economies might be re-created. (Further reflection on local economies can be found in chapter 20, "Creation Care, Food Justice, and a Common Table," and chapter 25, "Developing Common Work and Ministries.")

WHAT GENERAL OBSERVATIONS CAN WE TAKE FROM THIS QUICK REVIEW OF "VOCATIONS"?

In every age there have been renewal movements—persistent minority groups seeking to embody the calling of prophetic community life—living alternatives to the dominant state, culture, and church.

The net effect of changing from "city on a hill" communities to a focus on professions, trades, or lines of work has been to lose much of the discipleship content in "vocation." The context of this work has become increasingly secular, individualistic, materialistic, socially fragmented, and faster-paced to keep up with an information-technology-driven system.

Unprecedented economic prosperity has come to half the human race in a global economy that is proving inherently unstable and ecologically unsustainable. At the same time, once basic needs have been met, happiness does not grow along with increased consumption.

The economy is no longer on a human scale (the household or the neighborhood) whose goal is to solve the problem of poverty for the many. Aggressively expanding systems like the Roman Empire (or its imperialist colonial-era equivalents) have been replaced by an aggressively expanding free-market global economy that is designed to maximize return on capital investment. The Marxist critique of this system is only a recent (materialistic) version of a lament already sung by the Hebrew prophets, Jesus, and many Christian saints.

Wendell Berry summarizes this ancient wisdom with the immanent warning: "If you destroy the economies of household and community, then you destroy the bonds of mutual usefulness and practical dependence without which the other bonds [of gentle respect, marriage, and family] will not hold."

It is no wonder that people are seeking something new—which is actually something old! In every generation the Spirit calls Christians to make their vocation "discipleship of Jesus with community support" in seeking a world made new. This core vocation of Jesus followers relegates our jobs in the world to their rightful subordinate place. In this practical way we can exercise our faith, trusting God and the discipleship community for our survival. We are invited to invest our lives with Jesus, who calls us to "seek first his kingdom and his righteousness, and all these things will be given to you as well" (Matt. 6:33).

When the apostle Peter at Pentecost calls for his hearers to be converted, he does not scare them with hell. Instead he sums up his exhortations like this: "'Save yourselves from this corrupt generation.' Those who accepted his message were baptized, and about three thousand were added to their number that day. They devoted themselves to the apostles' teaching and to fellowship, to the breaking of bread and to prayer" (Acts 2:40–42).

The apostle Paul echoes this same call when he writes, "Do not be conformed to this world, but be transformed by the renewing of your mind. Then you will be able to test and approve what God's will is—his good, pleasing and perfect will" (Rom. 12:2). This calling of the Spirit to formation in community for work in the kingdom of God is a vocation for all of us and is credible in every age.

Whenever contemporary Christians are confronted with a call like this, the question soon follows, "Does every Christian have to live in community?" We might note how the question resembles an adolescent bargaining with a parent, "Do I have to?" Let's not despise the question but note, rather, that it represents a certain stage of life. The question begs a legalistic answer from an authority that one is already itching to resist and to leave behind. The question does not have a good answer at the level where it is asked. But let us step back and look at the question from a more adult or discipleship point of view. Let's move the question from fear of damnation to love of God.

Picture an ancient city where Father, Son, and Holy Spirit are leading a circle-dance of thousands in the central city plaza—a joyous expression of the rule of God, a unity in diversity with all good things in common. Somewhere there is an outer boundary to this land surrounded by hostile territory, although as humans we can't know exactly where it lies. We cross that line and enter this new land by saying yes to Jesus, by accepting his healing, forgiveness, and love. This is the line that Nicodemus hesitated to step over when Jesus urged him, "You must be born again." We hear many debates about exactly where that line is and what you have to do to gain the assurance that you are safe on the inside of the border. Often we hear variations on the legalistic adolescent question, "Do I have to?" "Do I have to give up my possessions?" "Do I have to join a community?" "Do I have to accept the poor as my sister and brother?" "Do I have to forgive my enemies?" Sometimes people ask these questions from a consumer's point of view. "What is the least I have to give up in order to possess eternal life?"

Instead, Jesus meets us at the border and invites us to become his disciples, to take on the disciplines of a long hiking journey, traveling with him through that land. On this journey we don't have to worry about the boundary anymore, but the commands of Jesus become part of our training as we journey with him to the city center. Even to the disciples who betrayed Jesus and failed him miserably, he returned and restored them to relationships of belonging and service. Instead of boundary issues they were invited to take on the character of the One they were following. "Love one another as I have loved you." This community with Jesus and his followers can take many forms, but these forms are chosen with the goal of helping us practice the things Jesus taught until they become our second Christlike nature.

Finally, we fully join the circle-dance by dying to self and being raised in the freedom of new life in God. This circle-dance is both the cross of Christ and his new creation. This dying with Christ and resurrection to new life can happen again and again in our life journey. We experience the promise of this eternal life every time we worship with sisters and brothers. This journey takes us from trusting not only that Jesus died for our sins but also that by sharing his cross we can be raised with him into newness of life that is eternal.

Of course, this image of a circle-dancing God at the center of a city plaza is far too simple to explain all of reality. Jesus is not just at the center but also at the edges and beyond the edges of the circle—calling, forgiving, healing, liberating, welcoming sinners home. One parable cannot convey everything that needs to be said about the kingdom of God.

But in this simplified version of the Christian journey we can discern three stages: (1) crossing the boundary with its legalistic "have to" questions; (2) joining with others on a discipleship journey where Jesus's commands become training exercises on the way rather than threats of judgment; and (3) dying with Christ so that we might rise with him in unity of Father, Son, and Holy Spirit. You might recognize the concept, explained in an earlier chapter, of theosis (God becoming like us so that we might become like God) in the second stage and perichoresis (joining the circle-dancing God) in stage three, which is our only vocation, now and forever.

We enter into the freedom of the circle-dancing God (perichoresis) by way of a discipleship community where our character is transformed into the likeness of God (theosis). This is the shape of our journey, our home, our hope for a world made new.

CHAPTER 6

Searching for Your Community:
Visits, Internships, and Mentors

Thousands of young people are awakening to a longing and a call to Christian intentional community. Their interest has been sparked by intense, if brief, experiences of community such as mission trips, attending a Cornerstone or Wild Goose festival, or summer camp experiences with youth speakers who talk about the church as community. They are in college trying out community in a variety of sharing groups and living arrangements. Perhaps they have read Shane Claiborne's *Irresistible Revolution* or Rutba House's *School(s) for Conversion: 12 Marks of a New Monasticism*, and they are exploring this calling by visiting communities or attending Schools for Conversion weekend retreats hosted by established Christian intentional communities. Most Christian communities welcome seekers for brief visits before extending invitations to move in and share life more fully. How do young people go about testing this call to community, what are their experiences, and what counsel can we offer in their search?

This chapter begins with the story of one such seeker, Amanda Moore, currently intern program coordinator at Koinonia Partners in Americus, Georgia. Although her experience of childhood deprivation was extreme, two themes we noticed earlier are present in her search— longing for the love of a healing family and an awareness of God's gifts blossoming within her to create community for others.

Amanda Moore's Story

I was raised in a poor, dysfunctional family. My folks were separated, and my dad died when I was ten. My mom, my older sister, my brother, and I lived with friends or relatives and in local shelters—many nights in cars. Early on I learned what everyone I knew had learned: that the only way to survive was sharing our lives, helping and supporting each other in whatever comes.

My mom was from a huge family of eleven, and there was not much stability in any of their lives. We spent a lot of time living with whichever relative had a house at the time, doubled up—more like a tribal existence.

My mom is bipolar and struggles with depression. When I was in seventh grade, we went into the most severe time with my mom in a mental hospital. We kids stayed with an uncle until he kicked us out. The only stabilizer in my childhood was a backwoods Appalachian Independent Missionary Baptist Church. I couldn't understand the singsong preacher, but I experienced the fellowship of God through the people. When my mom would swallow her pride and ask for help, they cared for us and never treated us like a lost cause. This shaped my understanding of church, and of Christ. This church was the only security in my life. Everything else was going to hell in a handbasket.

Even though I was the youngest child, in some ways I have always been "the responsible one." By the age of ten I was keeping track of our family finances. Already in elementary school I tried to listen to others, to reach out to them rather than just focus on "poor me, poor me."

My brother and sister tried to find help from people in the party scene, doing drugs, drinking—a very unsafe place for a kid like me. I started cutting myself, writing desperate letters to teachers and church people, looking for someone to rescue me.

My cries were actually heard. I had a teacher in seventh grade who became a very close friend. I was a smart student, but I just didn't care anymore. I remember one day I stayed after school to complete a makeup test, and my mom showed up insisting I come home right now. But the teacher confronted my mom (something no one had ever done) and showed her how she could change the situation by supporting my education. My mom did not "get it," but I did. I saw my condition through my teacher's eyes and let her be my mentor.

The next year, things with my family got even worse. I moved in with the principal of my school for a while. I had taken my mom to court, but the court deemed her a fit mother, so I had to go back home. But I refused to stay and landed in a mental institution and then foster care. In that mental institution, with people so full of pain, we did Bible study together, prayed, and really cared for one another. Even though it was not a Christian institution, we were church for each other.

My senior year in high school I stayed with a teacher. It was a time of rest that allowed me to be a child who did not need to worry about how we would pay the bills and if we would eat. I still go back and visit my adopted family.

I ended up going to Milligan College in northeastern Tennessee— half on scholarships and half on financial aid and student loans. At a Christian school, it was tough being surrounded by rich kids who had no material needs. Faith for me had been the clear understanding that God provides. But when I got a job and some income of my own, I had to deepen my understanding of what it meant to be a Christian.

At Milligan, I was introduced to an amazing community at the Hopwood Christian Church on campus. We lived a common life, scheduled our time to pray together early and to eat breakfast and lunch together, so that every day was bathed in prayer and Christian fellowship. For a time I lived with the pastor, Tim Ross, and his wife, Marsha, who were like surrogate parents to me. It was God who orchestrated all this, exactly what I needed.

I am sad for what I've missed in my life, but I've not wallowed in self-pity. I don't feel like a victim. Maybe that is because some people have really mourned with me. Andy Ross (the pastor's son) did this; he sat with me the way people do who are grieving in tribal settings, without needing to fix things or pull you through. He was present with me in that place of pain. I also remember a couple of nighttime adoration services at Milligan College, long times of silence where Professor Phil Kenneson held me in this time of deep sorrow, touching that anguish in its worst and most vulnerable state, acknowledging, "I see your pain and choose to sit here with you in it." That is the truest example of carrying one another's burdens, taking the humble position. Now that I think back over those times, I see how I was given the creativity of learning how to do this with others around me, too.

During my senior year, Andy Ross and other college friends were planning a trip to Koinonia Partners to attend a School for Conversion weekend. Phil Kenneson had shown the documentary about Koinonia called *Briars in the Cotton Patch*, and I knew I had to go. Being at Koinonia was an experience of falling in love. As I entered my twenties, I wanted to make decisions from a spiritually grounded place with other Christians to guide my path in the security that they were seeking God's will.

So after college I came to Koinonia for their three-month internship, planning then to go to Reba. Instead, my friend Andy Ross went to Reba, and I stayed here at Koinonia. Early in my internship I experienced the physical sensation of a calling. Something from the land soaked into the soles of my feet and filled up my spirit. I felt I had been claimed by God for this place.

❖

Amanda's story is extreme in some ways, but intentional communities who welcome young visitors must be ready for refugees from a society that no longer knows how to make commitments to family and community work. Amanda was raised by several mentors and by improvised Christian communities that awakened her to the knowledge that she was loved by God and surrounded by friends. With both feet, Amanda jumped into the opportunities for community that came along, both in receiving and giving love.

She was saved from a victim mentality, not by people pushing advice or good cheer, but by solidarity in her mourning for what was lost. It is fascinating to me, having also sat in mourning circles in the Congo, that this African healing tradition comes from a people with few resources, who must grieve calamities far beyond their capacity to prevent or repair. It is a tradition of contemplative prayer completely accessible to laypeople, a way of waiting on God to heal what humans cannot, and discovering bonds of solidarity and faith stronger than death. Amanda's desperate condition taught her to pray in an equally desperate way, and God has given her faith and love more than equal to the circumstances she has come through.

Amanda's official title at Koinonia is intern program coordinator, but she describes her calling as a "midwife of souls." We hear more from Amanda about the hopes, needs, and longings of her own seeker generation and of the interns she shepherds.

Amanda Moore's Story, Continued

I have read several articles that describe my generation well. In our society, the twenties are becoming an extension of our adolescent period. We're putting off major life decisions till we are thirty. This has been a historical trend over time. Once, young people attended high school, and they put off life decisions until after high school. Then it was until after college. Young people need some space to see where they are going, a time when there is not an academic arrow pointing to the next step. We look for experiences that test us—mission trips, AmeriCorps, time overseas learning another language, and internships in intentional communities.

Young people coming to Koinonia are looking for a lifestyle more challenging than what they commonly see. Most say they want to give back, to serve, to be in a place where they are not number one, where it is *not* "all about me." The way advertising works, it *is* all about *me*, the most important person in the world. There is something in us that knows this is not true, but we cannot envision how a life might work out another way. It helps young people coming to Koinonia to name that they are seekers, seekers of a calling and of community.

❖

Celina Varella came to Reba as an apprentice (Reba's nine-month volunteer program) in 2006, stayed on, married a fellow apprentice, and now is the apprentice program coordinator. Here is how she reflects on the persons who are coming to test their calling for life in community.

Celina Varella's Story

Some of the young people coming to Reba are hopeless about church being possible in the traditional way. They desire to live more simply and are critical of the culture as they've received it. Not everyone wants an intergenerational experience, but those who stay do want to be mentored by people with more life experience and wisdom.

Shane Claiborne's *Irresistible Revolution* is very attractive and has inspiring stories. But it tends to leave out some of the difficult realities, so some young people come with grand hopes that living in community will be the quick solution to every social ill. That is why I like Jean Vanier's book *Community and Growth* because he talks about the realities of just being with people. It is beautifully written, realistic, not cynical, but hopeful.

Last year, when some of our apprentices left before their terms were over, the rest of us read through Wendell Berry's *Sex, Economy, Freedom, and Community*. He explains how much we are shaped by consumerism— why certain people are looking for community as "something that meets my needs," rather than being transformed into a relational vision of what one's needs really are.

Some young people come hoping to find a place of healing. For those who want to work through the pain of family experience, they find this a supportive home. At the Patch, a Reba household of young adults, several of us were going through counseling of various sorts—professional therapy, Immanuel Healing prayer, meeting with mentors (see chapter 24, "Healing the Hurts That Prevent Community"). Supportive community helps the healing process. In this safe place I can be the same person on the outside with others as I am on the inside with myself and God.

❖

Celina recalls the importance of Jean Vanier's writings on her journey. In *Community and Growth* Vanier observes the need for "intermediate communities," places of healing and self-discovery between the parental home and the community to which young people feel called and ready to make an adult commitment of their lives. He writes:

Our world has more and more need of . . . places where young people can stay and find a certain inner freedom before they make their decision. They need somewhere where they can find their inner liberation through a network of relationships and friendships, where they can be truly themselves without trying or pretending to be anything other than they are. . . . It is only when they discover that they are loved by God and by others, and that they can do beautiful things for others, that they begin to get in touch with what is deepest in them. . . .

For a community to play this intermediate role, it must have a core of people who are really rooted there. Many people come to L'Arche [Vanier's community] having left school, university or a job which is no longer satisfying. They are seekers. After a few years they discover who they really are and what they really want. Then they can go to a more specific religious community, marry, go back to work or take up studies which now really interest them.

Others choose to stay. The community is no longer simply their place of healing, a place where they feel good and happy, but the place where they have decided to put down roots because they have discovered the call of God. . . . They too have personal plans—to stay in the community.

On the journey from the parental home and school to adult commitments, many young people spend stages of service in several communities until they finally feel the freedom to stay, or to take their experiences on to a new way of life and service in society. For this reason many communities have added internships and volunteer programs with various different names. Church of the Sojourners in San Francisco accepts "practicing members" for a year at a time. Koinonia Partners calls them "discerning members." This stage of seeking can be compared to looking over the field of marriage prospects, gaining some discernment, and growing in maturity till one is capable of commitment.

Thus far, we have observed two paths that often lead to community—the search for a healing family and the challenge of service. But mingled with these two is a third path that seldom leads to commitment. In the sixth century, Benedict of Nursia, in his Rule for what became the Benedictine Order, warned about certain monastic visitors called gyrovagues. These visitors have an unrealistic list of expectations that in today's context might look something like this: "I'm looking for a community that gardens, connects me with homeless people, with racial diversity, and no authority figures that remind me of my dad. I'm looking for a group that sings my favorite songs, thinks it is cool to rip off megacorporations, and where I can take a day or a month off whenever I feel stressed."

These community visitors remind me too much of myself, finding something wrong with every group they meet, taking a long time to discover that God calls us to love and serve in imperfect communities—the only kind there are. They want discipleship, but only if they are the ones directing the process. Lest we scoff at them, gyrovagues represent the highest virtue of our contemporary society, "keeping your options open."

Some of the issues they bring are best dealt with by saying, "We are not the community you are looking for." Some actions should be confronted as soon as they arise, while other behaviors should be borne with until relationships grow strong enough to face them. And if these restless souls stick around long enough, they may be ready for a season of sincere discernment about God's will for their lives. They might be ready to ask, "What changes do I need to make in my life to be ready for community?" And, "Does the love I feel here mean I am called to stick around as a novice member?" Questions like these will be the theme of our next chapter.

And now, a few words of counsel for seekers and explorers of a vocation to community:

- Find a mentor who has made life choices you can respect, someone who can listen and pray with you as your experience of community unfolds.

- Arrange to visit several communities or sign on as a volunteer. Give yourself fully to these experiences, which is how you will learn the most about the community and yourself.

- Don't be surprised when a community disappoints you or does not match up with your ideal. This will happen anywhere you go. Do your best to complete your service without gossiping about your disappointments. Rather, talk directly with persons in charge of your program or with someone in a position to do something about your concerns.

- It is okay to have a list of reasons why a community may not be right for you. But also keep a list of reasons why you are not yet ready for community. That is the list you should work on with your mentor, sharing group, or prayer partners.

- Don't hang out just with your peers. Talk to people who have loved a lot, lost a lot, and love anyway. Find out why.

Finally, here are a few questions that might help you know if you are one of the gyrovagues:

- Are you present as an observer rather than a participant?

- Can you listen to someone tell you your shortcomings and respond, "Thank you for caring about our relationship. I'll think about what you have said."

- Have you been checking out possible communities for more than two years and found them all lacking?

- Are your work habits useful as a community volunteer, or are you there mainly as a guest? If you are a guest, do you leave a donation?

CHAPTER 7
Novice Membership:
Testing Your Call Against the Community's
Questions and Your Own

A novice is giving her visiting friends a tour, and as they walk she talks about the community in terms of "us," "we," and "ours." A year ago she herself was a guest. What has happened? A mysterious transformation of identity involving pronouns and much more.

The previous chapter was about seekers reading up on communities, visiting, getting acquainted with different groups, and signing on as interns or volunteers. In the process, they come to understand their own sense of calling, gathering the experiences and the maturity they need to make a commitment.

For each seeker the call comes with personal questions attached. Karima observes, "I have learned to love these people who have loved me so well." Jolyn says, "I'm tired of connecting with people who keep moving on. I want to put down roots and go deep in relationships." Johnmark says, "I have this creative energy, these musical gifts. I think this is where God wants me to serve and be fruitful with them." Katie and Eric say, "This is where we want to raise our family, with people we respect, whose lives embody the values we hold dear." Josh and Candace say, "We feel called to one day start a community, but first we want to soak up some wisdom, so we can share what we have lived." They all wonder, "Does this mean we are supposed to join?"

The *novitiate* is a term borrowed from monastic experience, the last stage of testing whether the applicant is called to community membership.

The novice is saying, "I am done looking around. I think God wants me to join this community, but I have a few issues I still need to work through." Sometimes it is like a couple that is "in love," but nevertheless they are trying to ask the right questions, to be careful they aren't enraptured into a hasty marriage.

To understand this testing process better, let us look at a sample set of questions for novices from an imaginary community we will call Fellowship of the Beloved. The introduction and questions appear in italic type and will be interspersed with my commentary from other community experiences. I hope this chapter can be useful for novices exploring community membership, for the mentors who give them guidance, and for communities setting up their program for the novice year.

Fellowship of the Beloved: Questions for Novices

"I am my beloved's, and my beloved is mine." (Song of Songs 6:3)
"This is my Son, whom I love. Listen to him!" (Mk. 9:7)

Introduction: Just as Jesus gave everything for us, joining the body of Christ here with the Fellowship of the Beloved is our practical way of giving everything we are and have to Jesus. Liberated by the forgiveness of sins and empowered by the Holy Spirit, we are called by God to a transformed life in covenant with others, an expression of God's kingdom now, a foretaste of the age to come.

We live in a postdoctrinal age. A younger generation has little use for long belief statements crafted by the winners of old controversies. Rather, they appreciate the challenge of a community focused on a simple response to Jesus and his call "to come, and follow me." How do we become disciples in our time? Many novice groups start by studying Jesus's Sermon on the Mount, as did the catechumens of the early church. When we do, we discover the truth of Jesus's words: "I, when I am lifted up from the earth, will draw all people to myself" (Jn. 12:32). The period of novice membership is meant to move us from one world to another. We are resident aliens, created for citizenship in the kingdom of God.

The following questions point to a conversation we want to have with each novice to discern if God is calling you into covenant membership with us at Fellowship of the Beloved.

The novice period is a time of deep personal review to see how discipleship of Jesus engages each area of the novice's life. Jesus asked his disciples to renounce many good things: possessions, family, resentments, control of one's own life, and more. These renunciations are part of the good news, a way to make space in our lives for the kingdom of God. The novice questions are a way to make real this transfer of loyalty, behavior, and identity, which began at conversion. Some of these "questions" may raise no issues—they have already been "covered" in the novice's spiritual journey. But others may be a source of tension and call for further conversation and prayer. As St. Benedict says in his Rule concerning novices, "Test the spirits to see if they are from God."

Are you developing a spiritual life of regular conversation with God nurtured by common prayer, listening to the Lord, corporate worship, Bible study, and times of contemplation? In what personal spiritual disciplines do you want encouragement and accountability?

New Age spirituality grasps that certain meditative practices enhance the quality of life, but the self is still at the center, a selective consumer of new experiences. Christian formation, instead, is the way all of life is ordered from the center where we are in conversation with God. In our spiritual disciplines, many of us feel like we are always starting over, just learning how to pray, sometimes restless and sometimes deeply fed.

We are social beings who can sustain private disciplines much better when we are carried and carrying others on a common Spirit-led journey.

We grow in Christ by being in an environment where it is natural to ask one another, "What are you hearing from the Lord in your quiet times?" "What have been your desolations and consolations this week?" By asking questions like these and by listening well, we draw water for one another, reviving thirsty souls.

For most novices, a profound transformation is taking place, which Jesus compared to yeast that silently leavens a lump of dough, a field of grain that grows overnight. These images reflect how it is possible for someone to wake up one morning and discover they are at peace with a life committed to following Jesus with these brothers and sisters, come what may.

Is the practice of confession of sins, forgiveness, and reconciliation in relationships operational in your life? Do you understand Jesus's call to peace and nonviolence, including love of enemies?

The novice year is a crucial time to make an inventory of past relationships in order to reconcile what is broken. "As far as it depends on you, live at peace with everyone" (Rom. 12:18). This is especially a time for the novice to examine if she is carrying resentments forward into community life, or has she forgiven those who have hurt her? Does he practice gracious confrontation when someone offends him? How is the novice called to grow in courage and initiative as a peacemaker in this world?

Are you submitting basic life decisions to the spiritual discernment of your small group or people in the Fellowship? Are you willing to stay or be sent according to the Spirit's leading as discerned in the body of Christ at Fellowship of the Beloved?

We believe that "where two or three are gathered together" Jesus is there among us. Making decisions together creates a bond of solidarity.

If our deepest desire is to know and do God's will, then submitting our most important decisions to prayer and counsel with others increases the likelihood that we will not just make good decisions, but we will also be bonded to sisters and brothers who support us to live them out.

Given the hypermobility of our society and the high virtue it places on "keeping our options open," making an open-ended commitment to join an intentional Christian community sets off alarm bells in friends, family, and one's own individualized soul. For many young people, four years of college is the longest they've ever lived in one place. We've all been socialized as gyrovagues. The macho motto says well how some people feel about accountability: "When the going gets tough, the tough get going—right out of here!

Not running away from difficult relationships is definitely countercultural—we have to justify it, which is what Jonathan Wilson-Hartgrove has artfully done in his book *The Wisdom of Stability*. He writes, "Those on a spiritual quest for a place to call home are not alone. Benedictines, the Amish, Desert Mothers and Fathers as well as contemporary agrarians offer deep wisdom about what it means to commit to stability." Stability of relationships involves a willingness to stay the rest of one's life or to be sent in mission by the community, should God so lead. This vow recognizes that God's work is larger than the local community.

Do you accept Jesus's teachings regarding renunciation of personal possessions, and is this your intention regarding your own belongings? Are you ready to join in the community of goods, to live simply and be content with what you have, be generous and share with others, trust God for future needs, and receive everything with thanksgiving? Do you believe God is calling you to freely share your spiritual gifts and material resources, and do you understand how this works at the Fellowship of the Beloved?

Of the early Jerusalem church Luke writes, "No one claimed that any of their possessions was their own," and "there were no needy persons among them" (Acts 4:32 and 34). There are many different ways to administer these commitments of mutual love and care. At Jubilee Partners in Comer, Georgia, the covenant members receive a monthly allowance, and the other necessities are paid for from a common treasury. At Church of the Sojourners in San Francisco, the earners hold back an agreed-upon allowance from their paychecks and turn the rest over to the common fund for good works in and beyond the community. Other groups have a more informal way of sharing that honors the same commitments.

The novice year allows someone to ask their questions and to try on the economic disciplines of the community while observing how others make it work. By experience we learn to trust that others will care for us when we may be in need, which sets us free to care for others in their need now.

Do you understand how Fellowship of the Beloved works on a practical and organizational level? Do you know how to access shared resources either to give or to receive?

I remember talking with Eric who announced one day, "I feel like I belong here; I am part of the operation." He had found a niche of meaningful service, part of the community team. He felt free to invite his friends and to include them as volunteers in the bicycle repair co-op that he and other interns were starting up even before he became a member. Often the newest arrivals in a community are in the best position to connect with and welcome visitors and volunteers. It is crucial that everything is explained to them so that they can own what is happening. And if they have critical questions about why things are done a certain way, it is vital for them to have nondefensive conversations with the community where the novice is invited to become part of the solution. Of course, the community should not change its mission to please a novice, but novices can bring new insight and energy in pursuit of the mission. Neither the novice nor the community is a finished product.

Amanda Moore describes this important transition in her journey toward membership. "Most recently, in my prayers I've discovered that the very thing I want from Koinonia, God is asking me to bring. Koinonia is still learning how to be a community that runs a business rather than a business that happens to have a community. God is asking me to not wait for all that to come together before I decide, but to be a part of the unfolding plan that gets us there."

Do you seek to maintain sexual integrity in thought and behavior, whether in singleness or marriage, with support from the community, as taught by Jesus?

Our society's confusion about sexuality, resulting in an epidemic of broken families and scattered children, has scarred us all. At the heart of this confusion is the individualistic notion that how I live out *my* sexuality is *my* own business. All the "my's" in that sentence ignore the reality that I did not create myself or raise myself, nor am I capable of making myself happy. As long as my frame of reference is meeting my own needs, I will exploit others and remain emotionally alone.

Jean Vanier, founder of L'Arche communities (which have persons with mental and emotional disabilities at their core), has written with profound simplicity about the wound of loneliness that each of us carries, along with unique gifts from God to bless others. We cannot put our gifts and our loneliness together by ourselves. How can our characters be formed so that we become capable of intimate, life-giving relationships with integrity in the way of Jesus? We can only be fully human in some form of community, sharing our gifts to heal each other's loneliness in authentic friendships and celebration of God's presence.

Henri Nouwen writes about "chastity as a communal virtue." This is not some external rule to keep us apart, but the only way for us to live close together in mutual respect and freedom. In community both our behavior and our thoughts affect one another. Jesus is right in saying that the battle for genuine relationships needs to be fought in our imagination, and our behavior will follow.

"Support for celibate singles alongside monogamous married couples and their children" is the eighth mark of the New Monasticism, a fair summary of the teachings of Jesus and the apostolic letters to the early church. This is not a new legalism, but an offer of support for a particular way of life where brotherly-sisterly bonds of love can grow and make a loving home for persons in all stages and conditions of life, especially children.

> *Has a bond of trust formed between you and other Fellowship of the Beloved members? Do you sense that you belong to this people, to serve and be served, to give and receive admonition? Is it natural for you to talk about Fellowship of the Beloved as "we," "us," and "our"?*

How does trust grow? A newcomer has a conflict with someone in community, but they take time to listen to each other well and are reconciled. Trust grows by being tested and passing the test. Of course, we do not all come to community with healthy souls but rather come with a mixed history of wounds that have been healed and some that have not. This question encourages the novice and the community to review the barriers to trust that exist and to face them in a timely way. (See chapter 24, "Healing the Hurts That Prevent Community," for a deeper discussion of this theme.)

> *Are you in a personal mentoring relationship, and are you mentoring others in the way of Jesus?*

Benedict writes in his Rule, "A senior chosen for skill in winning souls should be appointed to look after the newcomer with careful attention." Young people come with their own worlds of ideas and experiences from various subcultures as their centers of meaning. Spiritual formation will involve extensive conversations—not to indoctrinate but to accompany as the Spirit helps newcomers sort out their authentic experiences of God from the false paths they have taken.

Spiritual direction, however, is not just for novices. This practice will make sense to novices if everyone in the community is included in the network of care. Mentors need spiritual direction, and novices, too, should be encouraged to pray for and care for others younger or more unsupported than they are. We often discover the neediness of our own souls and desire for spiritual guidance as we care for others.

We are a people in mission. Can you affirm the Fellowship's mission? Are you prepared to offer your gifts and passion, as God gives you grace, to seek the welfare of the people in this neighborhood where God has planted us, with special attention to the poor?

Some communities can welcome a wide range of seekers and shepherd them into fruitful participation, whatever their life stage. But other communities have a more specific charism, a gift or ministry at the heart of their common life. For L'Arche, this is sharing life with persons who have mental and emotional disabilities. For Jubilee Partners, it is running a welcome center for immigrants and peacemaking. It is fair for some communities to only accept members who can contribute to their mission, referring other seekers to communities that might be a better fit.

It is easier to belong, to make a membership commitment, when we are connected in friendships and meaningful work, but finally only God can be trusted to be there for us all the time. Jolyn Rodman, one of Reba's novices, wondered if she needed to know all the members of the community well before joining. "As an introvert, I realized this was never going to happen. But I came to trust that they all wanted to follow Jesus just as I did, and that God would speak through them too when we made decisions together." Joining a community of Jesus-followers is an act of trust in God, who has called us together, and nothing on the journey can separate us from God's love.

At Jolyn's membership celebration, she peeled an onion as she talked about the dry and crusty layers of self that had to come off, with plenty of tears, in order to reveal a fresh and savory person, free to blend her gifts in the rich and nourishing stew of community life. The joy shining in her eyes above moist cheeks and a sniffly voice filled in what words could not say. Then the novices had their feet washed by their mentors, and they washed their mentors' feet in return—what Jesus asked us to do for one another to remember him. To conclude the ceremony, one of our longtime members, Anne Gavitt, read a new poem, gently reminding us of the transition of relationships, human and divine, temporal and eternal, happening here before our eyes.

Membership Lines

We can't welcome you aboard
because you've been sailing among us
for quite some time

And we can't open the door for you
because you already dwell in the
house of God

We can't gather you into the family
 because you have been encircled in the
arms of God since your first "yes" to Jesus

But the "yes" which you now say
draws you into this particular
peculiar
circle of dance

Tonight you can
set down your suitcases on the bunk
unpack your things and
settle in to your new berth

We look around at each other
with hope—the sure kind—
that at the next port of call
you will still be with us
and we will still be with you

PART THREE

BEFORE YOU MOVE IN TOGETHER

CHAPTER 8

Dreaming the First Steps of a New Community

Marijke and her friend Kara wanted to meet with me concerning their leading to start a new community. Marijke said that she read the first chapters of Acts in high school and determined that she would one day live in such a community. When she got to North Park University in Chicago, she confided her longing to Kara, who not only shared the same dream but also knew of some communities like that. Marijke had no idea they existed. They were both eager to sign up for philosophy professor Greg Clark's class "Christian Intentional Community," which meets on Monday nights following a Reba Place Fellowship potluck—which is where we met and how I heard their story.

Dreams of Christian community can begin early.

So, how does a dream like this move to reality? The crucial developmental tasks and the order in which they should be faced depends upon a group's prior community experiences, the gifts within the wannabe community, and the context in which they are called to live out their mission. But for the sake of clarity and simplicity, I have gathered these topics in subsequent chapter headings under part three, "Before You Move In Together," and part four, "The First Year of Your Community." And there is much to learn ahead in part five, "Growing Tasks for a Young Community," and part six, "How a Mature Community Becomes Soil for God's New Seeds."

But before you start a new community, let's take a look at what might lie ahead by continuing the story of Luke Healy (begun in chapter 1) and a group at Kansas State University hearing the call to plant themselves in Kansas City, in the zip code with the highest population of murderers in Missouri prisons.

Luke Healy's Story

When I shared about the location with our campus pastor, he remembered a ministry years ago where he had volunteered in the area. He brought us to this giant limestone church building to meet with Pastor Howard, head of an African American congregation, the New Rising Star Missionary Baptist Church. We were there only for a few minutes when the pastor said, "We have thirty thousand square feet here, most of which we're not using. So if you want to base your ministry out of here or live here, you're more than welcome."

After seeing the space we were very excited, but also moved to pray about it for a time, till we all felt confirmation. We were given the third floor of the building—offices, classrooms, meeting spaces—but no one had ever lived there before. We had to build out a bathroom and kitchen, run plumbing up from the basement, add electrical work, and enclose bedrooms. It was a lot of work, but three months later, in June of 2008, we moved in.

For the first month we still had no hot water, which led to somewhat unclean dishes and brisk showers. We spent the first six months without a stove, making endless trips up and down three flights of stairs to the church basement kitchen, carrying food for nine people. It was mid-February of a brutal winter before we got the furnace and ductwork installed to half our space, including the kitchen and bathrooms. You won't believe how cold a toilet seat can get!

Through the process of our relocation, we talked with others we knew who had a heart for the city and a desire for community living. This led three others to join us before we moved in, and a few more within the first year of our existence. At the same time, half of our original community from K-State ended up leaving, due to differences between expectations and reality, and changes in life situations. We've had two weddings. The cast of characters keeps changing.

These first two years have called for a lot of patience and grace, a season we named "Introduction and Preparation." It's been an introduction to this neighborhood, where we come in humility—not assuming we can splash in and fix things; introduction to being the outsider, the minority in a completely different racial and social landscape; introduction to a new way of living in community—dying to self and the strong inclinations ingrained in us toward an independent lifestyle. For us it has been a time of preparation in making our space livable; preparation for what our work in the neighborhood will be; preparation in prayer to be led by the Holy Spirit so that our lives might flow from intimacy with Christ; and preparation to learn more about our neighborhood, about community— its pitfalls and opportunities.

We are still searching for concrete expressions of work in the neighborhood. We know we want to be a place of peace. We have the beginnings of a small urban farm as we transform old overgrown asphalt parking lots into places of life and nourishment. And we continue to search for a lifestyle of grace with each other, as well as life-giving rhythms of worship and prayer that work for us all.

❖

The story of this emerging community illustrates the need for a new group to come to unity on a huge number of issues, some of which they have begun to face—mission, location, diversity, learning to pray and worship together, reconciling relationships after conflicts, discerning leadership gifts. Many other issues are still before them, such as settling on a rule of life, agreeing who is inside and who is outside the group that will make long-term decisions, orienting and offering formation to new members, and deepening partnerships with leaders in the neighborhood.

It is impossible to just dream about community because the dream immediately calls for "experiments in truth" toward a common life. Mark Scandrette has written a book for this stage of community development, *Practicing the Way of Jesus: Life Together in the Kingdom of Love.* Scandrette observes that we don't read or think our way into a new way of living, but as we practice together with others what Jesus taught, making a series of experiments with our lives, we are transformed into a new way of living and thinking as well. Scandrette and his widening circle of friends have conducted a decade of such kingdom of God experiments. His book tells the results with instructions for others to conduct similar experiments with their friends, time, and possessions. Such experiments can be a way to gather tools for the kit of "community in mission." However, there is also a great temptation to keep on collecting community-like experiences without actually being transformed by laying down your life with others on a committed journey of faith, without looking back.

Launching a new community from scratch can be a lot like crossing the ocean while building your boat, a perilous undertaking at which many—actually, most—groups fail. But guidance from the experience of other communities that have "made it" thus far, by God's grace, can also make a huge difference. Drawing from the wisdom of their experiences I will give three reasons why launching a community from scratch is impossible—and nine ways you don't have to do it from scratch.

WHY IT IS IMPOSSIBLE

Too many issues to agree on. A new group needs to come to unity on a huge number of issues: mission, diversity, location, a common way of resolving conflicts, polity (your manner of making decisions), gender gifts and differences, as well as thinking about how to worship and pray together, recognize and trust spiritual gifts, work out financial support, determine who decides these things, all while becoming each other's primary social group. Trying to do all this without accompaniment from more experienced communities is like being the midwife and the baby at the same time.

Lack of practical wisdom. Most of us have little previous experience of deep community, and so we lack the apprenticeship, the tool kit, the shared experience with "masters of the craft" that prepare us to make good judgments about common life. These habits and skills, for the most part, cannot be learned from books but need to be absorbed from shared life experience.

People eager to start communities usually have high motivation and are flush with the ideals of community but are deficient in what Aristotle in his *Ethics* called "practical wisdom" (*phronesis*). Guidelines and recipes are useful, and this book offers a few of them, but we are always dealing with situations that, although like previous experiences, are different. They fit certain rules, but never exactly. Practical wisdom brings together general principles, reflection upon life experience, empathy, and a keen awareness of what is unique about the present people and moment in a way that, over time, becomes second nature to us.

Most of us are capable of practical wisdom, but not right away. Participation in communities of various sorts and wide reading are helpful, as are mentorships and committed relationships. For Christians, our wisdom ultimately comes from discipleship to Jesus, in a personal relationship nurtured by prayer, inspired and guided by the Holy Spirit. Our wisdom grows by discerning and exercising our spiritual gifts, by practicing the things Jesus taught and by sharing a life of mutual love and forgiveness as we grow to maturity with other Jesus-followers.

Personal transformation needed. Contrary to what you may have heard about intentional communities, other people are usually not the problem. We come into community having internalized many of the world's values and vices—of which we only gradually become aware as they cause conflicts and tensions within the group. We need to be resocialized from independence into interdependence, something that normally takes new community members several years of visits, internships, and novice membership to grow into.

An early Reba leader, John Miller, once named three idolatries of our age—mars (Mars was the Roman god of war), mammon (money), and me (individualism)—that oppose community both from without and also because we carry them within. To these idolatries we might add a few other barriers including sexism, racism, and classism, as well as defensiveness from past experiences of broken relationships. As we learn to graciously confront and forgive each other in such matters, a space opens up for healing and conversion of life to happen. It was in this spirit that an early Christian monk also once compared community to a bag of rough stones shaken together until its members become polished gems.

YOU DON'T HAVE TO DO IT FROM SCRATCH

A new community is most likely to thrive if a mature existing community births it. (See chapter 28.) But God works by other means as well. Here we will briefly list ways a newly forming group can increase its prospects for sustainability. Such a community:

1. Sees that the primary purpose of its life is to become disciples of Jesus, dying to self so that they may be raised into a new way of life that takes on the character and mission of the One they follow together. In other words, they already have a leader.

2. Takes adequate time (at least a year) to work on its relationships, mission, and spiritual unity before moving into a common life.

3. Has significant previous community experience among its members.

4. Has a mentoring relationship with a pastor or coach from a more mature community.

5. Has a pattern of visits to and from other intentional Christian communities so that the members can imagine other ways of doing things than their own. (See chapter 16.)

6. Has a relational connection to the larger church of Jesus Christ. (See chapter 17.)

7. Has a modest but focused mission that fits its members' gifts, location, and discerned leading of the Holy Spirit. (See chapter 18.)

8. Has a core of members with a vowed long-term or lifetime commitment.

9. Affiliates with a larger association of communities in a covenant of mutual care and support. (See chapter 27.)

So, if you are called by God to begin a new community, be prepared for an intensely educational, personally transforming, relationally bonding season of life covered by much prayer. What is impossible for humans is possible for God.

CHAPTER 9

Transforming Conflict into Solidarity

Many frustrating community meetings can be traced back to unresolved conflict between members. We need to learn to face conflict and turn it into solidarity. When we are intentional about confessing and forgiving sins—whatever we might hold against each other—a desire for unity follows, making community meetings a joy, filled with the tangible presence of God.

In his Sermon on the Mount, Jesus says, "Therefore, if you are offering your gift at the altar and there remember that your brother or sister has something against you, leave your gift there in front of the altar. First go and be reconciled to them; then come and offer your gift" (Matt. 5:23–24).

In times of conflict—and it is important to note that *conflict* is not always bad—our initial reaction, depending on our personality type, is usually fight or flight. For some of us the first temptation is to get even, to gossip and build up a power base of support with our friends so that we can win when the conflict comes to a head. The opposite temptation is to protect ourselves by increasing our distance in the hurtful relationship, or to take the spiritually superior attitudes of "forgiving in our heart" and perhaps even "suffering for righteousness' sake." But Jesus has given us a third way, which the Thirdway Community in Minneapolis has claimed as its provocative conversation-starter of a name.

In Matthew 18:15–20 Jesus outlines a three-step redemptive process for his disciples to follow whenever conflict arises in the church community. By putting this "Rule of Christ" into practice, communities soon accumulate a storehouse of practical wisdom and memory of reconciled relationships that inform further practice.

The first step is simple and straightforward: "If your brother or sister sins, go and point out their fault, just between the two of you. If they listen to you, you have won them over" (Matt. 18:15). We have all experienced someone coming to us with a beef, letting us know that we have hurt or angered them in some way. We have probably encountered people who do this in aggressive outrage, blind to their own part in the dynamic. And we know people who come to us from a more humble concern for the relationship, something like this: "David, I am troubled and hurt by something you said yesterday and want to talk with you about it some more. Here is what I observed. . . . I wonder, how do you see what happened? Help me understand how we can make things right. I want a better relationship with you." With such a conversation opening that avoids judgment and shame, mutual confession, forgiveness, and reconciliation usually follow. The Holy Spirit is active in such moments, moving us both to see our faults and to desire unity. This process is easier in community if we have already studied Jesus's teaching in Matthew 18 and agreed that this is how we want to handle the inevitable conflicts that come up between us.

I've lived in community long enough to see others model for me how to listen well when someone is outraged and abusive in sharing his hurt. Here at Reba, Julius Belser is remembered for walking into the home of a hysterical neighbor who was shouting threats and brandishing a gun at the police outside. After half an hour, the two walked out together with the gun in Julius's hand—a standoff diffused. Here is someone I can learn from. He is my mentor.

"The first challenge," Julius explained, "is to just listen, and to keep listening without rebuke until all the emotion has been heard out, until the speaker has gotten to the bottom of his concern and feelings. Ask humble questions until you can repeat the main concern and feeling of offense to his own satisfaction." Some conciliation experts have described this stage as "arriving at accurate empathy."

"Having validated the speaker's concern," Julius continues, "then I can take my turn to speak about the way I experienced events and to suggest how we might repair what has gone wrong. It is amazing how God is present in moments like that to draw us together in forgiveness and a new vision for living at peace. However, if after doing our best, one of us still feels like we have not been heard, it may be time to bring in one or two other persons that we trust, to help us mediate the conflict."

This brings us to the second stage of Jesus's process for reconciling relationships: "But if they will not listen, take one or two others along, so that 'every matter may be established by the testimony of two or three witnesses'" (Matt. 18:16). Sometimes, we have learned, it is acceptable for the process to start at this second stage. Perhaps one of the parties to the conflict is too afraid to talk without a support person at her side. Or the conflict seems so complex (like the story that follows) that everyone agrees to start with a mediator.

Tensions had been growing for the Mustard Seed, making community-planning meetings an increasingly frustrating experience for everyone. As they talked with each other in my presence, I learned that Eric and Betty (a couple) often met with Ruth because they lived next door to each other. From these spontaneous conversations they would go out for coffee or to share a midnight snack, building an intimate friendship and coming to agreement on directions they hoped their fledgling community could take. Martin (the designated community leader) and Eloise (his wife) were never included in these spontaneous relationship-building and conviction-forming conversations.

As we talked about this polarizing dynamic and the feelings of estrangement that had grown up around them, the conversation went a bit deeper. Eric, Betty, and Ruth all assumed that Martin and Eloise wanted to be left alone because they were newlyweds. Martin and Eloise acknowledged that this had been their wish at first, but now they felt ready to widen their circle of active friendships. Furthermore, Ruth and these two couples are the only ones who had made a long-term commitment to this young community, while others who came to the meetings had not. The five came to see their unique leadership responsibility to the larger group. Their lack of unity was affecting everyone.

After apologizing and forgiving each other for contributing to the estrangement, they were amazed to suddenly feel a tender closeness of spirit with one another. They were eager to build on this moment of reconciliation by getting together on Friday nights and dreaming together about the future of the community at times when undecided participants and guests were not present. They also agreed to fill in the rest of the group about this meeting and their need for it.

Notice how many things are going on at the same time in this story. It is not apparent that anyone was deliberately doing wrong, and yet estrangement was growing. No matter who feels it first, any source of tension or conflict is reason to enter into dialogue with reconciling intent. Furthermore we cannot know, before we talk, who might be in the wrong or what needs to be repaired—good reason not to gossip or make judgments. By talking together, new information comes to light, and ethical discernment becomes possible about the right action for these persons in this specific moment. By talking directly with each other, the community grows in practical wisdom about how to reconcile future hurts. God is really at work in the scene, revealing truth, forgiving sin, healing hurts, restoring love, and giving human beings authority to act in God's name to build up the kingdom. We see how the inevitable conflicts of community can be socially useful when we put Jesus's instructions into practice.

Some of us cringe when we read the third step of the reconciliation process in the Rule of Christ: "If they still refuse to listen, tell it to the church [or the community meeting] and if they refuse to listen even to the church, treat them as you would a pagan or a tax collector" (Matt. 18:17). This is not a "three strikes and you are out" policy—a quick way to kick out troublemakers. Rather, as long as a community member is willing to talk and listen, the process goes on in whatever creative ways the community can devise.

In my experience of forty years in community, I have not seen anyone asked to leave by a united community vote. Rather, when someone no longer listens, they have usually decided they do not want to belong, and it is helpful for everyone involved to acknowledge this. Sometimes, in a more established community with a long history of relationships, people who want to leave feel trapped because they do not have the financial means or the emotional support to do so. It is best, in such circumstances, to graciously offer the support they need to go, leaving the door open for further dialogue whenever they wish to return. It is essential for a Christian intentional community to be a place of freedom where everyone is present voluntarily.

That said, there are still ways in which communities need to set boundaries for their members and then insist that their members uphold these values. For example, households dedicated to radical hospitality have some special challenges as they take persons into provisional community who have not had a full orientation into the life and teachings of Jesus. They often live under a rule that advises residents as follows: "Being under the influence of drugs or alcohol, violence or threats of violence, will be cause for exclusion." A Reba household recently asked someone with a bipolar mental disorder to leave when he refused to take his medications, which rendered him incapable of listening to others about his abusive behavior. Disruptive individuals who refuse to listen to counsel should not be allowed to destroy the community that they say they want to be part of. It is important for the core community to be united on the approach they will take and who will implement it when problematic behavior begins. A few communities are equipped to live with persons off the streets, but most are not. This is okay. We are not the Messiah.

Jesus concludes his teaching on the three steps of conflict resolution with this summary: "Truly I tell you, whatever you bind on earth will be bound in heaven, and whatever you loose on earth will be loosed in heaven. Again, truly I tell you that if two of you on earth agree about anything they ask for, it will be done for them by my Father in heaven. For where two or three gather in my name, there am I with them" (Matt. 18:18–20).

The best brief exposition of this way of redemptive conflict resolution I have found is in the first chapter in John Howard Yoder's *Body*

Politics: Five Practices of the Christian Community before the Watching World. He writes,

> We have here a fundamental anthropological insight into the relationship of conflict and solidarity. To be human is to have differences; to be human wholesomely is to process those differences, not by building up conflicting power claims but by reconciling dialogue. Conflict is socially useful; it forces us to attend to new data from new perspectives. It is useful in interpersonal process; by processing conflict one learns skills, awareness, trust, and hope. Conflict is useful in intrapersonal dynamics, protecting our concern about guilt and acceptance from being directed inwardly only to our own feelings. The therapy for guilt is forgiveness; the source of self-esteem is another person who takes seriously my restoration to community.

Yoder suggests the Rule of Christ in Matthew 18:15–20 should be considered a sacrament. It is indeed something that God has promised to be present in and active through. What we bind on earth will be bound in heaven. What we loose on earth will be loosed in heaven.

The primary spiritual disciplines of traditional monastic communities are common work, common prayer, and submission to an abbot or abbess. However, for noncloistered communities with families and single people together, the disciplines are more relational in mutual service and economic in mutual support. These disciplines over time are meant to transform us into the character of Jesus. Our character is shaped in a Christward direction by our commitment to love and serve one another with all we are and have, to reconcile and forgive every offense between us, maintaining the peace of Christ. Such a commitment will lead us to better know ourselves and one another, and to experience more and more of God's mercy.

God has taken a terrible risk with us, that we will abuse this forgiveness. And we do abuse it again and again. Still, God has condescended to our level in Jesus, allowing us to hurt him, trusting that, in the end, all this forgiveness will change us, and we will pass on this amazing grace to others so that they too may be changed. God has given up trying to control us in order that we might learn how much we are loved. And in receiving this love, we are empowered to love others in the same way. When a community does this, it is heaven on earth.

CHAPTER 10

Commitment, Membership, and Mission

Many of the intentional communities that have been around for decades began with some instructive failures concerning commitment, membership, and mission. We begin this chapter by hearing about a promising community that did not make it.

WE NEVER REALLY BECAME A COMMUNITY

"Josh" tells of his community's demise—an account of several stories merged into one, with names changed to preserve anonymity.

Thanks for calling to ask about Roycemore Community. I'm sorry to disappoint you, but I should let you know up front that I've decided to leave. A lot of hype has gone out about all the good things we were going to do in mission to the city, but after two years, we've pretty much fizzled out.

As you know, about a dozen of us from our college moved to the inner city and set up two houses on Roycemore Street—one for us men and another nearby for the women. We had read and talked a lot about New Monasticism, Christian anarchism, Wendell Berry, and Shane Claiborne, and we had visited several communities, so we thought we knew what we were doing.

Back in college we were always frustrated because we could never get enough time with each other for our vision to gel. We thought that by moving together we would have more time to make community happen, to talk things through and agree on a rule of life, to make long-term commitments to each other and the neighborhood. We wanted Christian intentional community to grow naturally. But that's not how it worked out.

At first we all met weekly—the households taking turns hosting a potluck for our neighbors. And once a month we'd hold a "clarification of thought" evening like Catholic Worker houses do, with outside speakers—or one of our members would talk about some local social justice issue. In each house there were common prayers in the morning and a weekly household business meeting. Some of us got together as an informal steering committee, to give leadership to the project, but we were never actually affirmed as community leaders. We just did it because we felt committed, until we stopped doing it. Early on, it was apparent that some were less committed than others—a few only showed up when their busy schedules allowed, or when they wanted to.

We were doing lots of interesting things across the city. Most of us volunteered in social services that supported the poor or homeless in some way. That first summer we got a grant to do some urban gardening and community organizing around that. But no one figured out how we could invest in our local neighborhood—which is something we all agreed we were going to do when we moved here. All our different jobs, schooling, and projects made it really difficult to coordinate our schedules. After a while no one was available to host the potlucks, so that stopped. We tinkered around with different times and formats for household prayers. Now it's just two or three of us who meet in the morning with our cups of coffee, since the others head out early for their jobs.

At first it worked for us to make all our household decisions by consensus, with the meeting-convener role rotating among a few who were willing to do it. However, in these two years, some people have left and others have moved in who were not part of the original planning sessions. So now we are stuck with an expectation of consensus and inclusion of folks who rarely show up, and when they do we have to fill them in on previous meetings. We can't agree on how to change our rules, which we never actually wrote down, so people remember them differently. You can see which side of the anarchist argument I'm on.

Our social life has, in my opinion, been a mess. A few of the men and women are in courtship relationships with persons outside the group. It is pretty obvious that their partners do not share a calling to intentional community, so we are in this awkward place of having people in our houses whose hearts are no longer "with it." But they are our longtime friends and we don't want to kick them out—and, besides, we need their help to pay the rent. We've given up talking about sexual ethics, which really bothers me but not some of the others. This affects all of us, not just those who are moving on.

We've hosted some parties that have gotten out of hand, not so much because of our household members, but because of friends in "the movement" that some of us have invited. One neighbor called the cops after midnight because of the noise. The police were cool—they asked us politely to wind it up and send people home. We have not been able to arrive at consensus on how to set limits and who will confront the people who ignore them. Some people called us "that Christian frat house on Roycemore Street," which hurts but is true—a lot of talk about being radical, but not much commitment to actually doing it. We've become a vaguely Christian cohousing arrangement.

Now that I'm leaving the house, I have to decide if I will stick with my job as volunteer director for the local shelter, where relationships with the men mean a lot to me, or if I'll go to join a community upstate that has already figured out the things we can't manage here. I've also been talking to the pastor of the church some of us attend. He has taken a concern for our group and for others like us in the city. Maybe he can pull the remnants of this community experiment together and help us make a new start in a rundown house the church is trying to buy. I'd stick around if that could happen.

❖

I am struck by the way this group was too busy and fragmented in college to focus on a clear commitment and how the same pattern persisted to prevent a core community from uniting after college. Renunciation of many good things is needed to break our bondage to the fragmenting forces of our society, which most of us have internalized, as if busyness on many fronts were a virtue instead of a vice. Community does not happen naturally when it is up against social forces like ambitious careerism and individualism. In order for it to exist in this environment, community must be intentional, countercultural, and covenanted in response to God's call. Practically speaking, Jesus calls us to renounce whatever prevents us from making the discipleship community our primary social group.

An anarchist critique against leadership at Roycemore meant that servant leadership did not emerge. Dorothy Day and her Catholic Worker cohorts espoused a version of Christian anarchism that worked—except when it didn't. During the 1930s Great Depression, the Catholic Worker movement launched a number of houses of hospitality to welcome and serve the homeless poor. According to their personalist philosophy, individuals in the house would see what needed to be done and personally take responsibility. And if they did not, the task would not get done—with very educational consequences. If a house of hospitality did not have the support (or maturity) it needed and died, so be it. But in reality, Dorothy Day often stepped forward in crisis moments and took command. "The Catholic Worker is an anarchist movement," as her contemporaries were fond of saying, "and Dorothy Day is its chief anarch."

The apostle Paul teaches us (1 Cor. 12) that the Holy Spirit gives each member spiritual gifts of service to bless the church body, and when these gifts are discerned, affirmed, and active, the body will thrive. In this scenario, everyone has a leadership role and everyone learns how to follow in certain areas of life.

In the absence of designated leadership, a group is locked into consensus decision-making with persons who have not made a long-term commitment. The Roycemore community nevertheless had leadership—rather than being led by persons with faith and a sense of calling, it was led by the lowest common denominator.

SEPARATION AND GATHERING IN SCRIPTURE

Again and again in the Hebrew Scriptures we see both separation and gathering as the characteristic way God works. Creation was a separation of the dry land from the waters beneath and above, creating order out of primordial chaos. Time itself was separated—the Sabbath from all the other days so that communal holiness might be revealed. Abraham was told to separate himself and his descendants from all other peoples, to be a holy nation of priests on behalf of the world. The law created a people separated from the Gentiles. This separation is what holds back chaos and allows a distinct and a holy people to exist.

Jesus followed a similar pattern. One way to see this is to ask, how many disciples did Jesus have? There was a changing number of those who voluntarily followed Jesus in his itinerant ministry, including both women and men (Lk. 8:1–3); Jesus selected a circle of twelve whom he named apostles and trained for servant-leader responsibilities (Matt. 3:14); there were seventy whom he sent out in mission two by two (Lk. 10:1); and there was a smaller group of three companions with whom he confided most closely (Matt. 17:1). About a 120 Galileans went with Jesus on his final journey and stayed together in Jerusalem following his resurrection (Acts 1:15). Beyond these circles of disciples there were the crowds who came and went, with whom Jesus also spent time healing and teaching. Each of these circles received Jesus's attention—uniquely identified as a focus of his mission.

How should we view these differences in discipleship commitments? The disciples saw them judgmentally, as differences in status and power. They fought over "who was the greatest in the kingdom of God," and Jesus rebuked them. The privilege of a calling does not make us better, but it does change our primary social group, our responsibilities, and our need for the Holy Spirit's help.

In several ways, the Roycemore story demonstrates how a group without clear boundaries and a committed core is paralyzed. Persons without formation in the values of the community have entered the decision-making circle without espousing its mission. Without a long-term membership commitment, a group cannot make long-term decisions and cannot sustain a distinctive ethical way of life that embodies good news for the world.

Of course, we don't like to be labeled a sect, an in-group, accused of living just to ourselves; we want to be inclusive, diverse, missional, making a difference in the world. Inclusion and diversity are indeed virtues. Being included is the way many find their way to follow Jesus. Even children (of all ages) feel a surge of energy when they are allowed to learn by doing and belonging. Although inclusion is a virtue, it is not an idol to be worshiped. Taken to extremes, it will destroy community by starving the core. Long-term decisions should be made by persons who have made a long-term commitment. Persons who have not made such a commitment are still thinking about when they will leave on their own terms. This is a foundation of sand on which a durable community house cannot be built (Matt. 7:26–27).

Some communities have learned to get the best of both worlds, commitment and inclusion, by including everyone in the discussion phase of issues but allowing only long-term members (or covenant members) to vote on community policy or agenda with long-term consequences. Perhaps it helps to picture the virtues that nourish and focus the inner life of a community as the left foot and reaching out to others in mission as the right foot. If either of these virtues trumps the other, we are soon walking in circles.

In order for the Roycemore Community to be truly voluntary, they needed to make a distinction between those ready to covenant together for a disciplined way of life embodying the things Jesus taught, and those who were in it for the experience but not with a call. A covenanted core can then start to practice what it hopes to become as it works out the community's purpose, location, and initial rule of life. This core group needs time alone to clarify the vision that they can then invite others to join.

Consider other examples in recent intentional community history. The Camden House community in Camden, New Jersey, was greatly strengthened at its inception because a core group made a five-year commitment to pursue together what God wanted of them. Although this commitment did not solve all problems, it raised a bright flag that drew others for shorter (and longer) commitments.

The Kedzingdale Community in Chicago lives in a three-flat apartment building, with thirteen members (at the time I visited in late 2009). One of them, Tricia Partlow, explained to me their reasons for a sabbatical from "ministry."

> We had a lot of turnover last summer. We've been doing some good things but we want them to come together better. We've decided to stop our open-house community meals for a while, stop most of our outside activities to take time to pray and focus on community goals and purpose. (We still have a commitment to keep up "Food Not Bombs," a free food distribution project.) We used to have weekly house meetings, but now we are just praying—not doing business, hoping to draw closer together in God's love. And we feel the need for some outside wisdom on the way ahead.

The community's decision to take an extended prayer retreat from ordinary business is a sign of wisdom, a time to regroup and integrate with newer members, before they are scattered so far that they could not find their way back home. Someone with community experience from outside the group can be very helpful in assessing what it takes to keep the inner and outer life in balance. I am hopeful for their future, and so are they.

Social engagement without separation characterized the Roycemore Community until there was no center left, no unique witness, nothing serious to invite others to join. As Jesus warned, "Salt is good, but if it loses its saltiness, how can it be made salty again?" (Lk. 14:34–35). In the Roycemore Community, it is probably too late to put the salt back into the saltshaker. At the end of the story Josh avails himself of a pastor who might mentor the remnants of the community group into a new beginning. The Holy Spirit has given Josh some hope. We can't help but wonder how this community's story might have unfolded if a mentor had been recognized and welcomed by the whole community from the beginning.

In 1972 Joanne and I belonged to the Bridge, a community in Newton, Kansas, that folded after eighteen months, for reasons much like the Roycemore Community story. Some people from that community returned to a more conventional existence while the rest of us were left with a hunger for a deeply shared life, this time more clearly centered on Jesus. The Holy Spirit gathered the remnants of two such fizzled groups and brought us together. With some guidance from the Shalom Association of Communities, and a little wiser because of our experiences, we were led to build a more durable "house" on a rock foundation (Matt. 7:24–25) that we named New Creation Fellowship.

Most of the communities I know are blessed with a few wise persons who came as "refugees" from earlier community experiments that did not make it to the point of clarifying commitment and membership. But our failures do not stop God, who, as the saying goes, often "writes straight with crooked lines."

CHAPTER 11

Where Will You Put Down Roots?

Context and calling are huge. You have to deal with them." This is the advice I received one day from Mark Van Steenwyck of Missio Dei Community in South Minneapolis, when I asked what chapter topics should appear in a book of counsel for people forming new intentional communities. Where we put down roots speaks loudly about our hopes for peace in a world that has already made enemies for us. We may hope to be agents of reconciliation, as Van Steenwyck tells in his community's story later in this chapter, but the place we choose will surely change us and our mission.

"Putting down roots" carries a double meaning—committing to long-term relationships and to a neighborhood. When we look to Jesus, he has much to say about fidelity in community relationships, but at first glance it might appear that there is no guidance about where we should live. In fact, Jesus's ministry was relentlessly itinerant—uprooting his disciples from ancestral homes and moving about as a communal band, proclaiming and demonstrating the arrival of the kingdom of God. But this was not about self-centered mobility, seeking adventure, career advancement, or a more upscale neighborhood. Jesus's ministry was especially directed to "the lost sheep of the house of Israel," a people with whom Jesus and his disciples were deeply rooted. His was a mission of reconciliation and good news, going first to those who had lost everything under the crunch of empire and religious establishment.

One day a lawyer asked Jesus that crucial question about roots, "Who is my neighbor?" Jesus answered with a story (Lk. 10:25–37) about two persons, a Jew and a Samaritan, who would never be neighbors. Society had already organized and socialized them to suspect, if not hate, each other. The "problem" with Jews and Samaritans being neighbors is that they might end up liking each other, might come to see God's image in each other, and begin to unravel the historical myth so crucial to national identity—that we are better than somebody else. In Jesus's parable, the Samaritan behaved in a neighborly way, not because of geography but because of the compassion he felt on seeing himself in a wounded and helpless man beside the road. Does this story say anything about where we should live? What did the disciples make of it? How and where did they become neighbors?

For the twelve apostles, Jesus's call led them to first put down roots as shepherds of the persecuted church in Jerusalem. But history and legend tell us that Peter eventually became bishop of Rome, where he was executed. Thomas planted the church and gave his life in India. The other apostles founded churches in distant lands where they stayed and died as martyrs. With their planted lives and the death threats they refused to flee, the apostles interpreted for us the words of Jesus, "Very truly I tell you, unless a kernel of wheat falls to the ground and dies, it remains only a single seed. But if it dies, it produces many seeds" (Jn. 12:24). This is about putting down roots.

The apostle Paul often reflected on "the mystery hidden for long ages past but now revealed" (Rom. 16:25–26). Whenever he reflects on this mystery, it has to do with the inclusion of the Gentiles with the Jews in God's mission of reconciliation (Rom. 1:9–14; Eph. 3:1–6; 1 Col. 1:27; 1 Tim. 3:16). This racial and ethnic reconciliation is the foretaste of all things in heaven and on earth coming together in Christ (see Eph. 3:1–6). If the mission of God is reconciliation with all racial and ethnic peoples, then where God calls us to put down roots will always, in some way, be on the other side of the lines that separate human beings in this world, starting at the bottom.

This calling goes way beyond the sunny individualistic advice to "bloom where you are planted," as if one place is just like another. This calling to put down roots on the other side of the dividing lines that nation, class, race, and history have created asks us to become indigenous to a place not our own, incarnations of the good news of Jesus. In our day Jesus's call to die to self may not look like heroic martyrdom, but it is calling many to invest in obscure places and people, so that the kingdom of God can bloom where our seeds die to other personal futures and possibilities.

A lot has changed since Jesus's time, when expectations of support and loyalty to family and clan were strong (for better and worse), and most people could point to a tribal or ancestral home as roots. We are seeing the accumulating effects of Enlightenment individualism, of automobility, of a rootless society where most places are heedlessly exploited and going to rot because no one loves them, because no one cares and sticks around to be the neighbor. We consume places till they become toxic and violent and then move on. As an African American pastor friend keeps saying, "We've got to put the 'neighbor' back into the 'hood.'"

New communities often have a story of God's choosing their neighborhood for them. Luke Healy, in chapter 1, told of the *Kansas City Star* article titled "The Murder Factory: 64130," which convinced his community that God was calling them to move into the zip code that had produced more murderers in Missouri prisons than any other.

In 1973, in Newton, Kansas, Joanne and I gathered with a few families and singles for a weekend of prayer concerning where our would-be community should land. The Holy Spirit had given us a love for each other, a calling to be a daily church dedicated to peacemaking and especially to resisting the war in Vietnam. We were tired of driving across town to meet as a small group. We believed God meant us to live within close walking distance of each other, a place where our children could share community, a hub for daily work and prayer, a support base for welcoming the stranger.

We met in one family's home for a weekend retreat. During a break we took a little walk and saw a big house half a block away with a for-sale sign just posted that day. This "corner house" was large enough for two families if the carpenters among us would build out the third-floor attic. Within a couple of months we were walking to our daily meals and meetings, and our children could find playmates on their own. Community became real for us in new dimensions of sharing through common work, help at a moment's notice, gardening, a base for peace-movement organizing, a common purse, and the seeds of a new church. None of this could have happened had we not moved together. In our case we did not move across some ethnic boundary, but we ourselves had become aliens on home turf by all these Spirit-led changes.

Fifteen years ago, a group from Reba felt called to plant a church community in the North Chicago neighborhood of Rogers Park. For years they rented meeting space from another congregation. One day, a drive-by shooting left a young man dead on the corner of Pratt and Ashland. Everyone lamented another act of senseless violence in the "hood." But a few teens began a weekly candlelight prayer vigil on that corner, inviting neighbors and friends to join. After a month, adults began to stand with the youth, and a conviction grew that "God has called us to the corner." After many difficult negotiations, with the support of several partner organizations, Living Water Community Church purchased several storefronts "on the corner" and built out a worship space and ministry center that has become the home base of a vital community and multiethnic congregation.

So, here is some counsel for groups looking for their location: do your research, take prayer walks, knock on doors, check out for-rent and for-sale signs, and count on God to draw a circle for you on the map.

Once a community is planted, you can also count on God to keep opening up new reasons for this location far beyond what you could ask or imagine. Mark Van Steenwyck tells of Missio Dei's calling to South Minneapolis, along with some consequences for their church community and their neighbors.

Mark Van Steenwyck's Story

Our driving charism is hospitality in South Minneapolis. This means we must be culturally attentive to our East-African Muslim neighbors. Dogs in the house, for example, are a problem. So we decided to host Saturday outdoor meals with an open invitation to our neighbors.

Our neighborhood has many progressives and immigrants. We've allowed our neighbors to radicalize and make activists of us; their issues have become ours. At times we have taken the lead in things that matter to our neighbors. People now come to our meals because they have met us at protests. That's how our context has shaped us.

We also have this Anabaptist impulse to be a countercultural community that takes our inner life seriously. We don't want to become an anarchist collective, an activist community that happens to be Christian. This is the struggle that Catholic Worker groups often face. In their activism, they sometimes lose their spiritual anchor. Other communities have a high sense of calling to a common life but are not engaged with their context. Both of those are problematic for us.

We are surrounded by professional activists. We can't outdo them. How do we do community organizing in a Christlike way that makes a difference? We are present in a lot of demonstrations, but as peacemakers we try to be the loving voice that is often not present. The fact that we do hospitality adds integrity and gains some respect.

We've had a few people go on Christian Peacemaker Team (CPT) delegations. We hope to have all our members go through CPT training so that we could be a regional CPT support group. Through CPT we are getting involved in aboriginal justice issues in Ontario and have awakened to indigenous rights concerns here in Minneapolis. This is a convergence of our context and calling. We join the Lakota and others for protests at Fort Snelling. Land that used to be a garden for the Lakota people has become a war memorial for whites. We want the state of Minnesota to tell the truth about the 1860s Indian concentration camp at Fort Snelling. This would mean turning it into a memorial of a different sort or tearing it down, as the Lakota people would like.

We can't get on board with every local justice issue. But rather than criticize from a distance, we encourage a few people in our community to get involved and get a feel for what is happening. Eventually, if we all come to unity as a community, then we make a stand. Lots of issues don't come to that kind of convergence. But the indigenous struggles have been a pretty obvious one for us.

We give reality tours with InterVarsity Christian Fellowship students and other college groups. We hop on the light rail, with soundtracks telling the Lakota story to guide these tours. When apprentices spend time with us, we go through our core values, and when "resistance" comes up, we tell about the Lakota people and take their tour. It is a quick way for making our context and its history of oppression real.

Mainstream Christianity has either ignored the Lakotas' pleas or tried to apologize their way through them. The apologies are a good beginning, but we are encouraging Christian groups to enter into conversation with local tribes about returning land they are holding, doing something costly and meaningful.

Lakota spokespersons have reminded us that when a people is being wiped out, Jesus is more present in them than in the victors. What do we do with this overwhelming sense of immobilizing guilt? It brings up deep emotions that don't really have a way to go somewhere. But this is also an opportunity for God to do something new.

Like Missio Dei, many communities have done their research and developed "reality tours" that share with visitors an awareness of the neighborhood's ethnic makeup, history of exploitation and resistance efforts, local assets, and justice initiatives. They point out that destructive long-term structural forces can only be tackled by long-term commitment. "Abandoned places of empire" have been visited by enough mission trips and then forsaken so that locals are justified in their suspicions. It is not right to start a program, befriend lots of kids, and then move on to greener pastures whenever personal fulfillment beckons. We must become indigenous to a place in order to form nonexploitative relationships. If a new community wants to be taken seriously by its neighbors, a group of people must put down roots, find out "what God is up to" in that place, and plan to stay.

I've heard the story of a generous soul who asked a Bible translation society to send her a dictionary of some remote language group so she could help them translate a few books of the Bible in her spare time. How naive, we think! And yet, this story is not much different from those who imagine they can translate the good news of Jesus without intimately knowing him in community and without becoming in some measure indigenous to the place where they are planted.

This chapter on roots speaks especially to two marks of the New Monasticism: "relocation to abandoned places of empire" and "geographical proximity to community members." We want to add a few words about geographical proximity.

Many congregations are promoting "community" among their members, which usually means small sharing groups or mission teams—both good things. But there is an existential difference between thin and thick community. Thin community is when you go to church rather than be the church concretely in your own neighborhood. It is when you go somewhere else to do mission work. If community is a place you have to get into a car and drive to, then you might be giving the world of individualism, hypermobility, and consumer-based choices more power in your life than the church. Thick community is living within easy walking distance of other members, which is essential to sustaining a daily shared life. If we are not willing to put where we live on the altar, this thin "sense of community" will have little power to transform our lives or our world. Like logs stacked together for a campfire, intentional community brings us together so that spontaneous things can happen, so the Holy Spirit can light a sustaining flame.

PROVISO: NEW MONASTICISM,
WITH CHILDREN ADDED

"Moving to abandoned places of empire" is costlier for families with children, but with adaptations is richly possible. When some original members of The Simple Way community in Philadelphia arrived at the life stage where they wanted to raise families, they ended up leaving the intentional community on Potter Street and moving a mile or two miles away, or to the next town, where they do not hear gunshots at night. Shane Claiborne's continuing commitment, with a few others, to live on Potter Street has made it possible for an extended community to keep their neighborhood relationships alive through potluck dinners, summer programs for children, free food distributions, a few college scholarships, and other local benefits of these wider connections.

At Camden House (now Camden Houses) two families now have babies, toddlers, and live-in volunteers. Six years ago the community began with a focus on friendships among the prostitutes, addicts, and other neighbors on the edge of homelessness. It was a neighborhood featuring the most egregious industrial polluters in the state—a kind of ecological racism that dumps on minority neighborhoods with little power to fight back. Now with infants in their homes, the Camden community has focused its creative energy on supporting the schools, children, and families around them, all the while sharing hope and good food through summertime gardens involving lots of young hands. Changes in life stages will change how a community can engage their neighborhood with the good news of the gospel.

Catholic Worker houses of hospitality have usually tried not to mix families with children and the sometimes volatile behavior of persons with street-life habits. These houses of hospitality have often brought together young volunteers and singles of all ages in intensive ministry and shared life with persons who want to make a new start in life, and with those who don't. As these young people get married and start families, they often cluster in homes in less violent settings nearby and remain part of the Catholic Worker extended community. There they regularly volunteer to serve a meal with their children, who learn a more radical way of life by joining in the works of mercy. The extended community is crucial in raising funds, sustaining "Clarification of Thought" evenings, and putting out the newsletters that keep alive the stories of saints old and new. The Catholic Worker farms have been a more stable environment for families with children, communities often in close partnership with their sister houses in the cities.

At the Last Supper, Jesus summarized all his teachings with a new commandment. "Love one another. As I have loved you, so you must love one another. By this everyone will know that you are my disciples, if you love one another" (Jn. 13:34–35).

The biblical epistles to the churches likewise assume that Christians are already connected in this same kind of "one another" community. Here are a few samples from about forty such sayings in the writings of Paul, Peter, and James: "Live in harmony with one another, admonish one another, have the same care for one another, be servants of one another, bear one another's burdens, comfort one another, be at peace with one another, bear with one another lovingly, be kind and compassionate to one another, be subject to one another, confess your sins to one another, be hospitable to one another." A serious question for Christians should be, "What living arrangements and commitments would make these 'one another' counsels feasible?"

Moving in together does not automatically make us holy and compassionate people. Neither does reading the Bible make us good. But if our deepest desire is to learn how to give and receive love in the manner of Jesus, how can this happen except in a shared life? Practically speaking, amid the scattering forces of our surrounding society, Jesus calls us to move our "logs" together and invite others into that same transforming flame, so the world can see what its future might look like.

CHAPTER 12

Racial Reconciliation—
Listening, Submitting, and Collaborating

The Christian intentional community movement is largely a white phenomenon with some exploratory exceptions to which we want to give attention in this chapter. As a white person with experience of privilege, I have been sheltered from some of the hard social realities that lead to wisdom. However, I have some wise friends whom I want to quote at length in this chapter. So, let us return to the story of Leroy and Donna Barber (begun in chapter 1).

Two decades ago the Barbers, an African American couple in Philadelphia, discovered that the way they had been welcoming struggling neighbors and friends into a common life of discipleship had much in common with the Christian intentional community movement taken up by whites on a path of downward mobility. The Barber family story shifts to Atlanta, where Leroy and Donna invited others to join them in multiplying the number of ministering households, laying the foundation for a sustainable and diverse intentional community that could work at racial reconciliation and neighborhood development across all of life's stages. Leroy continues.

Leroy Barber's Story

In 1997 I began working with Mission Year in Atlanta. Then, after a few years, I was named director of the program nationwide. In South Atlanta we started doing community in a new way by inviting Mission

Year volunteers to come into neighborhood-focused households as a strategic plan for local economic development. Our nonprofit was called Community Fellowships. This took on some new dimensions beyond what a single family like ours could do. It was patterned somewhat after the Christian Community Development Association (CCDA) model that John Perkins and others have developed. I'm part of CCDA, on the board, and that has informed a lot of what we do. But in our community we bring a number of differences to our approach. I've pushed a lot harder on the relational component, something we let everyone know about up front.

Mission Year is pretty central to the way young people get formed in this new way of life among us. The introduction piece is where racial misconceptions are intentionally broken down and individuals are pushed into relationships beyond their own ethnic group. A new consciousness is built up through these personal interactions. We talk about structural racism, but the solution is embodied in relationships of different ethnicities together in community. This strong intentional year of service is like a rite of passage, a year of formation into a new way of life, learning to reconcile relationships as we go.

Now, in recent years, here in Atlanta, we are exploring what a church can do to help folks be strategic neighbors. There are three stages of our life together. The entry point is Mission Year. Young people come for a year to live together intentionally as volunteers in the neighborhood. Then Mission Year alumni dedicate their lives, living in covenanted households of single people, in connection with the local church. This pretty much fits the twelve marks of the New Monasticism model. The third stage is families living out their faith and justice involvement for longer periods of time—through all of life's stages. These families are accountable to each other, sharing prayer times, meals, engaging in the political needs and services of their neighborhood, school district, city, et cetera.

When you get to the third stage you are raising kids, and the whole way of life is informed by these relationships of different peoples together. Having done this for many years, I see that families often fall away from their radical commitments when they have kids unless there is a covenanted intentional community for them. I know that other mostly white communities like Church of the Sojourners in San Francisco have done similar things. We're exploring how to do interracial community in more diverse environments.

Our church is small—about fifteen families and some singles—about half white and half of color. We worship together on Sundays. But we have many other connections. One family runs thrift stores, another family trains entrepreneurs, another member is a computer designer and works with kids at a bike shop, another works with a baseball league. There is a community house with youth groups, sports stuff, and a summer camp. The distinct things these groups of families do all converge in the church. Of course, not everyone who is involved in these projects is part of our church, but they are part of the overall community that happens. We're not planning to grow big, but we do want to grow in depth of relationship and commitment.

❖

I asked Leroy if he knew of other long-term intentional communities with a similar African American participation and concentration of leadership. He replied, "I don't know of any. We are rare birds."

In *School(s) for Conversion: 12 Marks of a New Monasticism*, the fourth mark is "lament for racial divisions within the church and our communities combined with the active pursuit of a just reconciliation." The New Monastic communities I know have a few persons of color, but usually not people in leadership who might attract others. The racial diversity among them is the result of mixed marriages, adoptions, recent immigrations, or individuals attracted by the support network available as they go through a hard time of life. But there is a hurdle that most communities can't get over to arrive at substantial diversity. I asked Leroy, "How can intentional communities become more racially diverse?"

Leroy Barber's Story (continued)

That is a pretty big question. If the organizations aren't willing to make some real structural changes I don't see it happening. The depth at which you are connecting with people in the communities that are being formed assumes a familiar culture, common education levels, and sometimes familiar worship styles. These are dimensions of very strong identity for people. If an organization is not able to look at and rework these things, they will not get very far. People of color generally have a high identity attached to their culture and the history of the way people of color have been treated in America.

Where people of color have joined white-majority intentional communities, it is usually people for whom color is a low identity marker. High-identity people of color have usually gone to predominantly black schools, black churches, and that is where their worldview largely comes from. Attracting those individuals, especially the ones with leadership capacities, will take a major shift in how a community is organized in ways that makes it possible for persons with high identity to be at home.

Our strategy for drawing African American young people to Mission Year includes visits to historic black colleges and a once-a-year table discussion with a circle of African American pastors who encourage their young people to consider Mission Year. When we visit Christian college campuses, we connect with their multicultural affairs offices. I also speak at a number of African American churches through the year. Mission Year ends up with about 75 percent white recruits and 25 percent people of color. This allows for racial diversity in every local Mission Year community house.

Attracting high-identity folks over time is possible; it is not overwhelming. But it is rough for organizations to go through all the changes they need to make in order for this to happen.

For persons who want to start a diverse intentional community from scratch, you must begin with diversity in the initial relationships. You have to look deeper into that diversity. Are all the people of color in it persons with high or low identity? Do they all come from an Anabaptist background or from other points of view? Are there young people of color who have decided to make some strong steps toward simplicity? You have to look deeper into your diversity to see how diverse it really is and whom you are likely to attract.

Sometimes young people in the New Monasticism movement have a hard time admitting that their social contexts and that their relationships lack deep diversity. The window for learning about this is not always as open as it ought to be. Listening is the first step.

There are many ways that Christian intentional communities are working at diversity. Anton Flores-Maisonet and his wife, Charlotte, founded Alterna, a nonprofit in LaGrange, Georgia, with a loose intentional community at its core. LaGrange is a small city with about two thousand recent Hispanic immigrants. Anton is Puerto Rican, born in New York City but raised in Atlanta, with years of experience as a professor of social work and as a community organizer. He moves easily between Anglo and Hispanic cultures. The mission of Alterna is to serve Jesus in the area's Latino immigrant population, many of whom are undocumented.

At the time of my visit in spring 2011, the core Alterna community included the Flores family, four immigrant families, and two Mission Year couples who live in Alterna-owned homes within walking distance of each other. Anton's week can include a Spanish-language Bible study in the local jail, a trip to Atlanta to organize a Holy Week pilgrimage for immigrants' rights, a potluck party for Alterna members and friends, laying out community-service tasks for the Mission Year volunteers, and counseling and praying with a dozen immigrants in various kinds of trouble with employers or the law. Anton's advice to newly forming communities interested in diversity and action for justice is similar to Leroy Barber's.

Anton Flores's Story

I would say that if you want to end with diversity, then you need to start with a diversity of relationships already in the dreaming stage. The ideal of Christian intentional community that many of us carry comes from a position of privilege. We have possessions, power, and access to resources, which Jesus is asking us to lay down in order to seek solidarity with the poor and dependence on God. In building community with the poor we need to first come to authentic relationships before we import our idea of community. The community that is given to us probably will not look like our ideal. It needs to grow out of our experience of God together.

Martin Luther King called racism, militarism, and materialism America's besetting sins. This is a critique that comes from Scripture and has something to say to both whites and people of color. The Beloved Community that he talked about will be Good News for both blacks and whites, for people of all ethnic groups. But we need to explore that together rather than come to the conversation with our minds already made up about a model of community and what that will look like. Together we can study Jesus, our own and our neighbor's needs, and act as we are led.

❖

There is an underlying theology driving the church to become more diverse and more reconciled. Jesus came from heaven to share our circumstances, to suffer with us, and to invite us into the life of Father, Son, and Holy Spirit—which is community in diversity. Jesus began his movement crossing many social boundaries. The initial Twelve, although all men, represented the renewal of the twelve tribes of Israel. They seem to also have been chosen with some diversity in mind including a zealot and a Roman collaborator, some fishermen, and men of both city and peasant background. The Gospel of Luke especially highlights the ways that Jesus engaged with women, the poor, foreigners, the sick, and social outcasts often labeled "sinners"—all welcomed in his extended discipleship band.

In the book of Acts we witness profound structural changes enacted in the movement, first to incorporate Greek-speaking Jews into leadership of the newly founded church. (Notice the Greek names of all the deacons in Acts 6:5.) Later, under the action of the Holy Spirit, the apostles approved new guidelines and practices so that Jews and Gentiles could have table fellowship and community of goods across all their differences in a new and reconciled humanity (Acts 15:28–29). And when we think about diversity, let us remember all the changes made in order to welcome us Gentile Christians into the Jewish family tree of faith. Ethnic differences embody God's gifts to humanity and especially to the church. As we discover and bring these gifts together in humble service to one another, the mystery hidden for ages of God's intention to reconcile all peoples in Christ becomes historical reality (see Col. 1:26).

Anali Gatlin expresses this calling to become a new humanity in Christ on behalf of Hope Fellowship (Waco, Texas). "We are especially aware that the gospel doesn't come to life in its fullness if we all look and think alike. The Good News comes from different stories and backgrounds. Getting the gospel in all its dimensions comes from diversity. The structures we create will limit who is welcome, what diversity can happen. How can we be intentional about this? At Hope Fellowship we have chosen to be bilingual—to translate everything into both Spanish and English—at every meeting. Having a common purse did not seem like a good place to start because some of our members send remittances to their families back in Mexico, and the families who feel this responsibility couldn't imagine how to be part of a common purse. But now there is more sharing in such matters. We first had to overcome some trust barriers because of racial and cultural divides."

Chris and Lara Lahr illustrate another strategy in the work of racial reconciliation. They are affiliated with that "conspiracy of friends" called The Simple Way in Philadelphia. They included me on a recent food distribution run, picking up a vanload of day-old bakery and still edible produce that an upscale Jewel store had waiting for us at the back door. As we drove across town to make some deliveries, I asked Chris about the Hispanic congregation where their family has participated over the past decade.

"Lots of white folks," he began, "want their church to become more diverse, which usually means, keep the same structures and wish that people of color will come and join them. But most people of color," he continued, "don't want to go where whites are in charge. If you want to be part of a diverse congregation, go to an African American congregation or a Hispanic congregation, lay down your power, and learn from them. As you stick around and they come to trust you, they will probably ask you to help. Let it happen naturally as you become one people." There is a whole theory of submission and incarnation in those words, but instead of talking theology, we started to haul out the groceries as mothers and young men from Chris's touch football league spread out the goods for their neighbors across the street from the meeting house of a church that is becoming what its name says, "Iglesia del Barrio."

A similar pattern of submission and transformation is illustrated by the Oak Park Community (whose formation story Luke Healy told in chapter 1). The community began among white students on the Kansas State campus in Manhattan, Kansas, with a call to be planted across the color line, in the "murder factory" of Kansas City, Missouri, whose zip code was 61430. The members were offered space in a Baptist church building with an African American congregation, which they renovated into living and community spaces.

Luke Healy's Story

Though I grew up in Kansas City, I had rarely ever driven around in those neighborhoods that scared me, even in the middle of the day. The certainty in the calling of the Lord gave us the initial courage, but the actual experience revealed many of our fears as smoke and mirrors. This was not a neighborhood with gunshots ringing out all the time (although we do hear them occasionally), where someone will pull out a gun on you just for looking at them too long. The dangers do exist and crime happens—often close to us. But I believe as followers of Jesus we need to examine our theology of "safety." Is not the safest place for us to be right where God wants us?

Living above an active church and participating in its worship life also has its challenges. Trying to explain New Monastic intentional community to a seventy-three-year-old African American pastor has its gaps. The congregation's grace and welcome with us has been astounding, even as we're pretty sure that they don't know exactly what it is we're doing, and we don't understand all of what they are doing either. Reconciliation takes on further challenges when there is a large age gap as well as very different expressions of worship and church life. We are striving to learn how to work well together, how to bless one another, and how to understand each other—but it is far from easy. Sometimes it seems harder to form familiar relationships with those of a common faith than with those who are our neighbors! I used to think reconciliation just took humility and forgiveness, but there is so much more to it. We continue to pursue, process, and struggle with our unique situation.

ORGANIZATIONS WORKING AT RACIAL RECONCILIATION IN OUR COMMUNITIES

The largest network in America of communities, churches, and nonprofit ministries working at racial reconciliation has come together under the Christian Community Development Association, led by John Perkins. An African American born into violent segregationist circumstances, Perkins fled Mississippi to "make it" in California, and succeeded. Only there he found Jesus and a call to return to Mississippi where, with his wife, Vera, and a growing family, he pioneered holistic ways of doing evangelism and community development with grace and integrity of leadership that people of all ethnic groups have come to trust. His vision for potential partners in ministry is summed up in the call to "relocate, reconcile, and redistribute."

The annual CCDA conference brings together a few thousand practitioners of the "three R's" who are working together under minority leadership or in creative partnerships of whites with people of color like the stories told in this chapter. Many New Monastic communities have found resources, elder coaches, and fellow travelers in the CCDA. At the Chicago 2010 CCDA conference keynote address, John Perkins, now in his eighties, returned the focus of CCDA again and again to Jesus Christ, our reconciler. "On Christ the solid ground I stand. We cannot base our movement on antiracism alone, not on white guilt, not on victimhood, not on political power struggles. . . ." The litany went on and on, concluding in the refrain, "My hope, and the hope of CCDA . . . is built on nothing less than Jesus's blood and righteousness. . . . All other ground is sinking sand."

For more than a decade, I have been privileged to participate in a CCDA-affiliated, church-based, affordable housing ministry called the Evanston Community Development Association (ECDA), which is led by several African American congregations. I have been welcomed and changed in many ways in this setting of common work for justice and reconciliation. Perhaps most transformative for me have been the many bear hugs I have received after long ECDA board meetings from the late Bishop W.D.C. Williams Jr., who kept affirming, "I love you with the love of Jesus, and there is nothing you can do about it." In America, with its grievous wounds of race, there are plenty of reasons why he might not love me. But because of the faithfulness of Jesus, we are already *one* as we collaborate, developing affordable housing and tackling the barriers that keep our peoples apart.

CHAPTER 13

Gender in Community—Conflict and Synergy

DAVID JANZEN WITH SALLY SCHREINER YOUNGQUIST

Over our cups of tea one afternoon, Sarah Jobe from the Rutba Community (Durham, North Carolina) reflected on gender roles and expectations in her community. "I find that Christian intentional community is good news for women and especially for mothers," she began. "Our household can host community events because others take their turns making the meals, because Matt (a single guy in the house) plays with our girls while I see that the living room is ready for those who come over for morning prayers. Yesterday I could take our girls swimming from 4:00 to 6:00 PM because others were making the common meal and setting tables in our house. Our girls go to Jonathan and Leah's home to play a couple of mornings a week while I go about my work as chaplain in the women's minimum security prison here in Durham. Community liberates me in many ways to do what God has called me to do," she said.

It does seem to be the case that women in the intentional Christian community movement face more subtle barriers to fully exercising their gifts. Women, especially mothers, still provide most of the "social glue" that holds family and community together, and they generally have more demands on their time than do men with wives. Jobe continues, "While community is good news for women, it is not yet all good news. I get frustrated because, as a woman, I've been socialized to see a lot of things that need doing that others, especially men, do not see—stuff like putting the pillows back on the couch and picking up the prayer books after our morning gathering, washing the windows once in a while, or cleaning the bathroom. I hear the comment that 'messy is good enough.' But there still is a gap between us, an unfinished conversation that should not be my burden to keep bringing up. There is also the assumption that if someone does these things they are doing them for me because it is my house rather than that they are doing it because this is what it takes to make community work for all of us."

I have observed at Reba Place Fellowship how the larger households appoint a "household manager," someone who charts the rotation of meal preparation and cleanup according to a common schedule, who "sees" and "hears" what else needs to be done so that it gets on a list that everyone knocks out on Saturday mornings. Organizing traditional "women's work" into common work can have life-changing consequences. Community becomes an intimate space of resocialization where men and women come close enough for honest dialogue in the concrete experience of bearing one another's burdens and seeking the common good.

At Reba, we often joke about the Clearing household's "marriage prep course" where a long line of young single men has learned the servant leadership skills of "seeing what needs to be done and doing it to someone else's satisfaction." It is a mysterious and wonderful process how, after a year or two of such "housebreaking," these young men become interesting to the women in the community, and even attractive, not to mention handsome! The problem with this tradition is that after the wedding celebration we have to start over with another candidate for the Clearing revolving-door "finishing school," someone else who gets to learn the art of "seeing what needs to be done" until someone else sees him doing it and thinks, "What's not to like about that?"

Meanwhile, the conversation with Sarah Jobe that day returned to new communities and what they are up against. The consensus of Sarah and the group was that even if everyone agrees that leadership roles are open to women, the momentum of male entitlement and assertiveness tends to be self-perpetuating unless the community agrees to proactively model another way. This calls for some new reflexes in both men and women—for women to volunteer for leadership roles and for men to give active support until new patterns are established.

For a closer look at the structural and personal dimensions of this transition, I asked Sally Schreiner Youngquist, current Fellowship leader, to reflect on the changes she has seen in gender dynamics over the years at Reba. From age twenty-one to fifty-one Sally lived as a single person in households large and small, with roommates, and by herself—and then eight years ago married Orwin Youngquist, inheriting three stepdaughters, and now, seven grandchildren.

Sally Schreiner Youngquist's Story

When I arrived at Reba in the early 1970s, I observed men and women relating as empowered, articulate equals in the house church and community meetings while dividing their labors in traditional spheres of work. Women used their creativity establishing this simple but beautiful aesthetic in homemaking, cooking, and hospitality and in raising creative, competent kids. A few women were also leading worship, music, and a nursery school. Single women contributed money from their professional work mainly as teachers and nurses. Men worked more in the areas of theological reflection, preaching and counseling within RPF, and in other outside earning jobs.

When the charismatic movement came through in the early '70s, there was a more deliberate effort to teach about distinctive roles for men and women, including male headship and submission of women. We recognized and named the elders operating in our midst and gave them authority to lead. Most heads of households were men, but some were women, and they all eventually became elders. But as the elders group became too large, we called out a core group of senior elders who were all men. There was a deliberate grooming of younger men to become leaders, sending some off to seminary. Younger couples were raised up to be heads of household. Marriage seemed a badge of maturity. Weddings were the focus of major celebrations. This culture created some dissonance with the growing secular women's movement in the larger culture around us. As more professionally trained women came to RPF, the Reba community struggled through many unresolved and sometimes divisive conversations on men's and women's roles in church leadership.

Personally, I struggled with the question, "If marriage and child rearing are the pinnacle, then what place is there for me? How does God want to use me?" I had shared leadership roles in the singles group, in my small group, and in a summer arts program for neighborhood children, but I felt there was more for me to learn and more for me to offer than waiting for marriage to validate my existence. I was ready for some vocational exploration outside of high school teaching. With my mentor's support and counsel, I sought an outside track of fuller engagement of my gifts with the Mennonite Central Committee's Voluntary Service Program and in going to seminary after that—all discerned and affirmed by the community as a "sent out" member.

❖

"Why didn't you leave the community?" I asked Sally. "You certainly could have found other places that welcomed your gifts and might have saved you some emotional anguish." Sally continued.

❖

During my time away, I did not consider leaving Reba membership because I valued Reba's deep modeling of radical discipleship, sacrificial service, and healing of people coming from traumatized backgrounds. I did not hear God calling me out of membership just because of some differences in how we saw women in leadership. I saw community as a good way to live and a place of long-term relational grounding for me as a single person.

When I went to seminary I gained the tools to study some of the critical Scriptures on gender for myself and made many valuable discoveries. I realized there are two creation stories in Genesis. In Genesis 1:27 maleness and femaleness together reflect the fullness of God's image. This has implications for leadership in the church. In the Genesis 2 account, the woman's creation after the man is not a subordinate afterthought. If you look at the order of creation in this story, the woman is the pinnacle. Naming the woman as "helper" uses a word sometimes applied to God, who is not a servant but a highly revered partner. These were "ah-ha" moments for me.

In the restrictive passages of the New Testament, we see Paul giving instructions for the missionary context where he was operating. Up to that time women were generally not literate and did not have theological training. Paul was also concerned not to have untrained women be cause for discrediting the Jewish-Gentile congregations. His instructions to the churches on restricted roles for women were not all timeless principles. In other Pauline churches women prophesied and led house churches, and in one instance a woman, Junia, was named among the apostles. It was important to understand if a pastoral leadership role for me was in disobedience to Scripture, and I concluded it was not.

Our community is now in a place of more relaxed recognition of people's differing gifts and potential to serve, regardless of gender. The two congregations (Living Water Community Church and Reba Place Church) where our communal members participate now both have women pastors. We have come to see that women might do theology in some different ways and with more practical applications than men. I remember a very pregnant young mother giving an Advent sermon on Mary that a man could never have given. Women seem to embrace paradox more easily than men. It's been refreshing to hear the Bible interpreted by both men and women. When women or people of other races and cultures read Scripture and interpret it, we receive more of the fullness and wholeness of God than if we only hear from white males. Yet I acknowledge a great debt of gratitude to male theologians and teachers who guided me on my discipleship journey in community and seminary at a time when women were largely absent from these roles.

Looking back over my years in church planting and twelve years of pastoral leadership of Living Water Community Church, I acknowledge operating out of much insecurity and lack of female role models. I did not always find it easy to deal with self-confident men who had strong opinions, but there was also a certain acceptance I felt because people recognized I was not there on a power trip. People who gravitate to the vision of community tend to have a lot of ideas and idealism, along with distrust of strongly directive leadership. I am not a strong visionary, but I called for a collaboration of many peoples' gifts and visions to reflect the kingdom of God in our urban setting. I tried to make it possible for diversity to function together without a need to homogenize it all. I expect the Lord's word to come to us in the midst of our life together. We have gone in surprising directions because of visions that others have offered or from responding to needs God brought to our doorstep.

In earlier generations, female religious orders provided a place where women could become strong leaders and develop gifts beyond child rearing. An all-women's community can be a good thing for nurturing gifts and providing support for singleness. I have been part of a translocal Mennonite Women's Support Circle begun to provide stability for single women called to long-term service roles in the church (particularly in overseas mission). One member has made a permanent vow of celibacy, but most of us were less clear about that calling. Over the years, several of the members have married and departed, while a few who have married have remained part of the group. The group continues as an important source of friendship and discernment for the dozen or so members who now live across the United States and in Canada.

The present generation of young women is more used to being in front of groups, sharing their gifts, and seeing older women in leadership as role models. I see the confidence my stepdaughters have gained growing up in an affirming community. For such empowered women, leadership is not so much of a climb. I'm hoping they can be less self-questioning along the lines of "Am I having this problem because I'm no good at what I'm doing, because I'm a woman, or because it happens to everyone who leads?"

And then, Sally continued to reflect on what she has learned and how it is relevant to today's younger women and men who feel called to start new communities.

❖

I would encourage them to find good ways to team it so men's and women's gifts can work in synergy together. Often women are more practical, pastoral, and better at organizing, while the men are more likely to ruminate on ethical, philosophical, and theological issues. The yin and yang of working these things out can be messy but fruitful. I realize it takes energy to work this out within marriage and within the community as a whole.

In pastoral care I have seen great value in men and women working together. Some men will confess more weakness to a woman, but the man should not mistake compassion for a come-on. Some guys need men to confront and call them to accountability. Some women need the safety of other women to share deeply. In a community whose mission is hospitality to homeless and marginal people, it can be hard to set limits. A lot of people coming to community have lacked good parenting. Men and women working together have a way of both healing and challenging, putting together confrontation with kindness and grace. It's not always the woman who plays the gracious role. In the Clearing household, Hilda is the straight shooter and Julius the one who can be too compassionate. In tough situations they work better together. Both my husband and I have benefited from the spiritual parenting we received at Reba from godly men and women role models.

What I appreciated about Reba from the beginning is that I saw many more men holding babies, changing diapers, being involved with their families than anything I had seen to that point in my life. Community makes possible job sharing and having both parents actively involved in the family. Dave and Neta Jackson wrote about this in *Living Together in a World Falling Apart*. This collaborative approach matters for women whose greatest aspiration might not be as the homemaker and child rearer.

Different life stages will look different. Baby boomers and younger women now come to community with more training and willingness to parent part-time and do other kinds of work as well. Once kids are in school and you have an emptier nest, there is more flexibility. Women in community have felt less isolated raising children where they can have more life together, childcare sharing, and more energy for doing collaborative projects with others.

Community is a place where life's hurts can find healing, where gender roles and the theology behind them can be examined in faithful relationships that hold fast even as we discover and work through differences of opinions and experiences. We can be known for who we are even as we become who God wants us to be. And as we find our identity in Christ, we have good news to share with our children, not just in words but in a shared and meaningful life.

PART FOUR

THE FIRST YEAR OF COMMUNITY

CHAPTER 14

Decision-Making, Leadership, and Paths to Unity

All the believers were one in heart and mind.

—Acts 4:32

Many people, when they hear about the number of meetings we have in community, groan and say, "I hate meetings, especially the ones where people butt heads trying to make decisions together." I have to say, in response, that many of the best memories I have of forty years in community are of meetings where we have faced every kind of difficult decision, listened to everyone in the group who had something to say, and then waited in stillness for what God might want us to do. Eventually, one person or another would speak what they heard from the Spirit, and we were amazed to acknowledge that all the rest of us heard the same thing, or are at peace with it. Unity, peace, a common way forward, the sacrament of God's presence in the miracle of consensus, tangible in shining eyes and joy in being together. We break out in song and celebration. Meetings—I love 'em!

From the witness of the New Testament, we cannot arrive at a single normative pattern for community decision-making and leadership. However, both leaders and followers are urged to exercise humility—which means careful listening all around rather than relying on eloquence or political manipulation.

The way many intentional communities worship and conduct their business has been strongly influenced by the Quaker tradition, where meetings are characterized by unscripted silence, listening to "that of God in every person," trusting the Holy Spirit to lead the group into unity. The Quakers and other more secular consensus-building trainers have gathered the wisdom and experience of this tradition and are worth learning from. (See, for example, Diana Leaf Christian, *Creating a Life Together: Practical Tools to Grow Ecovillages and Intentional Communities*.) But Quakers did not invent this way of consensus decision-making.

The Spirit-led consensus model is practiced in Acts 15:1–29, when the Jerusalem church leaders gathered in council to deal with a crisis brewing in their missionary movement. How can Jewish believers and Gentile converts have fellowship when they come from deeply conflicting traditions? After listening to Paul and Barnabas about what God was doing in bringing the Gentiles to faith, the council agreed they would not demand a "kosher" life of Gentiles. Rather, they would ask the Gentile Christians to observe a few essentials of the Jewish law out of respect for Jewish sensitivities and convictions. Their report begins, "It seemed good to the Holy Spirit and to us. . . ."

In Paul's letter to the Corinthian church (1 Cor. 14) he offers detailed instructions about what should happen "when you come together." John Howard Yoder gives the best brief exposition I have seen of this "Rule of Paul" in *Body Politics: Five Practices of the Christian Community before the Watching World*. "Paul tells his readers that everyone who has something to say, something given by the Holy Spirit, can have the floor." This corresponds with Paul's teaching in 1 Corinthians 12 how "every member of the community—certainly not only the men—has a gift, and many of the gifts he named called for participating orally in meetings."

It is not enough to aim for unity in community meetings, but unity of the Spirit is a way of life to be pursued at all times. Paul, writing to the church in Ephesus, names the core virtues of this calling. "As a prisoner for the Lord, then, I urge you to live a life worthy of the calling you have received. Be completely humble and gentle; be patient, bearing with one another in love. Make every effort to keep the unity of the Spirit through the bond of peace" (Eph. 4:1–3). What are these preconditions to unity, and how do we maintain them so we can arrive at community meetings free to deal constructively with just the agenda at hand?

The following preconditions for unity are neither systematic nor complete. Rather, they refer to issues that I have seen arise most often in visits to communal groups and in my own experience of community. You and your group, can surely add other examples.

STRIVE TO BE ONE BODY AND ONE SPIRIT

The basic precondition for unity is stated in Ephesians 4:4–6: "There is one body and one Spirit, just as you were called to one hope when you were called; one Lord, one faith, one baptism; one God and Father of all, who is over all and through all and in all." As we saw in chapter 10, on commitment and membership, the community's novice year is essential to assuring that this basic unity of calling and purpose is shared by all persons present in a members' meeting. Without this foundation of calling and commitment, it is likely that group members will be pursuing conflicting purposes. In some cases a community may wish to include short-term participants who are exploring membership so they can see what they are getting into, but only those who have made the commitment and who will live the consequences should be making the decisions.

Conversely, it is important for members to actually be present. "Mailing in your vote" does not work because the Holy Spirit is doing something in the deliberations, creating unity on the spot with the persons present. You have to be there to experience it. If community members cannot be present because of illness or other reasons, they need to trust those who are there to act on their behalf under the guidance of the Spirit.

"You actually go to every meeting?" some visitors ask. Yes, unless we are sick or out of town for some community-supported reason. Attendance is not a matter of outward obligation, nor is it just "when I feel like it." Participation in members' meetings expresses who we are, members one of another in the body of Christ.

HEAL MEMORIES OF ABUSIVE AUTHORITY

Many of us have been wounded by leaders who were distant, did not know how to listen well, or who acted in arbitrary ways to preserve institutional order and their own need for control. And so we are "on guard." We have vowed to defend ourselves against all leadership—with a load of emotion and sometimes with ideologies from (leftist) anarchist or (rightist) libertarian sources. There is no way to untie this knot by technical expertise in group process or by arguments about submission from Scripture. If this is the bind your group is in, the most promising way forward is to meet in humility and brokenness, and to hear from each one's experiences with authority, both the good and the bad, asking God for guidance and healing.

As a teen, I was part of a church youth group entrusted with teaching our own Sunday school class. We decided to depart from the given curriculum and acquaint ourselves with world religions. Our church was without a pastor at the time, so when an elder heard what we were doing, he shut down the class and took over as teacher. From that time on, I felt physically suffocated in this elder's presence and in many other home church settings. Years later, I realized—with the help of sisters and brothers in community—that I was resisting authority, both the good and the bad, in a way that troubled them and impeded our group. I read a book by Dennis Linn and Matthew Linn, *Healing of Memories: Prayer and Confession Steps to Inner Healing*, and as I followed the exercises in it, I was moved to forgive this church elder from my past. In doing so I discovered that God had also freed me from the stifling feelings that would rise up in the presence of strong leadership, setting me free to forgive others in my past and to acknowledge my own part in the conflicts.

This personal transformation did not release me from the responsibility to sometimes confront leaders about overstepping their bounds, but I was no longer "on guard." I could more nearly trust where trust was deserved and choose my responses with more humility. By that time I also had some leadership responsibilities in family and at work, so I knew more keenly my own need for forgiveness.

In a community visitation to Communality in Lexington, Kentucky, I observed a similar dynamic of fear and mistrust of leaders within their group. I felt moved to share this story from my own experience. The community chose to take the season of Lent to reflect on their own leadership wounds and, for Christ's sake, to forgive hurts of their past and of one another.

Often, intentional Christian communities, with their consensus models of decision-making and daily shared life that offers free access to leaders, feel like a safe haven for persons who have suffered under hierarchical models of authority. But if these wounds are not healed, they often bring with them fear and mistrust of leadership based on the past rather than present experience. Sharing our stories in small groups, counseling one another on how to repair what is broken in our experience and our attitudes, can open a space for God's liberating work of repentance, forgiveness, and renewed trust of one another.

In some cases, a more profound and deliberate process of healing from experiences of abuse is needed, which we will discuss with more depth in chapter 24.

RECONCILE CURRENT RELATIONSHIPS

Here it is enough to recall chapter 9, "Transforming Conflict into Solidarity." In memorable words, Jesus counsels, "Therefore, if you are offering your gift at the altar and there remember that your brother or sister has something against you, leave your gift there in front of the altar. First go and be reconciled to them; then come and offer your gift" (Matt. 5:23–24). This advice applies to community meetings as well as times of worship. Otherwise we are prone to oppose any suggestion made by someone with whom we are not reconciled.

SETTLE HOW LEADERS WILL SERVE THE GROUP

Once a group has decided to move in together, the pace of decision-making accelerates. Many communities that start with a consensus model get bogged down at this point, facing more issues than they can process in a weekly meeting unless they can entrust some responsibilities to leaders, task teams, and overseers of different areas of community life.

In our attempt to launch a community in Kansas in the 1970s, we hardly had time to deal with the immediate agenda. Garden season is upon us. The childcare schedule is broken down again. Do we make costly car repairs or buy a van? And who will talk with the visitor who disrupted worship last week? Longer-term issues such as working on our covenant, choosing a name, and deciding about incorporation were put off again and again.

By God's grace, we struggled enough that everyone felt frustration with our bogged-down decision-making process. We asked a team from a more experienced community to visit, to help us think through and talk over our issues. We already had a lively sense of the Holy Spirit's power to lead us, as often happened in our times of worship where various gifts were exercised by a variety of people.

A community visitation helped us see that, whatever we might wish were the case, leadership in a group is a fact of life. If unacknowledged, it is nevertheless at work. We noted that when Steve led our meetings, they were peaceful and productive; when I led—not so much. We had some gifted musicians with strong ideas, but Lynn, a modestly gifted musician, was especially gifted to shepherd the music group and all of us into harmonious worship. Irene had the gift of passionate prayer that named what was going on among us, and several had the gift of taking good meeting minutes. A leadership team began to meet to carry out group decisions, gather agendas, and prepare proposals that the whole group would reshape and decide upon in our weekly meetings where consensus still prevailed. Everyone had a role, and everyone had situations where they followed the lead of others. It took longer than one paragraph indicates, but we became a functioning body submitted to one another in the Spirit rather than a dozen heads trying to convince each other about the way to go.

John Howard Yoder, in his chapter "The Fullness of Christ" in *Body Politics*, explores the scriptural background and understanding for this way of operating:

> The Paul of Ephesians uses the term "the fullness of Christ" to describe a new mode of group relationships, in which every member of the body has a distinctly identifiable, divinely validated and empowered role. "His gifts were that some should be apostles, some prophets, some evangelists, some pastors and teachers, . . . for building up the body of Christ . . . until all attain to the unity of the faith and of the knowledge of the Son of God . . . to the measure of the stature of the fullness of Christ" (Eph. 4:11–13).
>
> The Paul of 1 Corinthians says literally that every member is the bearer of such a "manifestation of the Spirit for the common good" (1 Cor. 12:7). He prescribes quite detailed guidelines which run counter to our intuitions and our habits, for how this vision of the dignity of every part of the organism should lead his readers to ascribe the greater value to the less honored members.

While everyone in the community is responsible to pray and think about the common good, this works best if one person is called and commissioned to give oversight.

Julius Belser describes his role in the Clearing household at Reba in this way: "I pray for each person in our household family and look for ways to build up our life and work in the love of Christ." Our temptation as humans is to draw status and power to ourselves in such a role, so humility, wisdom, and a servant spirit are virtues we look for in confirming someone in an oversight role. Regular times of community review should also be built into leadership appointments.

How does a community close the distance and keep at bay the alienation that often characterizes leadership in the world? "Perfect love casts out fear." Our fear of leaders can be somewhat allayed by an intimate common life where daily love and mutual service bring us close to those who carry special responsibilities for the group. We also learn that community life goes better when each of us concentrates most of our energy on doing our part well for the common good rather than fretting over how others are doing their part. A new tradition was launched at Reba when Greg began his three-year term as overall community leader by personally meeting with all community members, so that each one's concerns were heard well from the outset.

DO HOMEWORK BEFORE THE MEETINGS

Proposals that have a major community impact, like a mission statement or a change in leadership structure, should take several meetings—and, perhaps, a weekend retreat. At the first meeting the leadership team lays out the issue and asks for questions of clarification and for improvements to the proposal. It is important to find someone to lead the meeting who accepts her role as a servant of the consensus-building process rather than the pusher of an agenda. An outside facilitator can sometimes be helpful. It is natural that some persons will want much more information and engagement, while others might trust the process or have other, more pressing concerns. Further information-sharing meetings and working sessions can be arranged outside community meetings for persons to pursue the topic as deeply as they choose. If a common direction seems to be emerging, it is helpful for the community leaders to set a date when they hope the proposal can be confirmed. This marks a season of prayer, reflection, and a final request for anyone with reservations to speak to the leadership team before the meeting. When unity is given, it is important to stop and celebrate, to give thanks to God and to those who have worked hard for the common good.

LISTEN TO EACH OTHER AND TO THE SPIRIT

It is a good spiritual discipline to hear from everyone who wants to speak on a proposal, shaping it until the best ideas are worked together, and then take some time of silence to listen to the Spirit.

I remember a time at New Creation Fellowship when we were deliberating about buying a house in our neighborhood where larger meetings could gather and a larger household of people could share life. We all were agreed to buy it except one person who felt the Spirit was asking us to wait. Without consensus to go ahead, we waited. A few weeks later a group of doctors approached the community saying they wanted to give us a large house if only we would move it off a lot where they planned to build a clinic. Half a year later "the Free House" was sitting on a new foundation in our neighborhood. In the basement we had a worship-meeting-dining space large enough for all our community and guests too. We should never block consensus without faithful listening and prayer. But sometimes one person hears the Lord better than all the rest, and consensus is still a blessing.

Listening deeply is an act of mutual submission, not in the sense of turning off my own mind and conscience, but in taking someone else's experience and wisdom as seriously as I would listen to myself. In this way no one is pushed aside, but we each become participants in concerns and hopes that now move us all. We do not need to convince one another. It is the work of the Holy Spirit to move free individuals, fully engaged, into unity of purpose and love.

LEARN TO RECOGNIZE THE FRUITS OF UNITY

The process of Spirit-led consensus may take a little longer sometimes, but the implementation is much faster and the decisions made hang together in a durable way. It might be hard to believe that five thousand believers in the early church at Jerusalem were of "one heart and mind" unless we have had repeated experiences like that ourselves. But if we have, it makes us look forward to more such meetings, which stand out as landmarks of God's presence and history-making work among us.

CHAPTER 15

Taking on Work Schedules and the Seduction of Careers

New communities are often pulled apart by conflicting work schedules and the demands of professional career development. One way to observe this fragmenting dynamic and its repair is to sit in on breakfast at two different households.

Household A: At 6:00 AM Jeff has already gone to his job, opening for a bagel shop—the only work he could find after a month of searching. At 6:30 Sherry puts on a coffee pot for those who will follow, packs her lunch, and takes a thermos of Java out the door for a crosstown commute. With her recently acquired MSW, Sherry is eager to prove herself and gain accreditation for a career in social work. At 7:00 Henry and Molly, a married couple, come down the stairs, make breakfast, pray, and eat together. Henry gathers his books for a long day of teaching at a parochial school, usually followed by an evening of paper grading. Henry is out the door with a kiss and a lunch provided by Molly, who leaves a little later to work as a receptionist in a doctor's office. Molly is pregnant and wonders how their schedules and finances will balance out once the baby arrives. Karl, a graduate student in policy studies, worked late last night on a paper and now tries to find his way out of the fog with a cup of coffee. Jonathan, who is unemployed, sleeps till 9:30, gets up depressed, and scans the web for any new job openings. Household A eats a "serial breakfast."

The community members have committed to eat dinners together three times a week and to host a Friday night potluck for neighbors and friends. But even this minimal common life is hard to sustain because of work demands and frequent schedule changes. The community is frustrated because they moved into a common household for the shared life, but they are finding little time to actually support each other and get to know their neighbors.

Household B: At 6:30 Gus is making soft-boiled eggs and raisin oatmeal for the household. The night before Chuck had already set the table. Joseph has been up for an hour helping Bob, who has muscular dystrophy, to get his shower and into his wheelchair in time for a 7:00 breakfast. The household eats early enough so that everyone with outside jobs can be present. Twelve persons assemble around the table with greetings. Peggy leads the readings this week from *Common Prayer: A Liturgy for Ordinary Radicals.* At the point in the liturgy marked "Prayers for Others," household members pray for each other's work and ministries, and for the world according to the thanksgivings and concerns they have lifted up. As they eat, one person speaks at a time so that everyone can hear a single conversation, often reflecting on the common readings. Breakfast done, each person carries dishes or leftovers into the kitchen. They check the chart that the household manager, Char, has created to see who is "on" for dishwashing. Those with outside jobs gather their things and move to the door, sent off with blessings for the day, each one primed to reflect on the same story from a saint and readings from Scripture.

What differences do you see between these two communities? And how did these differences come about? When I visit type A communities, I hear how they feel trapped by their own career expectations, school debts, and the demands of the money economy. Many would like to become a type B community that sustains a more integrated life, where all find meaning in roles of service to one another, where work, prayer, and Christian community service each find a rhythm in life. But how can they tame the "wolf at the door" and make him serve a common good? The money economy that the gospels refer to as Mammon has too many of us in thrall, both externally through the pressure of economic survival in the system, and internally as well, through the individualistic and materialistic values we have absorbed and live by. Obviously, there is no way a group can get from A to B in one step, but with patience and discernment, there is a path we want to explore in this chapter.

Most Christian intentional communities would like to minimize their dependence on the money economy, to arrive at common work or ministry that affords the freedom to set a community schedule for meals, times of prayer, community meetings, availability to neighbors, and other expressions of their mission. However, common work usually involves common training and major capital investment. Common ministry means raising money from an extended community of supporters. ("Developing Common Work and Ministries" is the topic of chapter 25.) In the meantime, most communal members will need to find jobs and function in a mixed economy, "in the world but not of it."

GOOD WORK—WHAT DOES IT LOOK LIKE?

When I visit communities, we often discuss the questions, What does good work look like? and When you are looking for work, what guidelines should you follow? Here are some answers and a few stories I've picked up.

Good work uses and develops our gifts as cocreators, made in God's image.

Early on in the biblical story we read, "The LORD God took the man and put him in the Garden of Eden to work it and take care of it" (Gen. 2:15). Something in us remembers the freedom of the Garden and longs for its wholeness restored—humans freely exploring, working with, and delighting in the creation of a God who observed, "It is very good." As any unemployed person will tell you, work is a blessing. It not only helps us survive, but it also enlarges our capacity while it gives our existence dignity and meaning by connecting us to others whose needs we meet by our labor.

I've seen summer workers return from Plow Creek Farm to their urban communities, bodies tanned and fit, eyes alive as they tell of growing and harvesting real food. They are glad they did it, but the long hours of toil also lead most of them to conclude they are not called to be farmers.

Work is good, but struggling for survival, as many in the world must do, can also feel like a long and unrelenting march to death. "Cursed is the ground because of you; through painful toil you will eat food from it all the days of your life. . . . By the sweat of your brow you will eat your food until you return to the ground, since from it you were taken; for dust you are and to dust you will return" (Gen. 3:17–19). Sin has corrupted our global economic system by organizing it to extract wealth for the few rather than to solve the problem of poverty for the many. This unsustainable economy of infinite expectations has plundered and polluted creation and racked up mountainous debts for the next generation.

I remember early on in our community experience in Kansas that when idealism did not pay the rent, I took a job in a recreational vehicle factory, pushing plywood through a table saw for mind-numbing hours and assembling doors for campers that I never saw installed. Despite my MA in history, for four months I was an alienated cog in a larger machine with bosses I never met. Besides a weekly paycheck, the main benefit I got from this job was a very personal experience of the oppression of the working class and a list of resolutions—things I would never do if I ever became a supervisor or an employer. I saw how workers toil all week at jobs they resent, to make money to buy some weekend distractions to numb their pain, and then do it all over again. Work is indeed under a curse.

But that is not the last word either. The apostle Paul writes, "Creation waits in eager expectation for the children of God to be revealed. . . . The creation itself will be liberated from its bondage to decay and brought into the freedom and glory of the children of God (Rom. 8:19–22). As we are being redeemed by God, we also get to participate with God in the redemption of creation, our local economies, and our work. After a few months pushing plywood through a saw, I found better work (for less money) advocating for victim-offender reconciliation programs and recruiting volunteers for prison visitation. I see this pattern often repeated in the lives of younger community members—a series of difficult jobs with significant life learning, eventually leading to work that more nearly fits their gifts and calling, work that reveals to the world in some way what the kingdom of God might look like.

As we look for principles of good work, we will keep discovering the truth of these three biblical insights: Work is a blessing; work is a curse; and God is working with us to redeem and renew all things.

Good work meets real and basic needs.

I remember talking with Jason Winton from Chico, California, a young unhappy social worker who, with his wife, Julissa, know their calling is to offer hospitality in community. His job provides enough income to support the household, but he doubts he can continue much longer. The funding sources for his counseling agency push them to meet only with clients who can be billed at top rates rather than take time with the people who have the greatest need. Jason had gone into social work because he wanted to come close to people with real needs, and he laments serving a corrupted system.

Tim Otto, from Church of the Sojourners in San Francisco, is a half-time home health care nurse and a community leader. In a spring 2011 *Conspire* article, Otto encourages radical disciples in alternative communities to avoid demanding professional careers and to instead go into the trades, where they are more likely to serve real human needs, and where part-time employment can pay the bills, leaving a significant margin of time for ministry. Like the apostle Paul, who supported apostolic church-planting with tentmaking labor, Otto advises, "Work for money and minster for free."

Good work is part of daily and weekly community rhythms.

This is the wisdom of Sabbath that God commanded at Creation, an insight that traditional monastic communities have cultivated over the centuries and that blesses New Monastic groups like Household B we read about at the beginning of this chapter. Human beings come fully alive when their spirits have time for both concentration and contemplation, for engagement and retreat. From such a base, persons can connect for a lifetime of sacrificial service in the world and not burn out, already participating in the life that is eternal.

Good work creates a surplus.

Doug Selph is a gifted computer programmer at Reba with the highest income in our community. But because he is a disciple of Jesus, he only takes on work that allows him to be near home and fully involved in our common-purse community. He is happy to support others who can express their gifts for ministry. With community support, he has learned how to say no to the personal wealth, lifestyle, and the career moves that beckon his professional peers. Instead, he does good work that creates a surplus, allowing him to be generous in support of his family, community, and those in need around the world.

Good work takes place in a healthy and loving spiritual environment.

In such a setting we can build relationships that express our real selves as witnesses to the good news of the kingdom of God. In community-owned businesses or ministries, this kind of environment is easier to sustain, but in the market economy, creativity is sometimes possible.

For many years my wife, Joanne, worked as a supervisor of assistants in one section of the Northwestern University library. Many of these assistants were lonely foreign students who were happy to find a "mother away from home" who listened to their woes and invited them to join our circle of friends in community. It became natural to say, "We'll pray for you and for your family" whether in Iraq, in the Congo, or in war-torn Lebanon. We had a life in community that we could share with others because of this workplace connection.

Good work promotes social justice and ecological integrity, participating with God in mending a broken world.

Not everyone gets to do their dream job, but after a few years of survival-type wage labor and gardening on the side, Bobby Wright, from the Oak Park Community in Kansas City, Missouri, won a grant to test the viability of raised-bed farming on a vast old church parking lot. Such meaningful, creative, and hopeful work often comes after a few years of ordinary wage-labor, simple living, and investing in serious cutting-edge learning. Patience and a sense of calling precede the kingdom of God breakthroughs that most communities can tell about who have stuck together for a few years.

Good work is chosen with the guidance and discernment of one's community.

Micah Waters is a member in Cherith Brook, a Catholic Worker community with a ministry of friendship, hospitality, and advocacy for homeless people of their neighborhood in northern Kansas City. Waters writes, "We are all discerning our call for the next covenanting year here at Cherith Brook. Last year we each made the decision on our own and presented it to the community. This year we were hoping to truly discern each one's work and calling in the midst of community and dialogue. If you have anything you could give to us, I would greatly appreciate it."

I observe that this deepening of community has become possible at Cherith Brook because they have chosen to share their income and expenses in a common-purse living arrangement. With shared finances, a community can say to an individual, for example, "We think you should quit the job that oppresses you with such a long commute and trust God and the community until you find work closer to home that fits a common schedule." Work chosen with the guidance and discernment of one's community can consider the needs of the community, the individual's gifts, and how the work participates in the community's mission. This is a process of growing trust and mutual submission. As the individual submits work decisions, the community also must look at each one's needs and gifts so that all can thrive in mutual service of the community's mission. When we discern our work together, it becomes common work, an expression of the body of Christ and his mission in the world.

Good work expresses our call to embody God's new economy breaking into our old distorted world.

In *The Road to Daybreak*, Henri Nouwen wrestles with a call to leave academia and become a member of a L'Arche community—a step he took by the end of the year that this journal covers. Nouwen describes an eye-opening covenanting ceremony of assistants who have lived and served in the community for some years. They are not so much making new vows or commitments, but rather a public statement of their discovery that they have, over time, become bonded to the core community members with mental and emotional disabilities and that they accept this as the work of God in their lives.

When I saw the men and women who announced their covenant with Jesus and the poor, I saw how real this downward way of Jesus is and how, if I go this way, I go not alone, but as a member of the "body of Jesus." Seldom have I experienced so directly the difference between individual heroism and communal obedience. Whenever I think about becoming poor as something I must accomplish, I become oppressed. But as soon as I realize that my brothers and sisters call me to go this way with them in obedience to Jesus, I am filled with hope and joy.

Many in our society have arrived at a distorted idea of vocation as a calling to work harder and longer to sustain a rising standard of living, seduced by Madison Avenue's vision that those with "more" have found the meaning and purpose of their lives. In our distorted economy where almost all the wealth flows to those at the top, this vocation of "more" is like frantically climbing the "down escalator." As we have seen in the stories of this chapter, there is a way off the wrong-way escalator by reducing our wants, finding contentment in fulfillment of our basic needs, and working with others like Henri Nouwen to become living parables of a broken world made new.

In every generation the Spirit calls Christians to make their vocation the discipleship of Jesus. In this practical way we can exercise our faith, trusting God and the discipleship community for our survival. This frees us to invest our lives with Jesus, who calls us to "seek first his kingdom and his righteousness," trusting that "all these things [good work included] will be given to you as well" (Matt. 6:33).

CHAPTER 16

Making Connections Among Communities

Christian intentional communities have been seized by a gospel vision so radical that they are countercultural within Christianity itself. They do not accept the authority of those who counsel assimilation back into the "Egypt" they have fled. But we should also be wary of any group or association so full of the truth that they need no one else. Communities that "go it alone" are likely to fail, while those that band together greatly increase their chances of sustaining growth to maturity.

The early Christian movement was Spirit-powered, controversial, and, as we will see, highly networked among its newly sprouted communities all around the Mediterranean Sea. To get a taste of this vital collaboration of friends and coworkers, I urge you to peel off a minute from this book and read the last chapter of Paul's letter to the church in Rome. . . .

Okay, you're back. What do you think? In Romans 16, amid Paul's many salutations we get a quick tour of families, house churches, and mission partners in the city of Rome. Paul greets no less than twenty-nine friends, relatives, coworkers, and acquaintances. These greetings, moreover, are extended by eight of Paul's companions in the gospel, including the scribe taking dictation, who sneaks into the Bible by adding, "I, Tertius, who wrote down this letter, greet you in the Lord." I am amazed that Paul knows this many "sisters and brothers" in a city he has not yet visited. Those Christian communities sure were connected!

Initial community connections can take many forms, three of which we want to explore in this chapter: partnerships between younger and more experienced communities; informal communities of communities that emerge among groups in the same area; and a community board of directors that provides oversight from outside the group.

The reasons for intentional communities to connect with each other are many and similar to the reasons why individuals join local communities—for fellowship and support in a countercultural calling, to grow in discipleship of Jesus by drinking from a larger pool of wisdom and good judgment, for mentoring and leadership development, for emergency care in times of crisis, and because it is energizing to make friends with others of "our own tribe." At the same time, this search for connections usually begins like a cautious courtship, building trust in little ways before deeper collaboration is possible.

We begin with a dialogue that explores such a community-to-community connection at its starting point. Imagine a partnership between a newer and a more experienced community that begins something like this.

David: Hi Tricia. I've listened to your message on our phone and I'm eager to learn more about your community. How did you get the idea to contact Reba?

Tricia: We got your name from Shane. We asked him for some advice about bringing a family into our community, and he mentioned that Reba is not far away and is available to pastor newer groups like ours.

D: Tell me more about your community and why you are looking for more connection.

T: We live in a three-flat with thirteen persons here in the Humbolt Park neighborhood of Chicago. We had some turnover last summer. We've been doing lots of good things but want them to "come together" better. We've decided to stop our open community meals and stop most of our outside activities to take time to pray and focus on our community goals and purpose. We feel the need for some outside wisdom. We used to have weekly house meetings, but now we are just praying on Monday nights—not doing business. We are still committed to keep "Food Not Bombs," a free food distribution project, going in our neighborhood.

D: What about your house? Who lives there?

T: We have a family with us—a dad and his two teenage sons we invited in about four months ago. We have another family with very small children. The rest of us are singles in our mid-twenties to early thirties. Three of us have been here since the start, two and a half years ago. We are social workers, social justice people, artists . . .

We came together through a church group where I attended. Friends invited friends to talk about community. About a year later we found a place. We started just meeting, praying about it. When we ran out of things to talk about we started a community dinner, inviting whomever, and a group started to form. We've gone through a Bible study focus, a social justice focus—as we felt led.

D: What are the areas of koinonia, of sharing in your life? What do you have in common?

T: We share food, meals together, rent payments, morning prayer sometimes, a commitment to the neighborhood, to sustainability, and creativity. We have a community gardening group. Others have started a business together.

D: Do you have a covenant?

T: Periodically, we've talked about "Who are we?" but never written it out. For our everyday life it has not felt pertinent.

D: Is this because you have resistance to putting yourselves in a box with words, or because of other reasons?

T: I think we see more of a need for it than we used to, especially when we think of the long term, but completing the covenant is not urgent for every day.

D: Are there outside folks who look into your life, like pastors or other communities?

T: We are ecumenical, go to different churches, so all our pastors came together to bless our house when we moved in. One pastor has said he would be available to us but has not actually been here since then. That's why we called you. We wonder if Reba could help us in this time.

D: I'd like to visit, just to get to know you better. When communities make connections for guidance and mutual support, it is important that there be a "blood type match," that you find a community that can really affirm your calling rather than try to undo it. I suspect that the pastor you mentioned cares about you all, but having never lived in community of the kind that you are, he is not sure he can give appropriate counsel. Our groups should get to know each other before we decide how we should be further involved.

T: That sounds good. We're not sure about coming under an outside authority but feel the need for support and partnership.

D: That makes sense. If I could come for an initial visit, how might this happen?

T: It would be great if you could come to one of our Monday night meetings. What about next week?

Since that initial conversation more than two years ago, this north-side Chicago community has named itself "Kedzingdale," merging the street names of Kedzie and Bloomingdale that intersect nearby.

Now, looking back over the dialogue we shared, I notice several things happening at the same time. The community had exhausted itself, like other new groups, trying to do more good things than they could sustain. They had wisely chosen to step back from overactivism to pray more and to look for supporting partners on their long-term journey. Like the child who insists, "I do it myself," they were at an important stage of growth. But, at the same time, the child is looking around for role models from whom she can learn even more.

I remember in the 1970s when our Kansas community, New Creation Fellowship, was just finding its way, we welcomed visits by Virgil Vogt and John Lehman from Reba Place, sometimes asking their spouses to come as well. We found immense encouragement in these connections and would visit Reba in return. All the issues that we faced in community they had already struggled with—whether it was renovating bedrooms to fit in more people, discerning Holy Spirit gifts, bed-wetting children, celebrating memberships, or mourning departures. These community visits made us wiser and gave us confidence in ways that we could never have managed by ourselves. Our leaders began regular phone consultations with their mentors in other communities. By talking over our community agenda with more-experienced leaders, we also avoided some major blunders.

We also ignored some of the advice we got because our reality was different, but folks from other communities did not cease loving and caring for us because of that. We had some struggles within our group between those who wanted more guidance and those who feared being taken over by outside authority. This way of "coming alongside" imparted wisdom and confidence without hierarchical structures. Looking back, I would conclude that all the how-to books (including this one) about community are not worth as much as good mentor relationships and a pattern of visits that build friendships between fledgling groups and more experienced communities over time.

Now, as part of the Nurturing Communities Project, my role is reversed and I am the one visiting new communities. I realize that even though new groups ask for wisdom, what they most often want is someone from the outside to listen, to ask good questions, to get to know their unique journey with God, and to affirm all that is going well. From such trust-building beginnings, further visits and exchanges of people will grow. Young communities usually want help to discern and affirm their charism—the particular gifts God has given them with which to bless the world—whether it is hospitality, peacemaking, guerilla gardening, friendship evangelism, art for kids, or engagement with the city through each member's work. I keep asking, What is the calling God has given to which a community should remain faithful in their life together, and where is the network of partners that can accompany them on this journey?

The decision to enter into a partnership with other communities or to work on its covenant (see chapter 18, "Covenant-Making in Story, Rule, and Liturgy of Commitment") signals that a community is taking seriously its identity and future, that living together is not just a youthful phase they are passing through, but that this divine calling and way of life for its core members is for the long haul. This communal life stage transition often coincides with making a home for children or welcoming persons who might be dependent on the community for existence—the point at which a growing community enters adulthood.

AREA NETWORKS

Brian Gorman is a "community builder" in Cornerstone Community, a transitional home for formerly homeless men in recovery who have HIV. He is also coordinator of a local network of communities in and around Washington, DC. "We meet once a month for a discussion group and prayer time for one another's communities. Most of the communities in our gathering are 'very new' to 'kind of new,' ranging in age from a few months to four years for some of them. For every community that sticks around and lasts into its second year, five disappear and re-form somewhere else with a different cast of characters." As Gorman suggests, one value of an area network of communities is to offer more committed and durable role models for groups still in the dreaming-and-finding-one-another phase.

These area communities of communities come together for special events—visits and tours hosted by each of the communities in turn, retreats on themes of common interest, learning from out-of-town guests with more community experience, or celebrating the publication of a book of vital interest to all the groups. Gorman reports, "We hosted Common Prayer parties, launching the use of *Common Prayer: A Liturgy for Ordinary Radicals.* It's been an honor to share this community resource with the different communities and even with some churches here. I've been thrilled to see nonliturgy folks showing up in droves to pray in a way many of them had given up on."

New York City also has an area community of communities with a tradition of quarterly get-togethers, often coordinated by Jason Storbakken. Storbakken arrived at Radical Living community in Brooklyn by way of a housing co-op movement in college, a spiritual conversion at the age of twenty-seven, and long talks throughout his life with his grandfather, an ethnic Hutterite, whose stories of communal living, martyrdom, absolute pacifism, and radical Christianity planted the seed for a life committed to Christian community.

"When I came to a serious faith," Jason continued, "I realized that I'd already been involved in intentional community. Vonetta and I married and got a house and opened it to community. There are four floors here. People started moving in and getting other apartments on the block. We have friends from the Bruderhof who were a big help when we began. This [2011] is our fourth year. We earn our living in many ways— social workers, school teachers, a college professor, a chocolate maker, a formerly homeless woman teaching daycare.

"We are a core group of about ten who are very active and a larger circle of about two dozen in all, trying to figure out how to grow in relationship to God and each other." Most recently, Jason has been ordained by the

Mennonite Church, an affirmation of his ministry at Radical Living and in the New York City Area Community of Communities.

"Amy Stabeno was the first to have a vision for the New York City Area Community of Community gatherings," Jason explains. "She asked me to help. We've had round-table conversations and skill sharings. At our last gathering we had fifty people come together—everyone from Franciscan friars to the Sisters of Mercy, Catholic Workers, and New Monastic communities. This last time we used a Liturgy of the Beloved Community, a text that Christine Sine and I wrote together. Our gatherings have been a beautiful witness of Christian unity, no one trying to evangelize the others."

Other cities, such as Kansas City and Minneapolis, have less formal associations of intentional communities. In Chicago the network gathers quarterly and includes housing co-ops as well as secular and religious communities. Beyond the immediate benefits of finding and knowing each other, such local associations help communities sustain their identities in a seductive and powerful empire rather than be digested in the belly of the beast.

FORMING A BOARD OF DIRECTORS FOR OUTSIDE OVERSIGHT

Some intentional Christian communities built around a core ministry, including Jubilee Partners (refugee resettlement and peacemaking) and Koinonia Partners (Christian discipleship, racial reconciliation, and earth-care), have 501(c)(3) status with the IRS as tax-exempt service agencies. As such, a board of directors must give oversight to the community and its ministries, and a majority of this board must be from outside the circle of community members ("interested parties"). Bren Dubay, who is committed to leading Koinonia Partners back to its radical discipleship and communal roots, has made a virtue of this legal necessity by requesting three other intentional communities—Jubilee

Partners, Church of the Servant King in Eugene, Oregon, and Reba Place Fellowship—to name members to the Koinonia board of directors.

I've been privileged to serve on the board with Koinonia Partners and at The Simple Way in Philadelphia. I observe that, in normal circumstances, a board of directors that only meets a few times a year cannot be "in charge" of community life and operations the way it falls to those who live and work there. But in times of calamity or when facing major decisions, the wisdom of a wider circle of responsible friends can make the difference in a community's survival and recovery from deep crisis. Not all communities are structured with a board of directors, but where this is the case, it is a boon to have other persons on it whose daily life in community gives them the wisdom of similar experiences and calling. This provides outside perspective along with insider's experience.

As trust grows between communal groups, as they share hospitality, take vacations together, pray for one another, see courtships flourish, and gather for special events and conferences, deeper tribal connections grow. (In chapter 27, "Becoming Accountable—Visitations and Community Associations," we will explore more formal ways in which communities establish associations with a common rule of life.) Without connections to a new tribe, a shared identity, and history of resistance, this new generation of Christian communities will be reassimilated into the dominant culture, back into conventional Christianity, or the solipsistic culture of the "me generation." Not all communities realize what they are up against. If they want to survive and thrive, they must come to grips with the nonconformist reality of the gospel that Flannery O'Connor pointed to when she wrote, "You shall know the truth, and the truth will make you odd."

CHAPTER 17

Stop Going to Church and Become the Church

I wish I could begin this chapter with an interview of John Alexander, spiritual leader of Church of the Sojourners in San Francisco, who has reflected more profoundly, systematically, and biblically on the calling of church-as-community than anyone else I have known. The problem with this wish is that John died of leukemia in 2001. However, he was considerate to leave behind a life's-work manuscript from which he read at length at many "Nature and Purpose of the Church" retreats hosted by Sojourners over the years. The title of his unfinished book, *Stop Going to Church and Become the Church*, however, provides the title for this chapter.

In my opinion, John Alexander has pulled together the most forceful biblical argument for intentional community as the shape of church that makes possible the transformation of character that Jesus and the apostles Paul, Peter, and John expected in the normal Christian life. His book is also a critique of any kind of church that we have to "go to" because if we must get in a car to go somewhere else in order to experience church, it is not our primary community—something else probably is. The kind of disciples that Jesus sent his apostles (and us) out to make can only be made in community—and not just any kind of community. It must be a life where we serve, love, correct, and forgive each other in daily interaction, where our true selves cannot hide from one another. That is the environment where we have a chance to grow into the full stature and character of Christ.

To summarize John Alexander's argument, the church is present wherever people:

- Love one another with all they are and have in lives that thickly overlap.

- Exercise the gifts of the Holy Spirit on one another, giving and receiving the love and presence of Jesus in this way.

- Experience the extravagant diversity of Jesus's followers, pursuing honesty of conversation and reconciliation in relationships.

The primary mission of the church is to be the body of Christ in this loving, intimate, sacrificial, diversity-serving-in-unity kind of way.

What then about outreach? Isn't the Christian faith about reaching out to others? Yes, of course, but the primary form of outreach is to love people with the love of Jesus, inviting them into fellowships of costly discipleship that form us into people capable of loving, serving, and dying to self for one another as Jesus taught.

John Miller, an early leader of Reba Place Fellowship, expressed this same vision of church as our primary community in a pamphlet called *The Way of Love.* "Everything that Jesus sought to communicate to his disciples in many months of teaching he gathered up in the new commandment that they love one another as he loved them. This love, which he likened to that of a self-sacrificing friend, is the one unique sign by which he wanted his disciples known in the world. Without exaggeration it can be said that the whole mission of Jesus was concentrated on one thing, the coming together of people who would love one another in this self-giving way."

In my community visits, I have met with activist groups who believe it is "outreach" that justifies their existence. When ministry comes first, then community is usually incidental. With this focus, their life with each other is often fragmented and does not convey the love that Jesus calls his disciples to live in. On the other hand, in the communities that focus on loving one another extravagantly as Jesus taught, there is often a joy its members have in being together that visitors experience as a breathtaking culture shock. There is little argument against being loved with the love of Jesus. As the apostle Paul writes of this experience, "Therefore, if anyone is in Christ, the new creation has come: The old is gone, the new is here!" (2 Cor. 5:17). Visitors get a tangible experience of how the whole world, and they themselves, can be made new, empowered by the love of Jesus.

My purpose in giving this extended exposition of John Alexander's ecclesiology (theology of church) is to encourage intentional communities to see themselves as primary cells of the church. A gathered life where people love, serve, confront, and forgive each other is the main thing about being church, the heart of the action. Even if we fail much of the time, this is the game we are supposed to play. By this New Testament understanding, most intentional Christian communities are more "church" than the places they go to on Sunday morning. But many of them do not know this.

The church, of course, exists at many levels. "For where two or three gather in my name, there am I with them," said Jesus (Matt. 18:20). This is the church at the cell level of the body of Christ. But the wider church also includes congregations, denominations, parachurch organizations of many kinds, extending to the worldwide fellowship of believers. All of these levels are church, and none are complete in themselves.

The question then arises: How shall intentional Christian communities relate to the wider church, beloved and chosen as it is by God, and yet often in a terrible mess of conformity to the ways of the world?

Dorothy Day, cofounder of the Catholic Worker movement, had her own caustic way of getting at the heart of things when she acknowledged, "The church may be a whore, but she is my mother." By this image Dorothy Day called attention to the way the Catholic Church hierarchy was often "in bed with" the military, with the powerful and wealthy of society, and in so doing, unfaithful to Jesus, her spouse, who made his home with the poor. Day's stance toward the church was not rebellion, but love and grief. Her comment is a reflection on her decades-long loving and tension-filled relationship of subversive submission with "mother church." Day's daily participation in the Mass and welcome for radical priests to offer retreats, to speak and serve Communion at community gatherings, were signs of her genuine submission. At the same time, her communities of solidarity with the poor and homeless, her pacifist essays and public acts of prophetic witness for peace and justice, presented both a critique and an example of what faithfulness might look like to the wider church.

PATTERNS OF SUBVERSIVE SUBMISSION BETWEEN INTENTIONAL CHRISTIAN COMMUNITIES AND THE WIDER CHURCH

Contrary to the pervasive spirit of rebellion in the community movement of the 1960s and '70s, this generation is in agreement with the fifth mark of the New Monasticism: "humble submission to Christ's body, the church." But this submission has taken a variety of forms, each with its own tensions, which we will explore in the remainder of this chapter. These tensions are inherent in any prophetic renewal movement. Jesus affirmed his submission to the law and the prophets by saying, "I have not come to abolish them but to fulfill them" (Matt. 5:17). By dramatic "street theater" Jesus cleansed the temple of its animal-sacrifice system and subversively inaugurated his Father's intention to make of it "a house of prayer for all nations." Yet he demonstrated his submission by allowing the temple authorities to arrest and crucify him for this act of divinely authorized civil disobedience. By becoming the sacrifice that ends all sacrifices, Jesus reveals God's new covenant long foretold: "I desire mercy, not sacrifice" (Hos. 6:6 and Matt. 9:13). Jesus models subversive submission—a dramatic witness revealing the nonviolent regime of God in human affairs, a new covenant that awaits a free human response.

Intentional Christian communities are designed to support a more radical communal expression of the life of Jesus with his disciples in the world than its members can manage as nominal members of individualistic culture-conforming congregations. Along with the demonstration of a more disciplined life comes the temptation to compare our communities to the wider church and to take pride in the differences. At the same time, communitarians can fear pride so much they hide their light under a bushel. There is no one right structural answer to this dilemma, which is both a relational and a spiritual issue.

We are called to boldly live (and sometimes speak) the truth that has been given to us, remaining in humble dialogue with the church, knowing it is unlikely that we are right about everything. Intentional Christian community does not make us holier than anyone else—it is just a way to live the life of Jesus with more intensity and devotion than we could manage by ourselves. "From everyone who has been given much, much will be demanded" (Lk. 12:48).

I have often pondered the most appropriate relationship between intentional Christian community and the wider church and have come to the conclusion that there is no one right model. Our contexts and our callings are dynamic, so the opportunities created by the Spirit need to be discerned again and again. They are not timeless categories that can be theologically deduced. That said, we still can learn from the strengths and weaknesses of various church community experiences.

A communal church. In many ways this is the model that most resembles the churches addressed by the New Testament epistles. The social template on which these early churches grew was their experience of the Jewish synagogue, a grassroots community base for a people in exile that could be formed wherever a minimum of ten families wanted to assemble. The synagogue was at the same time a center for worship, a place of study, a hub for all kinds of gatherings including decision-making about ethical issues, and a locus of mutual aid. The synagogue was not under any outside authority but was relationally connected to other such groups by frequent visits, traveling scholars, a common Scripture, and a shared salvation history performed in seasons of celebration. The early church, following the teachings of Paul and other apostles, built on this communal foundation wherever the Holy Spirit created a spiritual family of Jews and Gentiles, united in following Jesus.

Intentional communities that function as their own church would include Church of the Sojourners in San Francisco, Church of the Servant King in Eugene and Portland, Oregon, the Bruderhof communities, and Reba Place Fellowship and Plow Creek Fellowship in their first decades of life. There is simplicity in this arrangement because community schedules do not need to be coordinated with another church body. But it is also difficult for new emerging communities to cover the essential functions of church life that eventually must include teaching, baptisms, marriages, and pastoral care in times of crisis. The synagogue minimum of ten families is realistic about the range of gifts needed for healthy church life.

An intentional community within a larger congregation. At Reba Place and Plow Creek Fellowship, over time, the communal church attracted others who wanted to belong to the fellowship life but did not feel called or ready to make all the changes and commitments involved in a common purse and common household living arrangements. In other congregations, such as Englewood Christian Church in Indianapolis, a committed community core has come together with its own patterns of meetings and neighborhood ministry as the local heart of a larger commuter congregation. As we read earlier, the (white) Oakwood Community was invited to plant itself within the (black) New Rising Sun Missionary Baptist Church in Kansas City and participate in its congregational life as they were able.

What has emerged in these and other communities is something like a missionary order within a larger congregation, which has given the whole a more communal character but avoids the legalism that comes with insisting that all Christians must be communal or that "if you do not join our community disciplines, you cannot be part of this church." Over the years, as this model has evolved at Reba, it has proven crucial for separate leadership to be appointed for both congregation and the intentional community, and for those leaders to keep building a close and mutually respectful relationship.

Intentional communities where members participate in several congregations. Nehemiah Community in Springfield, Massachusetts, involves four families and single people living in three households and attending different congregations. Kedzingdale Community members living in a three-flat in the Humbolt Park neighborhood of Chicago attend several congregations to which its members have historic connections. Many Catholic Workers and L'Arche communities have a diversity of volunteers and core members who attend various churches where they are denominationally at home. Such arrangements make an ecumenical witness but also pose a challenge to an integrated community life because experiences of church are not shared and participation in them creates tugs in different directions with schedules that do not always mesh.

But the ecumenical witness of intentional communities participating in different congregations can be significant. During a community review at the Springfield Nehemiah Community (NC), I met with two pastors, Greg and Tracy, of congregations attended by NC members. "We see," they reported, "how NC helps its people fill their lives with good things from God rather than from the world. Nehemiah Community sets a pattern in our churches so others can see what an intentional Christian life looks like. They are the kind of people we hope our congregations can become—like Christians on steroids! We can show up with a van-load of young people at Nehemiah House and be welcomed to a meal and deep conversation about Christian community life." Greg and Tracy also spoke with great affection of their relationship with Patrick Murray, spiritual leader of Nehemiah Community, with whom "we have a Paul and Silas relationship." Such connections between community leaders smooth the way for mutually beneficial working relationships between churches and communities in the wider body of Christ.

Communities are part of a larger order. Monastic communities are characterized by a rigorous period of formation (as much as seven years) for all members in a common rule of life. Obviously, new Benedictine, Jesuit, or Franciscan communities do not spring up spontaneously but are founded by seasoned members sent out under the order's supervision. The orders are their own governing bodies with formal ties of accountability to the Catholic Church or other church structures. In addition to traditional Catholic orders, other examples of this way of doing church could include the ecumenical L'Arche communities built around core members with disabilities and the Episcopalian Community of Celebration in Aliquippa, Pennsylvania.

The strength of monastic and missionary orders has been a disciplined life that is able to sustain the Sermon on the Mount teachings of Jesus in community along with a high level of service to the church. The weakness of orders has been in accepting the honor of a special calling in the church for a life that is not expected of ordinary Christians. The orders have usually made peace with a less committed church by being affirmed, honored, and financially supported in their special calling.

Many New Monastic communities have learned from and adopted practices from monastic and missionary orders. The twelve marks of a New Monasticism have the potential to serve as an ordered rule of life, but the communities who identify with the New Monasticism have not yet matured and come together sufficiently to constitute an order of their own. Some networks of relationships are growing informally and a vigorous conversation is going on between New Monastic communities and the old monasticism that may yet result in new ways of being prophetic communities in subversive submission to the wider church.

PART FIVE

GROWING TASKS FOR A
YOUNG COMMUNITY

CHAPTER 18

Covenant-Making in Story, Rule, and Liturgy of Commitment

When a new community is born, its members may feel no need for a written covenant because they have talked, prayed, and struggled over their vision until it feels like a living thing given by God who has brought them together. They have an informal rule of life, commitments they know by habit and by heart. However, when others express interest in the community and ask, "What are you about? How does one join?", it is most helpful to have a clear, agreed-upon response. So how does the first generation of community go about clarifying their covenant for those who will follow?

A good place to begin is with a brief mission statement. This can itself be a lengthy process of several meetings and, perhaps, a time of retreat. It is time well spent that helps express in sometimes poetic form the community's calling and priorities. (A mission statement is also useful if the community has a corporate structure that requires by-laws.) At Reba we have described our calling as "extending the mission of Jesus by being a community of love and discipleship, and by nurturing other such communities as God gives us grace." Plow Creek Fellowship describes itself as "a global village practicing the peace of Jesus." Such concise statements both remind a community of who they are and explain to others enough to get a conversation started.

However, the heart of a Christian community has the shape of a covenant between God, the community, and each member in it. In the Bible, with its many covenants, we can discern three parts to the covenant-making process—story, rule, and liturgy of commitment. We will explore each of these with scriptural and contemporary examples.

THE STORY

When we think of a biblical covenant our minds might jump to the familiar Ten Commandments, as if knowing and keeping the rules is what matters most. However, that leap would start off on the wrong foot. Exodus 20 does not begin with the commandments but rather with a vivid, compressed story that makes all the difference between law and grace, between legalism and a grateful community. "I am the LORD your God, who brought you out of Egypt, out of the land of slavery" (Ex. 20:2). Here we are reminded that God has acted in history with a liberating deliverance, creating out of a quarrelsome lot of slaves a free people in order to bless them and to bless the world.

As human beings we are formed in culture and character by the stories that we are told and that we tell each other. And as the people of God we are participants in the biblical drama, not outside of it—shaped by a story that God continues to write in the power of the Holy Spirit.

Each community God calls together has a story to tell of deliverance that creates a people for a holy purpose. The place to begin the process of covenant-making is to tell each other and, while you are at it, to write down the community's story from the perspective of God's gracious and liberating action. This grounds the covenant in gratitude, in actual people and their experience of God's love rather than in grandiose visions of what the group proposes to do that will save the world, disconnected from present reality.

During a session focused on covenant-making, our visiting team asked Nehemiah Community (Springfield, Massachusetts) members to tell their story of God's deliverance—what "Egypts" has God brought you out of? The answers poured forth—alcoholism, idolatry to career, authoritarian experiences of church, failed and abusive relationships, dreams of a wealthy retirement far from any needy people, homelessness, despair, and more. This covenant-building story, it turns out, is also an exodus from many isolated "me" stories into a story of "we," a move from loneliness to family, from solitary dead ends to a people spiritually alive and responsive to God's intentions. We pondered how

God had called and bonded together this very unlikely group of people, and why. That was as far as we got in one weekend. But the process was launched. Ten months and a lot of common work later, the community invited a host of friends to join them for a celebration of commitment in the covenant that God had given.

The Bible has many ways of telling the story of God's action that leads to covenant-making and covenant renewal—psalms, liturgies, impromptu speeches, and celebrations. And, as we will see, for each generation the story must be updated in order for the ancient story to become their story and ours. If your community is working on, or reworking, its covenant, it could be useful to review the ways such stories are told in Scripture. Here is a partial list:

Exodus 20:2 (the shortest story of deliverance from Egypt and slavery)

Deuteronomy 6:20–24 (Exodus to occupation of the Promised Land)

Joshua 24:2–13 (Abraham to occupation of the land)

Psalm 78 (Exodus to King David)

Psalm 105 (Abraham to occupation of the land)

Psalm 135:8–12 (Exodus to occupation of the land)

Psalm 136 (Creation to occupation of the land)

Acts 7:2–50 (Abraham to Solomon, at which point Stephen, the storyteller, was stoned to death.)

Acts 10:36–43 (Jesus to the end of the age)

Acts 13:17–41 (Patriarchs to Jesus's resurrection and the end of the age)

What is true of these stories is true of Scripture as a whole: "The biblical story focuses on God's design for forming a covenant people," writes New Testament scholar Richard Hays in *The Moral Vision of the New Testament*.

Thus, the primary sphere of moral concern is not the character of the individual but the corporate obedience of the church. . . . The community, in its corporate life, is called to embody an alternative order that stands as a sign of God's redemptive purposes in the world. . . . Many New Testament texts express different facets of this image: the church is the body of Christ, a temple built of living stones, a city set on a hill, Israel in the wilderness. The coherence of the New Testament's ethical mandate will come into focus only when we understand that mandate in ecclesial terms, when we seek God's will not by asking first, "What should I do," but "What should we do?"

The New Testament is not so much concerned with the question of "How can I be saved?" as with forming us into a people, a "we" that can be the body of Christ. It is in the body that we are saved, that we find our purpose, that we become Christ.

Still, some communities ask, "Why do we need our own covenant? Are not all Christians under the New Covenant, which is sealed by Jesus's blood on the cross and celebrated by communion where we remember him? Isn't the story of Jesus and the early church also the story of our community's foundation?"

Of course, we are under the New Covenant, which Christians understand as the fulfillment of the Old. And this New Covenant is a living thing, a law written upon our hearts by the Holy Spirit. Nevertheless, the Holy Spirit keeps doing new things, extending the New Covenant that is the same for all followers of Jesus into "local covenants," which get specific about the unique story by which each group has been called together and the unique context in which God has called them to be faithful servants, with the unique gifts or charisms (giftings) of their calling in this present season of life.

We are all called to love our neighbor, for example, but faithfulness calls for a different organization of life if our neighbors are undocumented immigrants as at Casa Juan Diego in Houston, or if they are Duke University graduate students learning to live with African American housemates at Rutba House in Durham, North Carolina. Each community has been given unique charisms from God, of which they are called to be faithful stewards. At Reba this has meant "nurturing other communities," while at Plow Creek Fellowship the farm has given them an opportunity to offer retreats to burned-out city folk and to grow healthy food for farmers' markets.

A local covenant is likely to be revised as the community matures and finds new ways of expressing the Good News of Jesus. But it is always timely to tell our own particular stories as testimonies of God's grace in continuity with the biblical story and the traditions that have nurtured us. Like the psalms, these stories will include failure and restoration, but God is glorified in such stories even if we turn out not to be the heroes. The biblical stories can prompt our local communities to write their own psalms, celebrating God's liberating and people-creating actions as a prelude to the commitments that constitute part two of the covenant-making process.

A RULE OF LIFE

Vows, values, commandments, and shared practices all represent different vocabularies that communities have used to express the commitments and motivations that characterize their lives together. Many communities feel the need to write these down, to create a rule of life, but are also baffled by how to proceed. If we would write down all our practices, the list might be endless, and it could change with every community meeting. And how can you trust that someone reading the rule will take the words in the sense that the community has meant them? So much about life with Christ can only be caught, not taught.

A community's rule of life need not be perfect in order to be useful. Think of the local covenant as an outline of a conversation that you want to have with any novice approaching the community for membership, to see if God has given you all unity on the essentials of life together. The twelve marks of a New Monasticism might serve as a "first draft" that can be adapted to express the unity God has given your particular group.

Borrowing or referring to creeds or denominational statements of faith is fine insofar as they fit. The *Confession of Faith in a Mennonite Perspective* has proven a useful platform for some communal commitments.

A community's rule of life is not an invention so much as a discovery, a way to approximate in words what God has done and wants to do with this particular group. In this regard, it is similar to writing marriage vows. The community's rule answers the question, how shall we live faithfully in response to the story of what God has given?

So, how to get started? Rather than propose a model community rule of life, here are notes from one intentional Christian community's first meeting to discuss their local covenant. Castanea is a three-year-old community of two families, five children, and several singles in the Chestnut Hill neighborhood of Nashville, where their big project is to renovate two worn-out apartment buildings for their own dwelling space and for affordable housing. These are the notes from their first meeting aimed at creating a rule of life.

I. Vision: Castanea is an interdependent Christian community that embodies and shares Kingdom of God life, liberated for economic, ecological, and racial reconciliation:

Committing to a common life centered on sharing meals, prayer, work, study, play, and possessions.

Working toward a healthy food culture through urban farming and education alongside a commitment to sourcing food locally.

Caring for creation through conservation, alternative transit and energy, sustainable housing, and decreased dependence on fossil fuels.

Fostering solidarity across racial and economic boundaries of our neighborhood through hospitality, a commitment to localizing the economy, and the sharing of work, resources, advocacy, and celebration.

II. Covenant Areas of Castanea:

1. Jesus—deepening the knowledge and love of God, discipleship, creedal affirmations?
2. Common prayer
3. Support of the vision and mission statement of Castanea (the not-for-profit corporation)
4. Truth telling—peacemaking
5. Sexuality
6. Possessions
7. Mutual submission combined with submission to the church catholic or outside accountability
8. Commitment to know and love neighbors

As you can see, Castanea's rule of life began very much as a work in progress. Notice how the first section highlights its values as verbs in the present progressive tense—"committing," "working," "caring," "fostering." The community recognizes itself as moving toward a shared vision. The "Covenant Areas" are topics they recognize as crucial to their common life, issues on which they must come to unity but that still need to be fleshed out with more conversation and detail.

Communities who thought they had a common vision are often surprised by how long it takes to actually write and agree on a covenant. This process invariably flushes out differences of opinion, which is to say different experiences within the group. At Castanea some wanted to express "solidarity with the oppressed," while others asked, "Isn't it enough to love our neighbors?" Inevitably, we make assumptions that

200 | THE INTENTIONAL CHRISTIAN COMMUNITY HANDBOOK

only come to the light when we enter into deeper dialogue. Rather than press for ideological purity, as some of us are wont to do, a more humble and fruitful approach is to listen to the experiences that gave birth to each other's deeply held convictions. In this way each one's story becomes part of the community's common story. Finally it is best to express honestly the unity that has been given and not to claim more. Unity is a gift that God wants to give to all who seek with a humble and listening heart. Community covenants are miracles that keep happening where people persist in loving dialogue with each other and in following Jesus.

Space does not permit the display of a full-fledged intentional community covenant in this book, but Jesus People USA, or JPUSA (Chicago), has an excellent covenant statement with commentary on its website, as do Church of the Sojourners (San Francisco) and the Community of Celebration (Aliquippa, Pennsylvania).

A LITURGY OF COMMITMENT AND RENEWAL

Your covenant will play a central role in the community's formation and renewal for as long as you live together. On the day of their annual covenant-making worship service at Koinonia Partners, longtime community members and newly arrived interns (those who are about to make their first serious commitments to the community) all dramatically process from the Koinonia campus across the highway to the chapel where family members including children, friends, board members, and guests await them, all the while singing "Guide my feet while I run this race." Norris, the community elder and pastor, calls them all to worship with reference to the story of God's liberating action to bring these people together.

We have journeyed to this place called Koinonia from many different directions, along many different roads. For the most part we came alone. We have walked across the road to our chapel many times. But today is different; today we walk together hand in hand. We go to enter into a covenant with one another because we believe God has called us to walk not alone, not as individuals, but as one. Welcome to our newest partner and welcome to our community interns. We are happy that you feel called to walk with us a bit further down the road.

In the service that follows, they all sign (or re-sign) their community covenant and repeat the community mission statement together:

We are Christians called to live together in intentional community sharing a life of prayer, work, study, service, and fellowship. We seek to embody peacemaking, sustainability, and radical sharing. While honoring people of all backgrounds and faiths, we strive to demonstrate the way of Jesus as an alternative to materialism, militarism and racism.

The service continues with vows renewed for the other membership groups. It moves along with songs, prayers, Scripture readings, poetry, and testimonies. The time of worship concludes with Communion, remembering Jesus, and a foot-washing celebration where those who have taken lifetime vows wash the feet of the other members. They conclude the service with the benediction, "Let us go forth to pray, work, study, serve and fellowship together renewed by the Holy Spirit that dwells with us and in us. Let the love of God that will never let us go fill us now and forever more. Amen."

In Joshua 24 we read how Moses's successor, Joshua, summons the twelve tribes of Israel to Shechem for a covenant-renewal ceremony, and there he retells the ancient story of Abraham and his descendants, to whom God promised the land of Canaan, of their deliverance from slavery in Egypt, and of the step-by-step occupation of the Promised Land. Then Joshua reminds the people how often they and their ancestors have fallen away and worshiped the gods of the people in the lands where they were living. "Choose for yourselves this day whom you will serve," Joshua challenges. "But as for me and my household, we will serve the LORD." They promise, but that is not good enough. Joshua taunts them,

"You are not able to serve the LORD. He is a holy God. . . . If you forsake the LORD and serve foreign gods, he will turn and bring disaster on you and make an end of you, after he has been good to you." And the people reply, "No! We will serve the LORD." It goes on and on, louder and louder, this litany of taunts, angry denials, and exasperated commitments!

> On that day Joshua made a covenant for the people, and there at Shechem he reaffirmed for them decrees and laws. And Joshua recorded these things in the Book of the Law of God. Then he took a large stone and set it up there under the oak near the holy place of the LORD. "See!" he said to all the people. "This stone will be a witness against us. It has heard all the words the LORD has said to us. It will be a witness against you if you are untrue to your God." Then Joshua dismissed the people, each to their own inheritance.

The point of this story is that, like Joshua, we can be creative in devising liturgies of our covenants and commitments to one another. Then, like Joshua, what might it be like if we wholeheartedly shouted them to each other, to remind ourselves of God's gracious actions in creating community, recalling the commitments we have made to walk in faithful obedience? With God's help, may we be sustained in these ways of celebrating and renewing our commitments for years and generations to come.

CHAPTER 19

On Why Your Community Might Need an Onion

Imagine three scenarios.

Community A: Several people have announced that they will be leaving at the end of the summer. The reasons for their departures have been affirmed by everyone—a voluntary service term overseas, a call to lead a community-based ministry in another city, a two-year graduate program after which the person hopes to return. But when the community wants to talk about its longer-term plans, they feel uncomfortable excluding these three friends from the conversation. So by default, the community puts off that conversation until the summer is over and the "lame ducks" have departed.

Community B: Max has been a committed member since the community's beginning four years ago. He is now in a courtship relationship with Celia, a member of a similar community a thousand miles away. To explore their relationship and to decide where they will become members if they marry, Celia has provisionally moved to Community B. Now it is really awkward for Max and Celia to be in Community B members' meetings because they do not know if the two of them will get married and, if they do, end up at Community B or back in Celia's community.

Community C: The Clark family came with a strong interest in Christian community but a somewhat troubled history. Before they become covenant members, they have been advised by community leaders that they should take a year or more to focus on reconciling some broken relationships from their past, especially with their parents. After some struggles to carefully hear each other's concerns, the Clarks have agreed that this is their desire as well.

All three of these communities need the same thing: they need an "onion."

This is how the idea of a community "onion" got started. When The Simple Way (Philadelphia) was about two years old, the community gathered for an urgent retreat in Tennessee to talk over tensions concerning "foundations and functionality of community." They hated how their talk about visitors, sojourners, temporary members, and committed members involved "levels" of membership, suggesting that one category was higher, better, or more holy than another. So they came up with the image of an onion—concentric layers that describe the differences of participation and responsibility wrapped around the committed communal core. The Simple Way "onion" helped them talk about the steps by which someone might become part of the covenanted life if they so chose. It validated the several ways of being in community as appropriate for certain people at certain times, and it did this without triggering competition for status in a power hierarchy. This more egalitarian onion displayed on their website caught on, and other communities started talking about their onion of membership categories as well. Some have also noticed how fitting it is that peeling an onion involves lots of tears, but with persistence and God's grace, the onion can season a rich stew that nourishes everyone around the table.

The inevitable emergence of membership layers in intentional Christian communities and the temptations to misuse them for power-wielding, elitist, discriminatory, or victimhood purposes is perennial— already present with Jesus and his disciples. Like other areas of the Christian life, this is one where Jesus's teaching and example sets the world and our usual motivations on their head.

Now, to be completely anachronistic, let's ask, what did the onion surrounding Jesus look like? Starting with the "peeling" on the outside, there were the curious and miracle-seeking "crowds" who came and went (Matt. 4:25, Mk. 8:2 and 12:37). Then there was a band of disciples of which Jesus once sent out seventy-two on mission, two by two (Lk.

10:1). Those who traveled with him included women who also served and contributed to the common treasury (Lk. 8:1–3). Within this disciple group were the Twelve, whom Jesus specifically recruited and named "apostles." We also read of a more intimate circle of three friends—Peter, James, and John (Matt. 17:1 and 26:37). Those who accompanied Jesus on his fateful journey to Jerusalem and who gathered to wait for the Holy Spirit after his resurrection numbered about 120 (Acts 1:15). These "membership categories" were descriptive of the discipleship training process, which depended on intimacy with Jesus in community, but they were also functional in terms of responsibilities in his mission.

We also know that the disciples themselves did not picture their community as an onion but rather as something like a pyramid, a political/military hierarchy in which they competed for the hypothetical top spots, arguing, "Who will be the greatest?" This toxic brew of rivalry and resentment boiled over one day when the mother of James and John knelt before Jesus and begged him for a personal favor.

"Grant that one of these two sons of mine may sit at your right and the other at your left in your kingdom." "You don't know what you are asking," Jesus said to them. "Can you drink the cup that I am going to drink?" "We can," they answered. Jesus said to them, "You will indeed drink from my cup, but to sit at my right or left is not mine to grant. These places belong to those for whom they have been prepared by my Father."

When the ten heard about this, they were indignant with the two brothers. Jesus called them together and said, "You know that the rulers of the Gentiles lord it over them, and their high officials exercise authority over them. Not so with you. Instead, whoever wants to become great among you must be your servant, and whoever wants to be first must be your slave—just as the Son of Man did not come to be served, but to serve, and to give his life as a ransom for many" (Matt. 20:21–28).

Jesus's impromptu teaching did not do away with distinctions, or even with competition within his discipleship band, but rather, he urged his followers to distinguish themselves by service, by renunciation of privilege, and by laying down their lives for others according to his own example. They were invited to come closer to him by drinking his cup of suffering, by sharing his cross at the center of the onion. Although the way of Jesus may be hard, it excludes no one. Everyone is encouraged to journey with him, to join that inner circle of communion and sainthood where Jesus is present in the body gathered and with the poor.

This is why the onion works for intentional Christian communities today.

1. It names the reality of different layers of participation, responsibility, and commitment in community; the temptations posed by these differences; and the antidote of Jesus's teaching and example.

Although we may wish for a community with no distinctions of membership, such differences nevertheless exist and, if unacknowledged, exert their influence in confusing and unaccountable ways. By calling the community together and naming the rivalry for leadership and status among the disciples, Jesus could lance the infection and apply the healing antiseptic of humble servanthood by which his body on earth is to be known.

Distinctions of roles and responsibility are unavoidable, like organs in a body, but they do not need to be viewed as competition for scarce resources of power and privilege as in the world's domination systems. A community can never have too many servants, and there is no limit to how many humble people can come close to Jesus. It is important to remind ourselves that, despite some functional and experiential differences in community, these differences are secondary to the unity of love and mutual care that binds all together in Christ. They matter, but more important, they don't matter.

To see how this works, let's look at a sample community onion, the one I know best at Reba Place Fellowship. Its outer layers would include neighbors, a few employees, guests, and friends of the Fellowship. But the more ordered layers would be:

- *Apprentices*: Seeking to learn about Christian discipleship and community by sharing the common life of RPF for a nine-month term from September to May.
- *Practicing members*: Wanting an in-depth experience of community discernment and support while exploring God's call in certain life decisions. Practicing membership is for one year and can be renewed if appropriate.
- *Novice members*: Seriously testing a call to membership in RPF while practicing the disciplines of an "all things in common" life. This is for a year, which can be extended if needed.
- *Covenant members*: Committing to all practices and disciplines of Reba Place Fellowship in full-time service as disciples of Jesus. Covenant membership is for life, or until God calls elsewhere, which will be discerned in unity with the local body.

Each year, in the month of September, new apprentices arrive, and the other membership groups make or renew their commitments. Persons who leave are thanked and released with prayers of blessing. Those who join are celebrated.

Whatever the layers of the onion are called in different communities, they name a reality—it takes time, discipline, and commitment to become a functional disciple of Jesus, giving and receiving love in community. Those who have made a commitment to a particular community feel a unique responsibility for the common good and have usually organized themselves to serve that good in a way that newer arrivals have not. At Koinonia Partners these core members are called "Stewards" of the vision. They need to meet regularly to seek God's leading and come to agreement about longer-range community plans. Persons who have just arrived, who have not been similarly formed by communal values, and who have not yet made a commitment have their own agenda to pursue. One group is not better than another, but they have different responsibilities, and the support they need from the community is different. For example, here is an outline of apprentice commitments at Reba Place Fellowship and the commitments of the community to them.

What RPF can expect of apprentices:
- Participate in apprentice program activities, disciplines, and small group
- Attend weekly RPF member meetings, social events, and annual retreat
- Find work for twenty-four to thirty hours a week to pay personal living expenses
- Volunteer six to ten hours a week in some regular service

What apprentices can expect of RPF:
- Welcome into an RPF household with first month's expenses paid
- Oversight of the apprentice program
- Mentors and models they can engage with
- Opportunities for service and spiritual growth
- Availability for friendship and pastoral care

Similarly, for the other membership modes there are unique commitments of support to the community and also commitments of care from the community to those members.

At Casa Juan Diego, probably the most elaborate Catholic Worker community in the United States, the onion looks very different. In fact, it might better be pictured as a cluster of grapes of which the committed stem is Mark and Louise Zwick, now in their seventies, who have guided the development of this community for more than thirty years. Over this time many young people have volunteered a few months or years, often until they get married and settle in Houston close enough to continue as an extended community, contributing counsel and service for a few hours or days each week. The single male volunteers live in the men's house, a shelter with its own rotation of leadership among twenty to forty immigrants, who serve each other and the community in a variety of ways. The female volunteers live in the women's shelter, which houses many children as well. The women are often busy fixing address labels to newsletters that go out to sixty thousand readers, who stay informed about Casa Juan Diego and contribute to its 1.2-million-dollar annual budget. Then there are houses of care for other disabled immigrants, a free clinic, food- and clothing-distribution days for hundreds of Houston's poor. Local Catholic seminarians and laypeople add their effort because the works of mercy are essential to their spiritual formation. No one but God seems to know everything that is going on in this conglomeration of houses, dormitories, sheds, and gardens that cover a city block and more, but many of those doing it gather for a Thursday-evening Spanish-language Mass, where prayers and thanksgivings go up to the One who sustains it all week by week.

Whatever the shape of your community's onion, most community meetings, social gatherings, and work events will bring together all the different membership groups along with guests in one common life, and most topics are open for common discussion. But there are also times when each membership group meets alone in order to focus on their unique lessons, needs, and serving tasks. However many layers, it is important that the onion name the realities of the community it is supposed to fit.

2. The onion displays a clear path to the center by which persons can approach covenant membership as an informed choice and confirmed calling, so that no one is excluded but, rather, everyone is invited and offered a way in.

Rather than being exclusive, the layers of the onion provide a sequence, a way to become covenant members for all who are called and want to pursue it. Jean Vanier in his classic *Community and Growth* observes, "True growth comes as members of the community integrate into their hearts and minds the vision of the community. In that way they choose the community as it is and become responsible for it." This is the spiritual journey from "me" to "we" that most communities focus on in novice membership. (See chapter 7.) For some it is a movement from being in love with an ideal community to laying down their lives for a very real one.

3. The deeper purpose of the community membership structure then can emerge, to support a lifelong journey of training in "the mind of Christ," along with appropriate responsibility in his ministry.

By naming the different layers of community membership and responsibility, we have focused more on boundaries than the heart of things. To mix our metaphors once more, the way inward to the center of the onion is a descending path of self-emptying love (*kenosis* in Greek) that the apostle Paul identifies as "the mind of Christ" and commends to the church in Philippi.

In your relationships with one another, have the same mindset as Christ
Jesus:
Who, being in very nature God,
 did not consider equality with God
 something to be used to his own advantage;
rather, he made himself nothing
 by taking the very nature of a servant,
 being made in human likeness.
And being found in appearance as a man,

he humbled himself
by becoming obedient to death—
even death on a cross!

Therefore God exalted him to the highest place
and gave him the name that is above every name,
that at the name of Jesus every knee should bow,
in heaven and on earth and under the earth,
and every tongue acknowledge that Jesus Christ is Lord,
to the glory of God the Father. (Phil. 2:5–11)

This, then, is the answer to fears of the younger generation approaching community, and to all our fears of power-wielding, glory-seeking, privilege-claiming authority. The self-emptying path of Jesus is identity-changing and hope-inspiring, but lacking in specifics. For most people, it is helpful to break up developmental tasks into stages of growth as is normal to any discipline. You do not jump from addition and subtraction to differential equations. You have to learn basic math, algebra, geometry, calculus, differential equations, and then you are ready for whatever comes next—which is as far as I got before I dropped out with a math minor. That does not make the math major better than a fifth-grader in any moral equation, or in the eyes of God. But everyone is responsible to keep growing and to help others grow from where they are.

John Cassian, who took the burgeoning monastic movement to Gaul and founded the monastery of Marseilles in the year 400, outlines his monastic "curriculum" according to the following steps in his *Institutes*.

The fear of the Lord: leads to
compunction of heart: leads to
renunciation of all that is the soul's own: leads to
humility: leads to
mortification of the will: leads to

driving out the vices: leads to
flowering of virtue: leads to
purity of heart: leads to
perfect charity.

Of course, spiritual growth is not this linear in actual experience, but such an outline gives a common vocabulary for community members to discuss and confess our growth challenges. ("#$X*?! Why am I always 'starting over' on love and patience?") The curriculum of monastic communities has traditionally worked with a list of seven deadly sins to renounce (pride, avarice, envy, anger, lust, gluttony, and sloth) and virtues to cultivate (prudence, justice, fortitude, temperance, faith, hope, and love). "Cultivate" is a good word here because the efforts of the gardener, though important, do not cause the growth, which comes by grace from God, often in ways beyond our understanding.

Becoming a committed community member does not automatically cause one to grow in all, or any, of the virtues. But without community these things usually do not happen, and with community, there is help. Peter Maurin, cofounder of the Catholic Worker movement, often described the purpose of their communities as, "To make it easier for people to be good." By sticking with and faithfully serving the ones God has given us to love, by receiving and sharing God's gifts on behalf of the body and the world, and by listening to the counsel of those who suffer with and know us best—we learn together the mind of Christ.

CHAPTER 20

Creation Care, Food Justice, and a Common Table

Our twelve-year-old granddaughter and her peers have picked up the essentials of Michael Pollan's bestselling *The Omnivore's Dilemma* and *Food Rules*. They've seen school videos about the sickness of factory farming that turns sentient creatures into egg, milk, and meat products. "We eat products? Yuck!" She and her friends already talk "ecology," "global warming," and "sustainability" as a native language, and they are making informed experiments in what they will and will not eat because of food justice concerns.

Meanwhile, in her parents' generation, more and more people are becoming allergic to environmental toxins, forcing them to eat organic just to stay out of the emergency room. The calorie-laden fare of industrial agriculture and franchise marketing is creating an epidemic of obesity, diabetes, and heart disease. Increasingly, these products are eaten alone and on the run in a society where households rarely sit down to a common meal. As Jonathan Wilson-Hartgrove observes, "We eat as individual consumers, not members of a body."

Any intentional Christian community today also must come to terms with how they will relate to food.

Our planet, our bodies, and our social fabric are all sick from endless growth, the only solution politicians and corporate CEOs can imagine for our political and economic crises. Earlier civilizations have exhausted their resources and died back to smaller, sustainable populations. We have seen where limitless consumption is taking us, and this time the consequences will be global. Will humankind learn the lessons of "equality" and "enough" in time to survive and thrive in coming generations?

Juliet Schor, in a video called "Plenitude: The New Economy of True Wealth," optimistically discerns where the social movement for ecological sustainability might take us. A key element in this vision is to limit our earning to four days a week, resulting in more jobs with reduced stress and consumption. "The plenitude economy . . . gives people more time away from work, expanded opportunities for low-impact economic activity, and a commitment to social connection and community. It's a way to reclaim the human scale to our economy, take responsibility for our lifestyles, and treat one another and the planet with the respect we all deserve."

The intentional Christian movement is exploring this sustainable future by growing food in a fascinating variety of ways, some of which may prove unsustainable, while others point a way forward uniting creation care, food justice, and a common table. In the remainder of this chapter we want to visit a few of these demonstration plots and also consider practices that support a common meal in remembrance of Jesus.

DEMONSTRATION PLOTS

Sustainable ways of growing food are closely linked to the given environment. We look at communal responses in three different settings—rural, abandoned urban spaces, and densely populated cityscapes.

Koinonia Farm near Americus, Georgia, has made an intentional shift from oil-consuming, tractor-driven, soil-killing, row-crop agriculture to permaculture—a way of sustainably recycling the contributions of animals, plants, and humans with minimal disruption to nature's web of life. Koinonia's plowed fields are returning to pastures, vegetable gardens, and orchards reborn under the care of farmer Brendan Prendergast, assisted by a stream of interns and volunteers. They are raising and preserving much of the food served at Koinonia's daily common meals, with some surplus for area markets. They have become a permaculture training center with frequent visitor tours and nine-day accreditation seminars.

For more than thirty years, Plow Creek Farm in Tiskilwa, Illinois, has been growing you-pick berries and healthy vegetables for sale in area farmers' markets, at their own sale barn, and in recent years through weekly Community Supported Agriculture (CSA) shipments to Reba and other friends in the Chicago area. But their most significant crop might well be all the children and summer interns who have learned hard work, gardening skills, and character that issue in a love for the land and a more wholesome way of life.

America has the most productive farming in the world and yet, as presently practiced, directly supports only two million farmers, whose average net income would be zero except for government agricultural subsidies. Many young people would love to explore more sustainable farming practices with direct links to eaters, but the hard work, low earnings, and capital required are daunting.

Bobby Wright, a member of the Oak Park Community in eastern Kansas City, is an urban gardening promoter—a profession that barely existed a decade ago but now is popping up both in prosperous cities and in decaying urban zones. Bobby learned the ropes working for Cultivate Kansas City, a nonprofit that promotes urban agriculture, runs an urban farm, and pursues farmer policy advocacy in the city. Now he is employed by Kansas City Community Gardens and is glad to talk about what he does and why. He recently explained it to me.

Bobby Wright's Story

I don't actually think a lot about food justice these days. I know the issues are there about industrial farming, how animals are abused, and how much it costs to store, process, and deliver food compared to the little that the farm workers actually get paid. I try to concentrate more on actually growing food in our community gardens and involving our neighbors in them.

I'm working with a teenager we have hired a few hours a week who has taken an interest in what we are doing. He is helping me reclaim more plots for urban farming. Working with him makes me a lot less efficient. We are going over basic math concepts—like how do you cut a pole into four equal pieces and make them into stakes to hold up vines. But we are not just growing food; we are also growing friendship and character. When our community went on retreat a few weeks ago, Marquise was able to gather eggs, feed our chickens, and make sure they were in the coop for the night. He got a lot of satisfaction out of this, and so did we.

Our neighbors are too close to the edge of economic survival to think much about larger food justice issues. But I can talk with Marquise and his friends about things closer to home. The other day we went to a store and he bought a dollar-fifty bag of chips. I asked him how much he spent on chips in a day. He said about three dollars. I joked with him, "That's a thousand dollars a year for chips, and it's not even good food. What could you buy with a thousand dollars that would be good food, would make you and your family healthy? Why, with that money you could buy a whole cow!" That's where we are at with food education around here.

Our community got a grant to buy a used concrete saw that allows me to cut rectangles out of the cracked up asphalt parking lots behind the church. Now, on an upcoming workday, volunteers can help us pull up the slabs to expose the gravel and sand underneath. Then we'll add composted soil to enlarge the "farming" space in the neighborhood.

I'm getting to know a few of the older African American neighbors who still remember what it was like to live as subsistence farmers and sharecroppers in the South when they were young. They have a wealth of experience to pass on about cropping and food preservation. A whole generation is missing in the transmission of farming practices. These older folks are a real resource that will not be with us much longer. I feel fortunate that my regular job with the city helps gardeners on their own plots to grow more food and to make urban farming more viable with local markets or food exchanges.

Not everyone in our intentional community is into gardening, but everyone helps from time to time, and it is exciting to see these vegetables arrive at our table or sometimes get passed on to our neighbors. We still have to buy lots of our food wherever we can find it cheap enough to fit our budget. It is tough enough trying to eat together and allow for the food allergies and sensitivities among us. But as we do the hard work of raising some of our food, we realize that when farmers and farmworkers are paid a living wage and when food is grown organically, it will be way more expensive and take up a much larger portion of our budget in years to come. We might as well get ready for that.

Many urban young people like the ideal of farming, but not so much the intensive work that goes with it. I just like to have my hands in the soil, to come back day after day and see things grow, to see people working together in raising and processing our food, and then feasting on God's goodness when the day is done.

Katie Rivers is a member of Church of the Sojourners in San Francisco, where there are no vacant lots and high land values squeeze out maximum rent. Katie told me about their commitments to creative food sourcing and a common table.

Katie Rivers's Story

We have all agreed to eat together in our households and with our whole community on Sundays as part of our worship, with our meal sandwiched between the bread and the wine.

Living in San Francisco we can't do much gardening, but each of our houses gets a CSA box from a farm about seventy miles away. One person picks them up for the whole community. This is something we can all do together for food justice. Each household has a $125 per person per month food budget. People have different food justice and creation care convictions, so that means each household has to figure out a balance between buying local food, supporting sustainable practices like organic, and getting some things cheap. For people with allergies, we prepare special options.

Like other cooks at Sojourners, I experience preparing meals for the community as a gift of love and a work of art. Sometimes the art is in satisfying diverse food needs, expressing our ethical convictions, while meeting a budget with beauty and grace. When Jennie and I recently shopped for the church retreat, we ended up compromising—buying some things organic and others more cheaply.

The discipleship issue that food raises for me is to let go of a need for control, which often leads to divisiveness. Our most important commitment is to eat together as the body of Christ and to hold our other values more loosely to make that possible.

❖

Growing most of our food in urban settings is not a realistic goal. But food, economy, and environment are serious justice matters. Christians have a responsibility to create God-honoring economies and to extract ourselves from the more violent ones. For community-minded people in the city, in addition to growing some of our food where we can, we should focus energy on *sourcing* food. Although it may not sound as exciting as raising our own produce, it is just as important.

The key is to do as much as possible on a community-wide basis because in life together, the whole is greater than the sum of the parts. Many communities are creating models of how to eat ethically in their own context by:

- Forming ties with socially conscious area farms to volunteer labor and to purchase food directly through CSA subscriptions, special in-season orders, and you-pick trips.

- Creating or supporting local food co-ops, which can start small and grow as neighbors are educated in ethical food habits and purchasing power.
- Organizing "freegans" (if it is free, we'll eat it) and "opportunivores" into the ministry of gleaning. This involves harvesting the amazing bounty available at the back door of local produce markets and bakeries, by dumpster diving, or by befriending store managers who would rather see good food not go to the landfill. This is reminiscent of mendicant orders in medieval times who begged as a spiritual practice and made a living on the food others did not want.
- Making common work out of processing, preserving, and storing food to share with neighbors and at a common table.

WHY WE EAT TOGETHER

One kind of poverty is "no food"; another is eating alone. Sarah Miles observes that we have a hunger that food alone cannot satisfy: to share our bread extravagantly. "We'll never feel truly fed if we're constantly competing to get our share; if we believe that love is scarce, and are afraid to give it away."

When Joanne and I lived in the Democratic Republic of the Congo, we learned from our poor neighbors how to celebrate with wholehearted communal joy at weddings, church holidays, and end-of-school-year feasts. We observed how people who normally eat a meager fare can get ecstatic over goat meat sauce and a double portion of greens with groundnuts on a doughy lump of *fufu*. After food, the feast was extended with soccer games till dusk, followed by drumming, singing, and dancing through the night. Our Congolese friends knew how to feast "with glad and joyful hearts" because their palates were not so jaded that to celebrate, they needed something more exotic than they had ever eaten before. They taught us the "more with less" lesson, that when our daily food is simple and basic, celebrations are less stressful to pull off and generosity can extend until all are included and satisfied.

Jonathan Wilson-Hartgrove helps us remember why God wants us to eat together:

> At the beginning of our story, God plants a garden full of fruit-bearing trees and invites us to come and eat. When God comes to Abraham and Sarah as three visitors, they have a meal together. In the early church, the sisters and brothers "devoted themselves to the apostles' teaching and to the fellowship, to the breaking of bread and to prayer." One of Jesus's favorite images of heaven is a wedding banquet—a huge dinner party—where God's people kick back and enjoy a feast. To remind us of what God's love looks like in the world, Jesus gave us a meal— bread to be his body and wine as his lifeblood, poured out for friends and enemies alike.

Above all, the wealth of experimentation among intentional Christian communities continues to grow, and sourcing and preparing food leads to the joy of sharing a common table in the kingdom of God. We conclude this tour by following Celina Varela's faith journey told in relationship to the tables where she has eaten, discovering more of Jesus along the way.

Celina Varela's Story

My family is of Mexican origin living in Texas. My parents were both schoolteachers, but every evening my mom would cook a meal for six of us to share at a common table. On Friday evenings we'd make pizzas and watch a movie, but it was still an experience of being together. I treasure that tradition of eating together and am amazed at how my mom made all those meals. When I became a teacher, all I had energy for in the evening was to grab a little food, watch the news on TV, and grade papers.

Later, when I went to seminary at Baylor University, my roommate and I read Wendell Berry and then joined the World Hunger Relief Farm, subscribing to their weekly CSA (Community Supported Agriculture). We decided to eat vegetarian because that is what we were getting in the CSA bag, and it seemed easier to eat locally that way. I found I really enjoyed this healthier way of eating. I'd never tasted kale, Swiss chard, or kohlrabi before. We discovered how to eat these new foods and find recipes to match. Sometimes we'd invite friends to help us eat these unexpected finds. We had fun with this new way of life and eating together that fit with what we were learning about the kingdom of God.

Then when I came to Reba, to the Clearing, the whole household decided to eat vegetarian just to accommodate me. Later, at the Patch household, everyone was more intentional about food justice and eating from local sources. We cooked for large numbers of people without trips to the store—just using staples on hand from the food co-op, CSA produce, and dumpster harvests. At first that was a challenge, but we learned to be more creative and thrived on it.

Now that Peter and I are married and raising little Mateo, we eat at a smaller table, but we share breakfasts and our evening meal together. Peter likes to invite guests, especially the youth of the church, but we have been hosted at other tables around here even more often.

I like what John Howard Yoder writes in *Body Politics* in his chapter on Communion. When Jesus says, "Do this in remembrance of me," "this" does not refer just to the Communion elements, but to the practice of regularly eating together. Jesus cared about the reality of what happens when we share food and conversation at a common table. The table is a representation of God's kingdom; it matters both who is welcomed and that our food is shared in common. When we give thanks for the food and eat it together, it is an act of worship.

I know that when I sit down to a meal that comes from our garden, there is a different spirit than if I'm sitting down at a restaurant meal. I know that God is our provider in both cases, but there is more a sense of gratitude and joy in the work and in the care that was put into the food. There is the joy of working and eating because the food has our participation in it.

When our food is a gift from someone in our community, this too is part of the thanksgiving. When the food comes from Plow Creek in a CSA box, we remember the actual people who worked to grow and get it to us. We are eating with a lot more people than those we see at the table, people who love each other because of Jesus, who bids us, "Do this in remembrance of me."

Amen!

CHAPTER 21

The Economy of God and the Community of Goods

Two economies run side by side in our world: God's economy of abundance ruled by Jesus's motto, "Freely you have received, freely give"; and the economy of money and profit (which Jesus called "Mammon"), where scarcity rules and everything has a price. In this chapter we will explore how intentional communities expand the Mammon-free zone of "all things in common," and we will share wisdom from the experience of groups that have practiced a common purse. Finally, with a little help from Wendell Berry we will see that "The Great Economy," God's economy, is actually larger than all the Gross National Products combined and is more real than the so-called real world.

First let's take a look at one community that has "taken the plunge," choosing to practice shared finances. In an article titled "An Uncommon Purse," Jodi Garbisson tells us both how and why the Cherith Brook Community has exercised their faith by practicing a community of goods. This Catholic Worker community is called to sustain a prophetic peace witness and hospitality for the homeless in Kansas City. Its "uncommon" name comes from the story of the prophet Elijah, who fled into the wilderness from the wrath of King Ahab, and there a flock of ravens fed and kept him alive at Cherith Brook (1 Kgs. 17:4). An excerpt from Jodi Garbisson's article follows.

There's nothing common about sharing money. It's quite unnatural. We each bring our own history, inherited perspectives and entanglements when it comes to money and spending. In fact, when Eric and I got married, people warned us that most of our arguments would center around money. If this is true, and for many people it is, why would we take the risk of including five other people in something that can be difficult for even two people to navigate?

Our common purse started as an experiment to deepen our commitments to each other, by living simply and by practicing solidarity. We wanted to live lives that more closely resemble Acts chapter 2, which states, "Because believers shared all in common, no one was in need and all had enough." The idea of sharing each other's burdens—even financially—seemed scary but we felt ready for the challenge. The idea was to live with a personal sacrifice and continue the downward mobility the gospel speaks of. To do this, we needed something besides our own perspective and limited vision.

We first sought advice from different communities we knew who had some form of common purse. We contacted Jubilee Partners in Georgia and Reba Place Fellowship in Illinois and they were kind enough to share ideas of how things work in their communities. After much discussion and prayer we decided to combine things we had learned and tailor them to fit our needs.

As a first step, each of us submitted a personal budget, which included fixed bills, monthly income and "wants." From that we tried to work through the differences between "wants" and "needs" and how to simplify the bills we had. We tried to imagine life without so many things and how we could cut back on things we have grown accustomed to. What could we potentially do without? This is where the ideal of common purse met the practical reality of day-to-day living. How were we going to actually implement our plan?

We agreed to find part-time jobs that would not require us to work more than 20 hours a week outside the community. This is important since we all understand our first call and commitment to be the work we share in common at Cherith Brook—the works of mercy, peacemaking and building community. We need money, however, for personal bills.

These are bills that wouldn't be covered by donations such as, bills for cell phones, cars and kids' activities. The money made from these part-time jobs would be our common purse—all of us would decide how it is used. It makes no difference whether you make $900 a month or $300 a month. We all have equal voice in the decisions, even though we all have jobs with different pay.

Once we worked through the bills we tried to determine a monthly stipend for each person. It's obvious that we are all at different life places socially and what we do with our time and money for entertainment varies from person to person. I might go to a movie for rejuvenation, Eric might buy a book or Nick might go to a concert. We came up with $100 for a personal monthly stipend. The way this money is spent is discretionary. The purpose of the stipend is not solely for entertainment. It is also to be saved for trips or for vacations throughout the year. Any need that arises beyond the bills is brought to the community to discuss. If anyone needs something like clothes or shoes or hygiene items, we first look through donations. Many times, exactly what we need is given or if we are patient, it might arrive soon. If we are unable to find what we need, then we discuss it as a group. The rub comes when not everyone agrees.

Is it working? It certainly isn't easy. We have struggled through many difficult conversations and we have all learned and grown from each one of them. Sharing money challenges the false sense of power and/or security we often place on money. We continue to need each other for accountability in order to move beyond selfish and careless spending. By releasing our tight grip on our money we hope to undo the culture's influence of consumerism and individualism. We have learned a lot from each other on how to challenge deep-seated practices of spending and yet still love each other.

Sounds like a miracle? Yes, you are right . . . it is a miracle! Several times throughout the last couple of years I've wanted to bail—

gather "my" money, count the losses and go my own way. It's certainly easier and cleaner to make decisions on my own. But is it healthier? Is it healing? Is it promoting the Kingdom of God and restoring possessions and ownership to their right order? When I'm tempted to run, I'm gently reminded that this common purse isn't just for us, the seven who share it. Our common purse is for the good of everyone, the good of others who read about it or hear about it. It's for anyone who is challenged by it and is inspired to try something similar. It's for the good of others who benefit because we have realigned our hearts to be sharers and not hoarders and to live in trust of God instead of fear. Our hope is to have more in common with no one in need.

Jodi's story reflects many of the reasons why Christian communities have chosen a life of "all things in common"—to embody the teachings of Jesus and the experience of the early church, to tame their "wants" and simplify their too many possessions, to focus more time on service to others and less on making money for themselves, to train themselves in seeking God's will on the larger decisions of their common life, to avoid legalism and the hassles of consensus concerning the small stuff, and to be a witness that might inspire others to trust God in similar ways.

Many communities have chosen this way of shared possessions because it represents the justice of God's economy. Some people living in plenty while others suffer want is not the will of God. Individualism and self-indulgence have become a way of life for millions, even among those who proclaim Jesus as Lord. Combining financial resources in a common treasury speaks prophetically to the church and offers a practical way for Christians to address poverty and inequality, which also gives them the integrity to call the world to a new kind of justice. Individuals can speak for justice, but it takes a community to embody justice.

Living out of a common purse, of course, can take many forms. Church of the Sojourners asks its members to live on a certain modest income level in their several households and to turn the rest of their earnings over to a common treasury for various kinds of ministry supported by the community. Many service groups like Jesuit Volunteer Corps and Mennonite Voluntary Service have volunteers turn in their paychecks and receive a modest monthly allowance, which allows the group to offer many hours of free service each week to their neighborhood. Other communities including Jubilee Partners (Comer, Georgia) have everyone working full-time in community ministries, which are sustained by outside donations.

This way of life is not as "uncommon" as you might think. The late John Alexander (former spiritual leader at Church of the Sojourners) in his previously mentioned, as-yet-unpublished book lists a variety of ways that "all things in common communities" have flourished.

It's no accident that the monastic movement started in the days of Constantine when church as family was being compromised or that Francis of Assisi recruited brothers instead of living out his vision alone. Nearly a million Catholic Christians live communally today as monks and nuns, using the language of brothers and sisters.

During the Reformation, Anabaptists stressed community, and one group (Hutterites, followers of Jacob Hutter) required living together. They started in Moravia and numbered 15,000 around the turn of the 17th century. Now, almost 500 years later, there are some 35,000 of them still doing this in the Western plains of Canada and the United States. They live in bruderhofs (brother houses), own farm land in common, and run businesses together.

Another group, the Amish, date back to 1693. They don't live together in big houses, but they live close enough to experience life together. They have learned to depend on each other dramatically. They don't need insurance because they cover each other. (Why don't all Christians do this?)

In 1920, Eberhard Arnold started a group in Germany that is similar to the Hutterites. They had to flee Hitler's Germany, but today that small band has grown to 2,500, mostly in the United States, but also in England, Australia, and Germany. They live in rural "hofs" of about 200 and have common work, common lunch and dinners, common child care. (Their lives are so much in common that individuals usually don't even have money!)

In 1948, other Germans who had opposed Hitler started Katholische Integrierte Gemeinde (Catholic Integrated Community) in Munich. It has around 600 full members plus hundreds of children, hundreds in the membership process, and many in a special category called "friends." It has groups throughout Germany as well as two in Tanzania, one in Italy, and fledgling groups in Austria and Hungary.

These examples do not even touch on the scores of communities in the United States and Canada that have been going for decades and thousands of younger experiments finding each other and discovering "we are not alone."

At this point in the conversation, I often hear multiple objections raised: "History has proven that socialism doesn't work. Capitalism, despite its persistent inequalities, is the greatest generator of wealth the world has ever known. And besides, the Jerusalem common purse was a failure since the apostle Paul had to rescue it from its dysfunction with an offering from the wealthier Gentile congregations."

Let us acknowledge that state-coerced sharing is a totally different animal than communities of believers, voluntarily joining together as disciples of Jesus seeking the future he promised. But Christians should not be surprised that the world will insist on coerced sharing to make justice happen if Christians have not solved these problems by personal sacrifice. It is not Karl Marx's fault that the goods of creation are monopolized by a few rather than shared for the good of all. The day of Jubilee was not invented by socialists, but reveals the will and nature of the God we serve. So it is not about what the state should do. It's about how we should live, we who have put our trust in Jesus. And by the way, the apostle Paul collected an offering for the church in Jerusalem because he believed this kind of sharing, from those who have to those in need, should characterize the church because it reflects the character of God (2 Cor. 9).

At the beginning of this chapter I mentioned that there are two economies running side by side in this world—the economy of God and the economy of money and profit that Jesus called "Mammon." And I promised to demonstrate that God's economy characterized by the motto "Freely you have received, freely give" is actually bigger than the Gross National Product (GNP) of all the nations on earth. In case you like numbers, those GNPs combined come to about sixty trillion dollars ($60,000,000,000,000) a year, or ten thousand dollars per person for the six billion people with whom we share this globe. Half the world lives on less than a thousand dollars a year, which is "balanced" by about a thousand billionaires on the other end of the scale. So where is this even more "humongously ginormous" economy of God?

Actually, that is what Jesus was trying to get his disciples to see with parables and sayings about wheat that grows when the farmer isn't looking, about rain that falls on the just and the unjust, about a father who gives away half his farm to a scoundrel son and then, when he has wasted it all, welcomes him back with forgiveness. In the kingdom of Mammon there is scarcity—only enough for those with money. In the kingdom of God there is free giving and receiving because God is the ever-renewable resource. Now where is that kingdom in operation? Where do we see this happening? Here are a few hints to get you thinking and seeing.

I like to ask college students, "What if the next time you came home your parents would give you an invoice for $200,000 saying, "This is how much time, effort, grief, groceries, clothes, and gasoline we put into raising you—not to mention all the wrongs we have forgiven"? What would you think if all that love had to be translated into the currency of money? But no, the young people object, our parents did it for free out of love.

Think of what a married couple might give and forgive each other over the course of a lifetime—for free, out of love. Think of all the meals prepared—what they would cost at a restaurant. Think of all the money earned and shared. Think of all the time spent listening to one another and what it would cost if a counselor did it. Even time spent in the same room is a gift. They've invested several million dollars in each other, don't you think?

Sometimes I ask kids why they study for years in school without getting paid. Some of them say they like to learn, while others just say, "It's what kids do."

I have a replacement hip that cost about fifty thousand dollars. Sometimes I wonder how much all my joints would cost if they had to be replaced. So how much is your body worth? And how would you pay for that?

Okay, so far that is just the small stuff. Now how much would the rain, the sunshine, and the air, the topsoil, the minerals underground, the water in and on the earth be worth in dollars and cents—which capitalist accounting just takes for free? Then we should also calculate how much nature is worth, not just to humans, but for all the two or four million other species that share and enjoy the earth with us. And that is just the earth and the sun, not counting the heavens. You get the idea. We're talking about what Wendell Berry calls the Great Economy on which the for-profit economy utterly depends and of which it is just a small fractional part. So, when someone wants to change the subject back to the "real world," which world could humans do without and which one is utterly essential?

The White Rose Catholic Worker community in Chicago has on occasion proclaimed a "Free-market day" in the tradition of Jubilee, where they give free services to their neighbors and invite their neighbors to do the same. It is a day of celebration with balloons, free haircuts, art lessons, garden produce, a chance to pet the chickens, a yard sale without prices, a potluck feast of mutual services offered in a park.

"Freely you have received; freely give," or as the New Revised Standard Version translates it, "You received without payment; give without payment" (Matt. 10:8). That is how Jesus summarized his commission to the disciples who are sent out to the "lost sheep of the house s of Israel" to heal, raise the dead, cast out demons, and announce the kingdom of God has come near. So wherever we share with the poor, whenever we give grace and forgiveness, we expand the Mammon-free zone of God's economy. Whenever we gather in communities of shared goods, we give witness to Jesus, who gave everything for us. Let those with eyes to see, see.

So why do more of us every year choose to live this way with all things in common, with a commitment to radical sharing? Because, once you get used to it, it is the most satisfying way to live. By walking in this way with Jesus there is relational intimacy, spiritual growth, a local demonstration of justice, hope for the world, the beginning of eternal life, and joy that the world cannot take away.

CHAPTER 22

A Spiritual Life for (and in Spite of) Community

T om Roddy is an eighty-year-old neighbor and a hearty friend of everyone at Reba Place Fellowship. This year I was honored when he asked me to drive him to Gethsemani Abbey in Trappist, Kentucky, where he takes an annual four-day retreat alongside the monks, both the living and the dead, including his favorite author, Thomas Merton. That's how we came to be there, sitting among the September oak trees turning color, overlooking the abbey where we had sung psalms with the monks and observed silence until this hour of evening recreation.

Tom looked at me with sudden seriousness and asked, "David, do you have a personal prayer routine?"

"Personally," I told him, "I am quite allergic to routines. Something in me bounces out of any scheduled box I've tried to pray in. Praying with Joanne each morning and times of prayer in community are all the structure I can handle. I would not make a good monk; but in my own way, I have found a routine."

About thirty years ago I heard a teaching from Jim Stringham, a psychiatrist and former missionary to China whose life was as disciplined, scheduled, and routinized in every way as mine was not. Jim's favorite teaching eventually was published in a pamphlet called *God Wants to Speak to You. Are You Listening?* Jim recommended a simple contemplative practice of daily quiet time, listening to what God wants to bring to your awareness and then writing down what comes. This practice of solitude is somewhat akin to Quaker silent worship, which had blessed me at times, so I was willing to give it a try. My commitment ever since has been that, at some point in the day, I will be still and wait on what the Spirit might want to show me—now with a laptop at my fingertips.

Prayer, I've found, is a two-way conversation that keeps renewing my awareness of God's love and gives me guidance that I have learned to trust for whatever comes up.

Then I asked Tom, "What spiritual practices do you follow?"

"When I was a young man," he replied, "I spent several years in the Maryknoll missionary order, where an hour of quiet contemplation was expected of us each day. Later, I left, got married, had a family, and all those personal routines fell away. Sometime in the '80s, I was in a small sharing group at St. Nick's [the local Catholic parish] where a young med tech fellow told us, 'You are not serious about your spiritual life unless you set aside time to pray every day.' This hit me really hard," Tom said, with eyes full of tears and his voice shaking. "I took it to heart and have spent half an hour every morning after my cup of coffee, quieting myself with prayer, a time of Bible study and some Zen breathing exercises. It has changed my life," he said with conviction. "I come here to the monastery every year to get a booster shot."

Daily solitude and contemplative prayer are of course good things to do for their own sake—it trains us in a heightened awareness of "the gift of all that is," both within and around us. And although prayer can happen anywhere, anytime, the communal Christian should cultivate a faithful practice of solitude for the sake of her own integrity—as well as for the community's welfare.

The monastic is often reminded to spend time in his own cell, to know himself as God does, to form personal habits of simplicity and good order, to cultivate solitude. Jesus, who had no house of his own, often "went off to a solitary place, where he prayed" (Mk. 1:35). Unlike the hypocrites whose cross-eyed prayers are aimed with one eye on God and the other on their reputation for piety, Jesus told his disciples, "But when you pray, go into your room, close the door, and pray to your Father, who is unseen. Then your Father, who sees what is done in secret, will reward you" (Matt. 6:6). What is this reward? Could it be that in solitude, we start to see ourselves the way God sees us, messing up all the time and yet beloved? In solitude we have a chance to lose our persistent habit of performing for others and accept our identity as children of God, whom we are eager to please out of love and gratitude.

It is good for the community to teach about and to encourage personal time for prayer, reflection, spiritual reading, and self-maintenance. But anyone who has tried to be faithful to the teaching of Jesus in this matter will find a spiritual battle on his or her hands.

FACING OUR DEMONS

The early Desert Fathers often tell of battles with demons who raged against them whenever they tried to pray. In our day, the first "demon" we'll probably encounter is that we have no time for prayer. Our lives in community are already full, full of good things. Our world considers busyness a mark of successful people, even as they complain about "no chance to catch up." We discover that, in order to make space for solitude, some order, simplicity, and integrity must come into the rest of our life. But as we ask God for the desire, guidance, and courage we need, a way opens up. Even if it is only for ten minutes a day at the beginning, this commitment can grow with us.

Henri Nouwen, a widely read author and popular teacher at Notre Dame, Yale, and Harvard Divinity School, confessed to an aching spiritual exhaustion that his reputation as a spiritual authority could not fill. After a year of retreat and several conversations with Jean Vanier, founder of L'Arche communities, Nouwen accepted an invitation to join Daybreak community near Toronto. *The Road to Daybreak*, his journal of this life transition, reveals the struggles of any beginner in community, but Nouwen reflects on these struggles with exceptional theological depth and pastoral sensitivity.

Which brings us to the second battle of the contemplative—the turmoil we find in our own unruly minds. Henri Nouwen writes:

> As soon as we are alone . . . chaos opens up in us. This chaos can be so disturbing and so confusing that we can hardly wait to get busy again.

Entering a private room and shutting the door, therefore, does not mean that we immediately shut out all our inner doubts, anxieties, fears, bad memories, unresolved conflicts, angry feelings and impulsive desires. On the contrary, when we have removed our outer distraction, we often find that our inner distractions manifest themselves to us in full force. We often use the outer distractions to shield ourselves from the interior noises. This makes the discipline of solitude all the more important.

The crazy voices in our heads constantly "grabbing the mic" of our inner attention cannot be shouted down without creating more chaos.

The bad news discovered in contemplative prayer is that we cannot defeat our own "demons." Every resolve we make to change by some kind of ego-project is made by the same ego that is the problem. But by waiting in stillness, patiently bringing every struggle to Jesus, the voices eventually quiet down. The good news is that Jesus has already won our victory by his faithful walk with the Father all the way to the cross. We really *are* saved by grace. As Nouwen puts it, "Solitude is the place where Christ remodels us in his own image and frees us from the victimizing compulsions of the world."

As a sample of how this works, here is a fragment from my recent journaling:

Ah, Jesus, I get an inkling of what was going on in your times alone in desert places. I expect you did not need to confess all the mess-ups of your life, but you did have feelings of futility and loneliness, of being misunderstood, of exasperation with disciples who did not "get it." And there, from the Father, your human struggles could be loved back into focus, that nothing could separate you from Abba's guidance and delight.

The self we get to know in conversation with God is more authentic than our constantly striving ego, which struggles to keep up a positive image before others and ourselves. We come to community with habits of fast-paced conversation because, in most settings, we have to compete to get a word in edgewise. But in a community that practices "listening to the Lord," we have the freedom to ask each other, "What have been your struggles this week and what have you heard from the Lord?" The resulting conversation quickly gets past social niceties to a space of intimate sharing between two souls in the presence of God. Nouwen reminds us of what we already know, "that without silence words lose their meaning, that without listening speaking no longer heals, that without distance closeness cannot cure."

I remember a community workday when we were washing windows, one person on each side of the glass. Several times I pointed to a smudge, assuming it was on the other side. My partner would scrub there to no avail because (guess what?!) the dirt was on my side. Afterward we talked about my self-righteous assumptions and the useful metaphor of window-washing in our efforts to reconcile relationships. Often in quiet times my conscience has reminded me of incidents where I needed to go back and make amends, of promises I had forgotten. The Spirit is at work within us, if we will listen, looking out for our integrity, helping us to reconcile relationships so the clear light of God's love can shine through the glass between us.

We go into our closet to pray not just to face our personal and relational demons but also for the sake of the broken world that God loves. Nouwen writes:

> It is tragic to see how the religious sentiment of the West has become so individualized that concepts such as "a contrite heart," have come to refer only to the personal experiences of guilt and willingness to do penance for it. The awareness of our impurity in thoughts, words and deeds can indeed put us in a remorseful mood and create in us the hope for a forgiving gesture. But if the catastrophical events of our days, the wars, mass murders, unbridled violence, crowded prisons,

torture chambers, the hunger and the illness of millions of people and the unnamable misery of a major part of the human race is safely kept outside the solitude of our hearts, our contrition remains no more than a pious emotion.

As we pray for the calamities of the world, God shows us that we can't do everything, but that we can do something. As activists we are tempted to respond to the latest crisis in the news, becoming moral nomads moving from one cause to another rather than sticking with relationships over the long haul, in which we might learn the mind of Christ. For example, the Church of the Sojourners (San Francisco) members once determined through their friendship with one of the "lost boys of the Sudan" to become cosponsors in Rebuild Sudan, a project to build a school in the hometown of their friend Michael Ayuen de Kuany. Here at Reba we've been in a sister-community relationship with a village in El Salvador for twenty years, walking in solidarity and deepening friendship with Valle Nuevo through several stages of economic, educational, and spiritual development, beginning with their return from refugee camps in the midst of civil war.

A few relationships faithfully discerned in prayer, which go beneath the statistics of calamity in our world—this is something communities can do better than solo activists who get their energy from the media and from the news. What is born in prayer will speak to others with conviction and a call that goes beyond "good ideas" of something we might do until something else beckons.

A DISCIPLINED SPIRITUAL LIFE IN SPITE OF COMMUNITY

Many come to community to escape loneliness; they come in the hope that, with other like-minded people, they will find acceptance and understanding friends to walk with them through the troubles of life. And often this does happen, but it cannot happen all the time and in all the ways that we will need it. Again, listen to Henri Nouwen:

I expected to live with and care for mentally handicapped people, supported by a deep friendship and surrounded by a beautiful network of Christian love. I was not prepared to have to deal with a second loneliness. . . . But I am coming to see the mystery that the community of Daybreak has given to me . . . a "safe" context in which to enter into the second loneliness with Jesus. There is nothing charming or romantic about it. It is dark agony. It is following Jesus to a completely unknown place. It is being emptied out on the cross and having to wait for new life in naked faith.

Our need for love is infinite, and what community can afford us is finite. We make an idol of community if we cling to human beings and hope in them to meet every need. Even in community, in fact sometimes *especially* in community, we must learn not to turn from our sufferings, but to name them the best we can and bring them to God. In the long run, community is only possible when its members have learned to wait like Jesus, on that one renewable resource at the heart of all things, God's resurrection love. Everything else is reflected light.

Teresa of Ávila, a brilliant writer on contemplative prayer and foundress of a dozen women's religious communities in sixteenth-century Spain, knew well the agony of this second loneliness and taught her sisters the motto, *Nada te turbe / Nada te espante / Quien a Dios tiene / Nada le falta . . . Sólo Dios basta.* ("Let nothing disturb you / let nothing frighten you / the one who clings to God / will lack nothing / . . . God alone is enough.") Understanding this wisdom in our guts brings us to spiritual maturity and prepares us for the worst that can happen in community, with the sure trust that God will bring us through.

I remember singing the chorus "Nada te turbe" with Tomasa Torres, dear friend and spiritual leader of our Salvadoran sister-community, Valle Nuevo. I observed, "It is easy for us in America to sing this song because we have not been tested to the edge of death. Does this song ring true for you?"

Tomasa waited a long time, eyes on her lap, and then slowly gathered herself to speak. "Yes, yes, many times we fled for our lives from the *militares*. Sometimes we ran in the dark stumbling over the dead bodies of our loved ones. Those were terrible times. We were crucified like Jesus," she said, looking up, eyes brimming with tears, "but we found that, indeed, 'Sólo Dios basta.'"

In the hard times when community is not there for us, or when we cannot experience the love that is there, nevertheless, we can know and trust the anchor of our lives and of our communities, "Sólo Dios basta."

CHAPTER 23

When People Leave

All departures are not equal in their consequences for the person leaving or for the community that remains. One community I visited was scrambling to recover from an incident where an intern did not show up for breakfast. A look in his room showed that he and all his things were gone. There was no chance to talk over what had gone wrong or how it might have been repaired.

Joanne and I left New Creation Fellowship in 1984 and moved to Reba Place Fellowship. This move (from Newton, Kansas, to Evanston, Illinois) began as a sabbatical year but ended up in a change of address in a peaceful discernment process between our family and the two communities over a couple of years. Both communities agreed that Reba was a better fit for our gifts and for the support that our family needed. Although we and the folks at New Creation felt sadness at this change, we went with mutual blessing. We have returned every year to keep up and even deepen relationships with our friends who remain at New Creation.

These two examples represent opposite ends of a spectrum of community leavings. In this chapter I want to share some of the wisdom gained from these departures—how to see them coming, what we can learn from them, and how to make partings a time of mutual blessing. I write mostly for those community members who stay, but as someone whose family left one community to join another, I also want to share experiences from the other side.

A FEW GENERAL OBSERVATIONS

Even when community departures are peaceful and celebrated with gratitude for all that was shared, they are tinged with sadness that must be named. Relationships will not be the same as before, since everyone will be giving attention to their new realities. And when someone leaves in anger with no opportunity to process the episode, the pain for both sides can be deep and enduring, but not beyond hope of reconciliation. In small and younger communities, departures tend to feel more threatening because the few persons who remain might fear for the community's survival.

Paradoxically, the freedom to leave is essential for the health of the community. We want people in community with us who are committed, wholehearted, thriving, joyful most of the time, and present voluntarily rather than under compulsion. When, for a variety of reasons, after a reasonable season of testing, persons are not thriving in community, they should be free, without shame, to go elsewhere. An intentional community should be the opposite of a prison—challenging to get into, full of enthusiastic participants, and easy to leave. Even in heaven, according to Revelation 21:25, the gates are always open.

THE PROBLEM OF LOFTY EXPECTATIONS

Most communities have learned to be attentive to the expectations of persons who arrive. New arrivals may have read Shane Claiborne's *Irresistible Revolution* and then discover that the community they've come to is not like The Simple Way. In fact, The Simple Way now is not like The Simple Way was when Claiborne wrote his book. If a community is alive, it will change. So there is a danger that people who come to community with grandiose visions or fixed expectations will soon leave because their hopes and needs were not all met.

Communities want to be welcoming and hospitable, so for younger and less experienced communities, the intake process might not be as careful or perceptive as for communities with some experience of unhappy folks leaving. Bliss Benson, from the Greenhouse Community in Minneapolis, says, "We have made it a practice when persons move into the House, we read the covenant aloud with them, not just hand them a piece of paper. We discuss each point as we go. Then, periodically, we reread the covenant as a whole community in case there is some slippage of our common understanding."

Also at the Greenhouse, when people leave they have a debriefing session to hear if those departing have any suggestions or counsel on how the community could function better. In this way they have accumulated wisdom for their own ongoing processes, and such conversation diffuses most tensions with those departing, leaving the door open for persons to return as visitors and friends—which they often do.

Allan Howe, a member of the Reba leadership team, speaks for many other communities when he says, "It is important to clarify before entry time that here we make major decisions together. We share our feelings and needs while we are still pondering them, open to conversation and seeking God's will together before we make a decision." It is easy to agree with such a commitment to shared decision-making when folks are falling in love with community. But after a while, it is easy for us to revert to the dominant culture's sense of individual autonomy unless the community continues to model this radical decision-sharing practice.

"Should I quit my job on which the community depends, and get more training?" "Our marriage has some persistent stresses. We would like to get counseling. Can the Fellowship help us pay for it?" Newer members are formed in the character and habits of discipleship as they see others in community vulnerably sharing their future options. It is transforming to engage in conversations that respect the personhood and experience of all, and yet wait for the Spirit to have the final word. If sharing decisions is the community's culture, then it is less likely that someone will surprise the community with a decision they have made to leave.

Provisional members, of course, are free to leave after their trial period, without shame or experience of broken promise. But what about covenant membership? A few communities see covenant membership as analogous to marriage—for life, with no possibility of an honest separation. If this is the dominant analogy, then departures are experienced as a divorce, a betrayal, making almost impossible ongoing relationships beyond the leaving. The result usually is two very different stories of what happened, a scenario in which both sides can end up feeling like victims.

I believe the marriage analogy overstates the character of a community covenant. Perhaps a better analogy is to compare community with the Sabbath, which, as Jesus said, "was made for man, and not man for the Sabbath" (Mk. 2:27). The purpose of community is to support its members to be better disciples of Jesus. The community is not an end in itself, the only way to give faithful expression to the kingdom of God. If someone can serve the Lord better in another setting, the home group should be open to processing this possibility. (Of course, there can be many less noble motives for leaving a community, which we discuss later in this chapter.)

If community departures leave us with persistent feelings of betrayal, it can be a signal that we have put our trust in the community rather than in God. In community we might have renounced personal possessions but still remain possessive of relationships, as if our security depended on them. Alas, in this life there are no institutions, no human promises, no contracts that can guarantee our security. Above the gateway to the Gethsemani Monastery in Trappist, Kentucky, are the words carved in stone, "God alone."

WHEN ALIENATION BEGINS TO SHOW

Long before people leave outwardly, there are usually signs of an inward withdrawal. This may manifest in persons not showing up for meetings, averted eyes, less than hearty greetings. Anyone should feel the freedom to respond with questions of personal care and concern to signs of alienation. "I missed you at the picnic yesterday. Is something wrong?"

It is important for a community to have pastors especially attuned to such needs. If the person feeling estrangement has enough maturity and self-awareness, she will mention such feelings to her pastor or small group. It is important that someone who is secure in the Lord listen to such feelings, someone whose first concern is the well being of the estranged individual rather than the welfare of the community. When people are wavering in their calling to community, it is good to recall with them the reasons they first joined and ask what has happened to those reasons, not with a goal of winning an argument, but with the desire to restore them to integrity and fullness of life.

When our family was at New Creation Fellowship in the 1970s, for a season Joanne was severely overburdened and discouraged, such that she began to drop out of community and family life. I continued attending community meetings as I could. However, this put a strain on our marriage, and mistrust grew between us until I felt the Spirit urging me to also step back from membership to express my solidarity with Joanne. The amazing thing is that the community accepted our change in status but did not cease to love and serve us. In reality, they increased their investment in our lives even though we could give almost nothing.

Irene and Jake met with us every Thursday evening for more than a year to listen to our distress, to counsel, and to pray with us. Others in the community watched our children on Friday evenings so that we could have a night out. Eventually, Joanne felt enough life and hope restored that she and I could rejoin as community members, which was duly celebrated on a memorable Sunday morning. No one can expect or demand to be loved like this, but it *is* part of our story—and without it, we doubt that our marriage and family would have stayed together. In many ways we left community, but community did not leave us. No set of rules can tell a community when to release people from their commitments and still keep on loving like this, but listening to the Holy Spirit will give them such discernment.

HELPING PEOPLE FLOURISH

Jesus said, "I have come that they might have life, and have it to the full" (Jn. 10:10b). As individuals learn the servant ways of Jesus in community, it is also the community's task to see that its members experience this abundant life. Sometimes, as in the story of our move, persons will find a better context for life in another community or another line of work, find healthier connections with family or service that God is calling them elsewhere. Such questions need to be uniquely discerned and not settled by a general rule. But it helps to remember that God's purposes are bigger than the local community. Our communities can help individuals and families discern where they can best grow and flourish in God's new creation.

Sometimes people in intentional community are not growing relationally and spiritually, and it is not until several years later, after they have left, that they can explain why. The reasons they give for wanting to leave do not "add up" for those who try to hear them out. It seems that solutions could be found for all their concerns, but they do not want to solve the problems; they just intuit a need to leave. Finally, we cannot give someone the "want to" that is essential to healthy life in community. Why people are called and why they leave are both somewhat mysterious to our limited ways of understanding.

Helping people flourish—in the sense that Jesus talked about—is not the same as our culture's autonomous search for personal fulfillment. Jesus spoke of the abundant life in the context of the parable of a shepherd who cares for his flock, not like the hirelings who run away when the wolf comes. "I am the good shepherd. I know my sheep and my sheep know me—just as the Father knows me and I know the Father—And I lay down my life for the sheep" (Jn. 10:14–15).

This abundant life is the same life Jesus has with the Father, a relationship of knowing and loving and giving everything for the other, even life itself. We are created for love and service, and when we can give ourselves wholeheartedly for others in the way of Jesus, this is life abundant. But it is a way of life that we can only receive and give away. We cannot possess it or make it happen for someone else.

One good reason for communities to be affiliated in a wider association or order is to help seekers find, as Frederick Buechner has written, "where your deepest gladness and the world's deep hunger meet." What Buechner fails to mention in this oft-cited quote is the communal part of the equation—that such questions are best discerned in community where you are known, and that can help you land in a place of service where you can belong. That means some people might be encouraged to visit other communities in the order or association and find a place where they can give themselves fully, where they might find a life partner, or where their service is uniquely needed.

SOMETIMES PEOPLE MUST BE ASKED TO LEAVE

Sometimes the community needs to confront a person about divisive behavior, accepting the risk that they might leave. Asking someone to leave is a very rare occurrence, but it is one that communities should be prepared for. Jesus suggests a process for such situations in Matthew 18:15–17. If there are signs of alienation, the person who becomes aware of it should go directly and try to resolve the breakdown of relationship. If that does not work, then two or three others should be brought in as mediators. If that fails to resolve the issue, then the whole community should get involved.

If it is clear that the person will not listen to the community, then he or she can be asked to leave. (This chapter is not long enough to deal in depth with all the variations of this sensitive issue. For more help see Marlin Jeschke's *Disciplining in the Church*.) The crucial issue for Jesus is not the size of the offense, but whether the person is willing to stay in dialog, to listen, to remain open to conversation and counsel.

Jean Vanier, speaking from the experience of L'Arche communities, says:

Only the people with responsibilities in the community and its long-term members can decide that someone must go. But in doing this, they too must recognize their share of guilt. Perhaps they did not dare to take the person in hand and set up a dialogue as soon as the first inkling of division appeared. . . . But a belated recognition of its mistakes should not inhibit the community from acting firmly. If someone is causing dissention among the members of the community, they must be asked to leave.

A community should not send people away simply because they are disturbing or have a difficult character, or seem to be in the wrong place, or are challenging it. The only people who should be sent away are those who have already cut themselves off from the community in their own hearts. . . .These people divide the community and deflect it from its first goals.

When facing this kind of situation, younger communities might want to ask counsel from a more experienced group. Springwater Community happened to have its first visitation (see chapter 27) at the time when a guest with "prophetic gifts" was privately encouraging several people to challenge the community on its "unfair" practices. Everything the visitor said had a grain of truth to it, and division was growing. But once the whole pattern of private conversations came into the light and benefited from the counsel of the visiting team, it was clear that the guest should be confronted about his divisive gossiping, at which time he chose to leave. Springwater members felt as if they had just dodged a bullet. Vanier continues:

> It takes much time and wisdom to build a community. But it can take very little time to break and destroy a community if a proud and destructive person seeking power is allowed to become a member. . . . If there are no strong people in the community to confront him or her, then it is likely that the community will break up and die.

What about the worst-case scenarios, when the reason for departure is that all efforts at reconciliation have broken down? In the Gospels we have such an extreme example to ponder in Jesus's relationship with Judas.

At that Last Supper, Jesus knows what is on Judas's mind and calls him out at a solemn moment of the Passover meal. Judas has already made a deal with the chief priests and temple police to betray Jesus when the crowds are not around (Lk. 22:3–6). What Judas's strategy and hopes were we cannot really know. We do know that the drama he set in motion for thirty pieces of silver turned out not at all as he had expected. And when Jesus was condemned, Judas repented, returned the money, and hanged himself. Centuries of scriptural interpretation have made Judas out to be the worst of villains.

But Jesus does not resist, humiliate, or publicly denounce Judas, who was, in a decisive and destructive way, leaving the community. Jesus grants him the freedom to do so: "What you are about to do, do quickly" (Jn. 13:27). Jesus speaks as someone who trusts that whatever awful things persons do with their freedom, God is able to bring good out of it. Maybe I am stretching the point, but it sounds to me like Jesus would have us say to persons who break their commitments in community, "Do, then, what you feel you have to do." It is not condemnation, it is not holding onto someone against the purposes of their own heart, and it includes trust that the worst thing that a human being could ever do—even killing Love Incarnate—God can redeem and use for good.

Sally Youngquist, a Reba community leader, once observed, "When people leave community without full reconciliation, there are usually two different stories told. Often the person leaving tells their story to whoever asks. The community, on the other hand, feels responsible not to go public with private information. As community leader, I often want to defend the Fellowship by putting out our version of what happened. But I realize that this will just add more hurt and distance to the relationship. It is better to stay relational, pray for reconciliation, and to stay open to whatever we can do toward that end."

Allan Howe, also from Reba, explains, "Our experience has been that we come out ahead by being generous with practical settlements to meet the needs of those who leave. Sometimes, a year later, people who left feel they need something else that was not clear to them at the time of departure. Without shading the truth, we try to do what makes for peace. Life is too short to accumulate enemies."

After a difficult departure, it is good for the community to spend extra time together sharing feelings, lifting up their own hurts and those who have departed in prayer. At such times Jesus is especially present, healing, unifying, and restoring us to love again. When we give, it is with the sure knowledge that we are plumbed into the fountain of God's love, which will never run dry.

MAKING FAREWELLS AS POSITIVE AS POSSIBLE

Most farewells are not anxious, tension-filled events. The reasons for the separation have been talked through and fully acknowledged. The lessons to learn have been spoken. It is time for a celebration. The things that need to be said at such a time (usually at a meal or a party) fall under a few simple headings: "Thank you," "We're sorry," "God bless you," and "Come again." When you have shared life deeply and then must say goodbye, sadness is a healthy sign that you have loved, that the relationship really means something. We can feel grief even while we give thanks for the gifts we have received in the relationship.

Jubilee Partners in Georgia welcomes batches of refugees for a few months of orientation before they depart for their new homes. During this time, deep bonds of love and mutual service grow. When the refugees leave, the community forms a hand-in-hand circle on the meadow with special mention of all the gifts that have been shared and a prayer of blessing. Then all the community members line the driveway as the van departs, waving their friends on with tears and shouts of goodbye into the next chapter of their lives.

THE ALUMNI CLUB

It seems that each community that has been around for a while has its own "alumni club." Bliss Benson says that many of the persons who have lived a while in the Greenhouse Community in Minneapolis now are part of their church, where she meets them every Sunday. "They keep coming back for Monday potlucks," she reports. In 2007 here at Reba, we had a fiftieth anniversary where hundreds of past members and guests returned to celebrate under a big tent in a local park, putting on a slide show of the five decades of Reba's existence with old faces, names, and events reconnected. Jubilee Partners hosts a grand Thanksgiving Day picnic in which hundreds of resettled refugees, past volunteers, and former members return for a family reunion in which everyone has a great day, except for the turkeys. Many communities have a newsletter sent out to all their friends, past members, former volunteers—the extended family—keeping folks in touch and welcoming them back.

Patrick Murray has the call and the gift of staying in touch with the young people who have been part of Nehemiah House (Springfield, Massachusetts) over the years and moved on. He remains the pastor of graduate students, medical residents, and service workers in many distant places. With Pat they keep on sharing their developing sense of call and, through him, stay connected with Nehemiah House with visits and phone calls. Some are planning to return and others have joined communities where they have landed.

Despite their departure from community, many ex-members share a common formation of life and a way of doing relationships that has changed them "for good." In different ways, those who come back for visits say they have been "ruined for anonymous church or for superficial relationships." Perhaps one of Christian intentional communities' best gifts to the world is people who have tasted and become addicted to relationships of depth and integrity, who keep looking for more until they find it.

PART SIX

A MATURE COMMUNITY BECOMES
SOIL FOR GOD'S NEW SEEDS

CHAPTER 24
Healing the Hurts That Prevent Community
DAVID JANZEN AND ANDY ROSS

Jesus is present at the heart of Christian community to help us heal the traumas of life and to walk with us into the freedom of maturity. Let me illustrate with a story.

After a community meal Olivia, an exuberant child at play, runs into a chair edge that stabs her knee. She sees blood and hobbles howling to her mother, who holds her close as she continues to wail. A nurse in the gathering comes to look at the wound and determines that only the skin is broken; it needs salve and a bandage, which she applies. Meanwhile her mother holds Olivia in her lap, whispering encouragement and a prayer for healing in her ear until the crying subsides. Teary-eyed Olivia limps around for a time, and others ask, "What happened?" and "How do you feel?" Before long, she is running and playing again with the other children, a little more cautious, but with joy fully restored.

Olivia has processed her pain with help from her mother's comfort and guidance, good medical care and information, and validation of the community around her. Olivia will have no lingering emotional trauma from the accident because there was enough love in the moment to cover it. This painful experience, fully processed, actually becomes a resource in her life, building confidence that she can handle hard times while staying relationally connected to others and to God, who heals.

By contrast, imagine a scene where the same accident happened, but instead of love and appropriate care, a parent berates the child for being so careless, the wound is neglected as punishment, and the child is reminded that "having you was a big mistake." With no one to help this child process the painful experience, it will likely be stored as a traumatic memory. The negative emotions from this event will get stirred up again and again by similar scenarios unless the memory is processed and healed.

Have you ever seen someone "blow up" or "melt down" with more emotion than the situation seemed to warrant and have no insight that he or she was overreacting? Have you ever gone from feeling joyfully connected to totally disconnected from others with the arrival of a seemingly insignificant word or deed? These are recognizable signs that past unprocessed memories are being triggered by present situations and exploding like land mines in the midst of community life. Unfortunately for all involved, the unprocessed memory root that is causing an overreaction can be hard to spot, leaving the unsuspecting people in the present to bear the entire blame for how the triggered person is feeling.

We all come to community carrying unhealed wounds that limit full participation in loving relationships and group belonging. What restorative resources does God have for us in Scripture and in the body of Christ? Is there a framework of common understanding that will equip our communities to be places of healing for our members and for those God sends our way?

Jim Wilder and other counselors at Shepherd's House, Inc. (lifemodel .org), distinguish between two types of relational and emotional traumas in a manual designed for communities to foster healing and growth toward maturity called *The Life Model: Living from the Heart Jesus Gave You*. Type A traumas come from the absence of good things we should all receive, things that give us emotional stability. These might include not being cherished as a child; no one taking the time to understand who we are; not receiving appropriate physical affection; not experiencing age-appropriate limits; neglect in the area of food, clothing, shelter; not being taught how to do hard things or no chance to develop personal talents.

Type B traumas, by contrast, are those "bad" experiences we weren't able to process. They range from extreme situations like experiencing or witnessing abuse, accidents, or disasters to seemingly small incidents (like a child suffering a bruised knee alone). By this definition, it does not matter how small or large an experience appeared; it becomes traumatic if we were not able to process it. As we saw in the anecdote about Olivia, three important processing tasks are staying relationally connected to others, navigating the situation in a healing way that allows us to look back and feel satisfied, and interpreting the experience with appropriate meaning.

In our journey of healing and maturity, Jim Wilder writes, "We need to know where we are, what we missed, and where we are going. Without a map, we will keep falling into the same holes."

Healing for Type A traumas often happens in a natural way over time in a loving community as deficits of love, care, and attention are filled in by relationships that complete what was missing from earlier stages of development. Metaphorically, we might picture this as "filling an empty bucket" with love till joy overflows.

Consider another brief example. Karima was a tenderhearted college student studying philosophy; she suffered frequent nightmares and daytime anguish. Despite an excellent intellect, she found herself emotionally bound and unable to trust others enough to risk close relationships. In a small sharing and prayer group following Monday night Reba potlucks, Karima experienced an urgent longing for the kind of adult relationship she had missed out on with her emotionally ill mother. Following graduation, she moved near the family of her college philosophy professor (a Reba member) where, for several years, she experienced something like a spiritual adoption. Her story, as told in chapter 4, is an example of healing from Type A trauma through giving and receiving love in family and community life.

Type B traumas might be compared to "holes in our joy bucket." These holes are "patched" by accessing troubling unresolved memories and processing them. For this task it is most helpful to have a mature companion (or a professional therapist) who is genuinely glad to be with you, who listens deeply, and is unshaken by what you share. As you will see below, there are also ways to welcome God to participate in the healing of these wounds. It is essential to remember that behind many Type A traumas are Type B holes. A community that tries to "fill buckets" with love and good intentions without addressing the related Type B holes will find their efforts drain out at an exhausting rate.

Louise Stahnke, who is a Plow Creek Fellowship elder and part-time baker from Tiskilwa, Illinois, tells her story of reprocessing abusive memories with loving community support.

Louise Stahnke's Story

I always struggled with a low self-image, lots of shame, and emotional grief. In the later 1980s, with the help of prayer counselors, I began to work with certain sexual abuse memories that came back to me from childhood. I let my small group at Plow Creek know what I was dealing with. That was a really good experience for me. Although it wasn't perfect, I learned I could let people know what I was facing and not be judged.

That opened the door for me, so that some years later when more memories, really heavy stuff about ritual abuse, showed up, I was still free to share with the community. I learned later how unique my experience actually is. Others I know who have experienced similar abuse felt completely isolated except for their counselors. That is a huge deficit to struggle with. But you do need to exercise a lot of discernment about whom you can safely share with.

My husband, Mark, and I went to two Thrive conferences to learn about Jim Wilder and his coworkers' approach to trauma healing. There we heard lectures on joy strength—how exchanged smiles between infant and parent and loving eye contact in childhood can build joy strength. Later in the lecture we heard, "If your capacity is up to a certain level, you will remember things that come up to your capacity level." In other words, you will remember trauma at the time when your inner strength is ready to deal with it.

I wondered how I could be remembering trauma when my mother had given me no joy or affirmation. But God had been building my joy strength for years in three ways: quiet times, listening to the Lord saying things like "My child, I love you"; thirty years of a good marriage, a supportive husband, someone who is glad to be with me; and I'd had twenty-five years in community where people were usually glad to see me, too.

Another huge gift from community: while I was remembering stuff that left me feeling a lot of shame and humiliation, people consistently reflected that I was valued, loved, and accepted. All along I had been trusted with community leadership. But when this crisis hit and the memories were coming back too strong, I took a six-month sabbatical from being an elder. I think if I'd told all my stories, some folks would have been "blown out of the water." But they still continued to respect and value me.

I was determined to not let this garbage affect my life any longer than I had to. It took me five years of intense work, but now, for the past year and a half, there have been no new memories. For this kind of abuse healing one definitely needs skilled, experienced help. I highly recommend the tools and the counselors that Karl and Charlotte Lehman [see below] have trained in healing prayer. Kind people with a good heart are important, but not enough.

For groups who want to be a place of healing, it is important for at least one person to become proficient in assessing and caring for community members. Do not assume you can solve everything in the world. Consult with folks from other communities with experience in the issues. You need to be realistic about what you can take on, not just for the community's sake, but also for the sake of the person you are trying to help.

❖

Contemplative prayer, a loving husband, and community support over time filled many of the voids caused by Louise's Type A trauma. Then when her repressed memories of Type B trauma surfaced, she felt enough support and joy strength to deal with what she called the "really heavy stuff." For this she needed the resources of focused prayer, professional counseling, and a support group to see the healing through. What Louise does not tell is the quiet joy she now radiates, the nonanxious leadership she offers in community, along with the wisdom and discernment God has given through her struggles, which have become resources for counseling others in times of crisis.

Andy Ross, a young husband and father in Reba Place Church, has heard a call to become "proficient in assessing and caring for community members," as Louise Stahnke recommends. He recently explained his experience.

Andy Ross's Story

I have been involved in formal and informal Christian community all of my life. I grew up in a communal culture among the Maasai people of Kenya. Our missionary team served as a large extended family with lots of "aunts" and "uncles" who liked to have fun together. After Kenya I participated in an ever-deepening way at Hopwood Christian Church, which celebrated by worshiping, eating, working, playing, and praying together. From 2007 to 2010, I was a practicing member at Reba Place Fellowship along with my girlfriend, Kristin. We got married in 2008 and currently live with our son, Gabriel, in the "Reba village."

As Kristin's and my friendship deepened, and we explored covenanting in marriage, we encountered serious conflicts over issues of trust, and whether I was giving too much attention to other women. After going in circles, we met with Karl and Charlotte Lehman, who explained that our past pains are sensitive to the slightest touch, like an open cut. Fortunately, we can resolve the past pain so that it becomes more like a scar that does not hurt when touched.

The Lehmans introduced us to a form of prayer for emotional healing called the Immanuel ("God with us") approach or simply Immanuel prayer. Through the Immanuel approach we gradually resolved some significant underlying pain, and our conflicts steadily reduced to the point that we felt confident to join in marriage. Kristin received healing regarding her parents' divorce, freeing her to trust me more. I received healing regarding rejection and loss in previous relationships. This helped me attain more single-minded devotion and overcome my fear of commitment. We continue to find the Immanuel approach essential for our own growth. I also facilitate sessions and teach the approach around Reba and beyond. For the past couple of years, I've been meeting with a men's small group where we take turns facilitating and receiving Immanuel prayer.

I think part of my calling is to help people recognize and resolve what hinders deeper communion with God and others. With encouragement from loved ones, and the help of a discernment team, I have entered a pastoral counseling program at Loyola University to pursue licensure as a counselor. Formal study has put me in conversation with a diversity of healing approaches that enrich the work I do.

❖

We have found that the Immanuel approach is a solid option in tune with many of the values of intentional Christian communities, in which trained laypeople can facilitate the healing of most of life's hurts in a prayer-group setting. Dr. Karl Lehman is a Christian psychiatrist who grew up in intentional community. With his wife, Charlotte (Reba Place Church pastor), the Lehmans have become internationally known as teachers and trainers in this way of healing. To picture how an Immanuel healing session proceeds, we'll hear a true story from "Collin" (name changed).

Collin's Story

I started as usual with a time of appreciation, recalling some times when I experienced the presence of God. I invited God to refresh my awareness of him, and soon I perceived God in the present moment. Then we moved to a time of waiting on what the Lord might bring up.

I recalled a recent incident where someone started to unfairly get angry with me. I got mad in response and snapped like I had to head off their anger with my own: like I wanted to protect myself. We paused to ask what God might want me to know about this incident, and then another memory came up from a time when I was about six years old. As I shared this memory out loud with the facilitator, the connection began to make sense. Our family was in a restaurant, and my dad lost control and started yelling mean things. I broke down crying, which made him even angrier. I felt ashamed because everyone in the restaurant was watching.

I asked Jesus what he wanted me to know about the memory. I recalled making a vow to do anything, *anything* I could to prevent a scene like this from ever happening again. Jesus seemed to want me to tell him about my feelings. I told him how I was angry at my dad for yelling at me and being so unfair, how ashamed I felt having people watch me while I was crying, and then how I became even more angry because I felt ashamed. When I waited for Jesus's response, the words came to mind, "Thanks for letting me be here. I've waited so long for you." As I relayed the message to the facilitator, it felt so true. Jesus then assured me that my anger was okay—who wouldn't be angry? I was able to feel connected to Jesus and feel my anger. I was also able to see that the people in the restaurant were not thinking I was a bad kid; they were feeling bad *for me*, not joining in my dad's condemnation. They did not think I was a "stupid crybaby." That changed my experience of the event so I could remember it now as an affirming memory rather than one of condemnation.

Another part of processing the memory was the new and more gracious perspective God showed me about my dad. I realized that he was under a lot of stress taking care of all the details for our family trip and he felt overwhelmed—and probably ashamed of what he had put me through. With this new point of view, I felt compassion for my dad and I could forgive him.

Since this prayer session, I'm less inclined to be defensive when someone is raising his or her voice at me or seems to be on the offense. I don't feel a surge of anger or a need to block the person. I tend to feel more at peace in tense and awkward social situations. This fully processed memory has now become a model for me about how to handle negative emotions. It reminds me that I can talk to Jesus about my feelings and ask for his perspective on situations that come up.

❖

As you can see, the Immanuel approach is a three-way conversation between a facilitator, an explorer, and Jesus. Sessions begin by reconnecting to God in the context of a positive memory when the person clearly perceived God's presence or goodness. The explorer then asks God to guide his or her thoughts. In our experience of the Immanuel approach, God's guiding presence often manifests itself like the "gentle whisper" Elijah encountered on Mount Horeb (1 Kgs. 19). What comes to mind may seem insignificant at first, but as we share it out loud it becomes clear that a brilliant healer is partnering with us in the work of renewing our minds. Sometimes it seems God just wants us to rest and enjoy fellowship together. Other times, God guides us to unprocessed memories that have been disrupting our relationships. As we invite his presence, he shepherds the healing process. The approach also has a safety net for the occasional times when someone feels stuck in an unhappy memory with no apparent resolution. In such cases, the facilitator can suggest that we return to the initial positive memory of God's presence or goodness, and we end the session with no harm done.

The good news is that most laypeople who are willing to work on their own wounds can be trained relatively quickly to become valuable facilitators of the Immanuel approach. This is not because we are so smart, but because Jesus is the one who guides the process. The best place to learn more is immanuelapproach.com.

Even with the highly effective Immanuel approach, our healing journeys will take time. As each of us waits for fuller healing, it is helpful to have a few practical skills available that limit the harm we do in relationships when our wounding causes us to overreact and disconnect from others. "The following practices, from Dr. Lehman's book *Outsmarting Yourself*," writes Andy Ross, "have been tremendously helpful for my marriage and friendships."

1. Perceive and own the fact that we are triggered and feeling more upset than the situation might merit. For a host of reasons, this can be incredibly challenging at first, but with practice it gets easier to say, "I'm really upset and I suspect that most of it is not your fault, but I need some space."

2. Embark on the journey back to joy and restored relational connection with
    *   Calming practices like deep breathing, relaxation techniques, music, or exercise.
    *   Deliberate appreciation when we remember, write down, or tell specific stories of thankfulness from our lives.
    *   Receiving emotional attunement by telling God or a mature person how we feel without being judgmental about it, and at the same time welcoming God, or that mature person, to be with us in our upset.

Although these practices don't heal the underlying wounds, they provide clear paths back to joy and relational connection until such a time when the wound can be fully healed and loses its power to disrupt our peace.

CHAPTER 25

Developing Common Work and Ministries

I was invited to participate in a review of the Greenhouse Community, home to ten adults and three children in Minneapolis. The Greenhouse is one of half a dozen loosely networked Christian households affiliated with the Salvage Yard church. To launch a discussion of the inward and outward dimensions of community, I drew a chart with a horizontal axis labeled "Community Gathered" and a vertical axis called "Community Reaching Out."

		Socially Engaged		**Jesus with his disciples**
	The Simple Way			**Taizé**
			Jubilee Partners	
Thin Community		**Rutba**	**Reba**	*Thick Community*
1	*2*	*3*	*4*	*5*
	Greenhouse			**Bruderhof**
				Hutterite Colonies
		Socially Unengaged		

On the horizontal axis we identified the following possibilities, moving from thinner to thicker community:

1. People meeting an hour or two a week who remain mostly anonymous. Example: Casual members of a commuter church.

2. Christians sharing a neighborhood with some fellowship structures. Examples: Localized parish-type congregation and Christian cohousing groups.

3. Community that shares lodging, meals, daily prayers, chores—a common schedule. Examples: Rutba House and some Catholic Worker houses of hospitality.

4. Christians sharing in community of goods, table fellowship, regular worship, childcare or elder care, and other tasks. Examples: Reba Place households and Jubilee Partners.

5. Full community of consumption and production, with common work and ministry. Examples: Hutterites, the Bruderhof, Taizé, and other monastic communities.

Then we considered the vertical axis of social engagement, which is more difficult to resolve into neat levels of "outreach" since these take so many different forms. The Greenhouse hosts a weekly potluck for neighbors and friends, their only form of communal outreach. So they locate themselves in the lower left quadrant.

A commonly heard caution to Christian communities is that communities with "all things in common" become insular and unengaged with the society around them—citing the rural Hutterite colonies or cloistered monastic communities as an example. However, this two-dimensional chart allows us to see that, indeed, close community and social engagement do not need to exclude each other. Jesus and his disciples, for example, were both intensely gathered in a common life and highly engaged with the people and the issues of the society they visited on their itinerant ministry. The two dimensions often reinforced each other, especially when the Holy Spirit (a third dimension we could picture as perpendicular to the chart) is active.

The early church in Jerusalem practiced "all things in common" as an expression of the Jubilee teachings of Jesus and as a witness to his resurrection, which threatened the authorities, who responded with attempts at containment and persecution. Nevertheless, many people took notice so that "the Lord added to their number daily those who were being saved" (Acts 2:47).

Shane Claiborne of The Simple Way (Philadelphia) has a prophetic ministry to thousands of young people at conferences and in campus gatherings, where he challenges them to join the "Irresistible Revolution," and yet his community back home has had its struggles with continuity. At times the Bruderhof has been about diligent work at home with a few visiting area jails or volunteering in the local fire departments. But in other seasons they will send out individuals and small groups to support the ministries of other mission communities around the world. By contrast, the Taizé community in France, with a core of about a hundred and twenty celibate brothers living a monastic life, welcomes about sixty thousand persons (mostly young adults) each year to experience community with them. These crowds of weeklong campers join the monks three times a day for prayers, singing the Taizé chants now known around the world.

Despite my very subjective placements of a few groups on the chart, it is clear that there are vital Christian communities with a variety of charisms in each of the four quadrants.

The members of the Greenhouse Community in Minneapolis all agreed on where they might pin their flag on the chart, but they also expressed hopes that they could move in the direction of a more gathered life and more social engagement. That began a serious discussion of the way God moves communities toward a more fully shared life and ministry. We agreed that the beginning point for such a transformation is common and persistent prayer for Holy Spirit renewal and guidance.

A next step for groups that feel called to move toward thicker and more engaged community life would be to visit a few such communities and to begin a mentoring relationship with a group of similar vision. This often inspires communities to see what is possible and to make Spirit-led changes that fit their circumstances. But before we look at how communities can make large steps toward common ministry, it is important to reflect on our attitudes and motivations.

WHEN OUTREACH BECOMES IN-REACH

"Doing outreach" sounds impressive, it makes us feel good, and tempts us to think that as "givers" we are somehow better than the persons who receive our ministry. We'd like to be one of those communities that stands out with a reputation for radical social engagement—and that is a problem.

When you can go somewhere away from home to be the missionary, it can enlarge the ego—what the apostle Paul calls "the flesh." But what happens when someone you "minister to" wants to become your friend, join your community, and receive your love on a daily basis? What happens when that person also starts telling you your faults, including "self-righteousness" and "hypocrisy"? That is when outreach becomes in-reach. That is when God is really pleased, and we want to run. At that point there is no glory in what we are doing because our own character is on the operating table. That is when we discover that God wants to save *us*. The only way forward is to desperately ask God for more love and mercy. And that is when we meet Immanuel, Jesus with us, the one who knows all this pain of transformation intimately, and who offers to live within and through us. This is what the apostle Paul writes about when he says, "I have been crucified with Christ and I no longer live, but Christ lives in me" (Gal. 2:19–20). So what began as outreach now is in-reach that saves us and glorifies God in the life of community, where people struggle to let go of the old self and learn to love like Jesus. But we can no longer brag about it. It has become the daily "one another" life of Jesus with his disciples.

In other words, the way to move toward more social engagement is usually to deepen the love between needy community members, bringing our private lives forward for healing and common discernment about our real gifts and needs. A thicker and more healed community becomes the base from which authentic outreach becomes possible, a humble way of serving for the long haul that glorifies God.

Jolyn Rodman is part of Reba Place Fellowship's common work that manages several apartment buildings in Evanston and the Rogers Park neighborhood of Chicago. Here is how she describes her job as property manager and community builder.

Jolyn Rodman's Story

The tough thing I'd like to run away from sometimes is my work in the 1528 Pratt building. But when I spend time with people, so often they open up to me in ways I never would have expected. I see that God has called me to this building and to the people he has placed here.

This fifty-one-unit apartment building is like living in a large household where no one wants to admit that they are in a community. For most people here, this building is just one step up from homelessness. Some people have been here for a while and become more stable, but most are very close to the edge. Their rent may be more than half their income. Some people are in programs to help them recover from addictions or mental illness. We are focusing on becoming a place of safety, comfort, and sharing.

It is tough being in a position of power—the one with keys and who collects the rent. But Nieta Jones and I live here in the building as roommates and soul mates. We offer ourselves many evenings, listening to whoever wants to talk. The more I share of myself personally, the more they let me see who they are. On weekends we go dumpster-diving and leave food out in the lobby for people to share. It helps blur the line between work and relationships. When I go to sleep these people are in my heart, and they are in my prayers when I wake up in the morning.

I hear people admit that they can't pay their rent because they gambled their money away. Someone else confesses that he has fallen back into drug addiction, so I sit and grieve with him. Another person calls me to say she has had ten days of sobriety, and then there is the pain of seeing her back "into it" again. I walk the tough line of keeping someone accountable to the rent payments and also deciding when to give grace. Sometimes I become a renters' advocate, helping them find other emergency sources of funding. God is working through all that. It is a gamble, knowing that someone may take the grace we offer and mess it up. Sometimes there is the pain of saying, "You can't live here anymore." One person using heroin is a temptation to others in the building. We wish them well even when they have to leave.

This building has helped me see the injustices and abuses of the system close up. When we bought the building, people were very angry and upset at us all the time. They were used to fighting just to be heard. Now the spirit of the place has changed. We've had a series of boiler problems and pipe leaks here in the middle of winter, and we have gotten no angry phone calls. People understand the way we work, and they care about us, too. They see they don't need to fight us to get decency and service. That is what keeps this place afloat. If we did not connect our faith with what we do, we'd have a lot more problems and angry people on our hands. Little by little we are becoming community.

Did you notice the "we" in Jolyn's last sentence? She is talking about a business that needs to break even to survive, a ministry that begins each day with the work staff gathered in prayer, and a diverse people that shares the same building becoming community. The economic discipline of everyone doing their share to pay the building's costs actually helps people to grow and to live in reality. The separation of status that allows us to talk about outreach is gone because it is all one life, a privilege to come close in whatever life brings, a "we" that sometimes looks like the kingdom of God.

EXAMPLES OF COMMON WORK AND MINISTRY

Most community groups aspire to depend as little as possible on the capitalistic economy, to find fellowship in common work, and to synchronize the schedules of members toward a fuller common life. But developing a successful community farm or business calls for special expertise, long-haul sacrifices, and start-up capital that not many communities are able to pull off, at least not at first.

William Cavanaugh, in his provocative book *Being Consumed: Economics and Christian Desire*, holds up a vision of Christians "called to create concrete alternative practices that open up a different kind of economic space—the space marked by the body of Christ." In the following pages let me share some examples of common work and common ministry that illustrate the variety and creativity that are possible in the economic space "marked by the body of Christ."

There was a time in Reba's early history (1970s) when most of the men worked as aides or supervisors in the Chicago State Hospital psych ward. They all drove up together in one van so they could experience community even in their commute to work. The hospital was certainly a neglected corner of the empire. The men quickly saw how the work could be reorganized to cut out abuses and humanize the environment for both patients and workers. And with what they learned on the wards, they soon turned Reba into a place of healing for many seekers with histories of trauma and family abuse. One of those who was involved in this work in the 1970s, Allan Howe, observed to me: "When you are overqualified for your work, and you function as a team, there is more room to revolutionize the environment."

Similarly, with community support, I was able to lead the growth of a community-owned business in the 1970s. Growing up on a farm, I had accumulated a range of construction skills without thinking much about a career. Then when we began our community at New Creation Fellowship (Newton, Kansas), to fill in some earning needs I worked as a painter and then in construction to fill some gaps in my skill set. After that I became a general contractor for our community's crew, New Creation Builders. By sticking together over a decade, a gradual start-up with a little investment each year in supplies, equipment, and a shop eventually made us a credible all-purpose small construction company. Our crew—made up of musicians, philosophy majors, visitors, underemployed friends, and what-have-you—was able to earn our keep and offer considerable flexibility to engage in other ministries that were our primary calling. And many folks hired us because they wanted to support those ministries.

There are many other examples. Another is Cherith Brook Community in Kansas City, which has a nonprofit service agency with a newsletter that gathers donations to support their ministry of welcome to homeless neighbors. Most members also have part-time earning jobs to pay for the common-purse community's living expenses. This kind of "mixed economy" is common for many communities that have been around for a few years.

Another start-up path is illustrated by Chris and Tammy Jele, leaders of Hope Center in Kansas City, where the nonprofit community development ministry was established first, and now the staff is moving toward more intentional community to sustain their long-term commitment to live in their challenging neighborhood.

At Jubilee Partners in Georgia, all community members work within their refugee resettlement and peacemaking ministry, which is supported financially by donations from a wide support base informed by periodic newsletters. By simple living, lots of gardening, and their own internal nonmonetary economy, they can live well under the income-tax level.

In general, communities that solicit donations under a 501(c)(3) tax-exempt status find they can sustain more ministries than communities that earn their own way. But they also depend heavily on donors whose lives are more tied to economic spaces not marked by the body of Christ. Jesus People USA in Chicago, by contrast, has chosen to support its common life and various ministries from its own members' earnings and a few common businesses, such as a roofing supply company and an elder-care facility. Like Reba, JPUSA is recognized by the IRS as an "apostolic order," a 501(d), characterized by shared life and common work within a religious purpose, which allows it to divide all community income into equal shares for minimal income-tax liability.

Most of the Church of the Servant King (Eugene, Oregon) members work for Wipf and Stock Publishers, of which John Stock (a community member) is a partner. Though Wipf and Stock is not community-owned, it is saturated with the community's values and ethos. Members serve as administrators, editors, bookbinders, and salespeople. They often take a vanload of books to sell at conferences, where the fruit of their labors is a prophetic resource for the event. Similarly, Paraclete Press (publisher of this book) is owned and operated by the Community of Jesus, an intentional Christian community in the Benedictine monastic tradition, whose main form of outreach is to publish and promote resources for a common life of faith.

The Bruderhof communities have supported themselves for decades now by common work in their "Community Playthings" workshops, producing quality hardwood toys and play structures for nurseries and kindergartens across the land. More recently they have branched out with Rifton Equipment, which produces a line of products promoting the mobility of persons with physical disabilities. Common work allows their communities to lead an integrated life with a peaceful tempo and also involve many guests in the loving work and fellowship, for which they have such a gift.

Finally, the chief gift of common work and common ministry is not in all the business structures and traditions of good service that have been built up, impressive as those sometimes are. Rather, these spaces exist so that the world can witness the attractive power of love and unity working in community, where persons flourish and their gifts serve a common good, a place where Jesus is alive in daily work and giving hope to the world.

CHAPTER 26

Sustaining Prophetic Vocations
and Families in Community

It is not so hard for young radicals to participate in heroic prophetic actions while still single. But without support from a countercultural community, most will revert to bourgeois lifestyles and values by the time their children need braces and beg for smartphones like their peers. So the question arises, how to sustain such a witness through life's various stages, especially the most challenging case of families with children? Stories from prophetic communities include courageous and creative answers.

Before the civil rights movement of the 1960s, Koinonia Farm, near Americus, Georgia, was the center of an epic struggle between violent white segregationists and a small rural intentional community that practiced table fellowship and common work with whites and blacks together. This vision of racial equality and solidarity came directly from the Gospels as translated into social reality by the farmer and biblical scholar Clarence Jordan. (For more information, see Dallas Lee, *Cotton Patch Evidence.*)

For years the community was under siege from drive-by shootings, bombings, and a countywide boycott where white merchants refused to buy or sell anything connected with Koinonia Farm. In response to this assault, Clarence Jordan spoke in colleges and churches across the land, wherever he could find a sympathetic ear, telling about their struggles to faithfully persist as a "demonstration plot" of the kingdom of God. In an end-run around the boycott, Koinonia launched a new mail-order business of selling pecan products to a wide and growing circle of friends. Clarence coined the marketing slogan, "Help us ship the nuts out of Georgia." His definition of faith was "not belief in spite of the evidence but a life in scorn of the consequences."

How did Koinonia sustain community and family life during a time of relentless persecution? At the height of the violence directed at Koinonia, the community children were objects of scorn and hostility in the public schools. For a time, Koinonia sent some of their youth to other intentional communities farther north, to Forest River Hutterite Colony in North Dakota, Reba Place Fellowship, and the Woodcrest Bruderhof in upstate New York. Meanwhile, these and other groups made visits of solidarity and rallied support as they were able. Dorothy Day visited Koinonia and had the dubious distinction of getting shot at and living to write about it in the *Catholic Worker* newspaper.

During these difficult years, Koinonia's resident community dwindled until only two families, the Jordans and the Whitcampers, remained. In a time of near despair, Clarence wrote Reba and offered to give them the farm. But eventually the tide turned. When vigilantes bombed a business in downtown Americus that was rumored to have dealings with Koinonia, the boycott was called off and an icy truce followed. Others came to volunteer time and support to the Koinonia community and witness. One of these young families was Millard and Linda Fuller, who began an affordable housing ministry at Koinonia, which eventually grew into the worldwide venture called Habitat for Humanity.

The collaboration and support of other intentional communities was crucial to sustain family and community life in a witness that had a profound impact, not only on Koinonia's neighbors, but also on the Koinonia children who grew up fully aware of God's calling on their lives. Now, two generations later, Lenny Jordan, youngest son of Clarence and Florence Jordan, says that though he chose a different spiritual path from his parents, he is proud to have been part of such a courageous witness for racial reconciliation, despite the animosity he suffered from school-age peers. Lenny has returned to his roots as the fundraising chairperson of Koinonia's seventieth anniversary celebration planned for the fall of 2012.

We could multiply similar stories from other intentional communities. There is Jonah House in Baltimore, founded in 1973 by Phillip Berrigan and his wife, Elizabeth McAlister, who have sustained a series of Plowshares actions, spending years in jail for symbolic destruction of nuclear armaments while other community members raised the children, who remained at home.

Jubilee Partners, planted by former Koinonia members in 1979, is made up of half a dozen families, singles, and three-month volunteers who have hosted more than three thousand refugees over the years. With community support, the members have at times committed civil disobedience in protest of the world powers that are the cause of refugees in the first place. (See Don Mosley, *Faith beyond Borders*.)

Since 1980, Casa Juan Diego in Houston has given shelter to mostly Hispanic women with children, underemployed men, and sick and dying immigrants, regardless of their legal status—simply because they are Christ present in the poor. (See Mark and Louise Zwick, *Mercy without Borders*.) The work is supported by Catholic Worker newsletter readers, area Catholic churches, local volunteers, and occasional police officers who drop off wounded and abused migrants that no one else will take in. The Zwick family home, a block away from the main action, has sheltered a growing family and now grandchildren who return to see Mark and Louise and to share the life with scores of persons in need of shelter.

Stories of communities like these demonstrate that ordinary people, when they band together, are capable of extraordinary courage and fidelity to the world-transforming gospel of Jesus. But behind the public scene is the long, slow work of God, of personal transformation and faithful persistence through the different seasons of life.

In all of these places and times, it has been clear that

- The inner transformations of the prophetic calling are like the submerged mass of an iceberg, sustaining the visible part that sometimes appears in public witness.
- There are different seasons of life with different emphases within the same calling.

- Children with a passion for justice who know they are loved are a gift to the world.

- If you want to go fast, go alone; but if you want to go far, go together.

WHAT, THEN, DOES IT MEAN TO BE PROPHETIC?

That is what I asked Mark Van Steenwyck from Missio Dei in Minneapolis, a community of three households whose charisms are hospitality to homeless neighbors and creative explorations of a sustainable urban food culture. Mark is an ordained Mennonite pastor, active editor of the widely read JesusRadicals.com blog, and parent, along with his wife, Amy, of three-year-old Jonas. He said the following.

Mark Van Steenwyck's Story

Prophecy is telling the truth that reveals what's really going on. The Hebrew prophet Amos is an example—he names the injustice that is happening no matter the consequences. Prophets pull off the blinders we are used to living with.

We try to do that as a family by living with others who are having a hard time with life, and doing it without guile or condescension. Our family doesn't live in Missio Dei's Clare House, where persons are often welcomed off the streets. But here in the Michael Sattler House, we have more long-term guests and members whom our son calls "uncle" and "aunt." We see no gospel reason why some people should live better off than others.

There are several levels of hospitality, and I've seen all of these in houses of hospitality: first, condescending nonhospitality where you don't do hospitality at all, just talk about poverty as a justice issue; second, condescending hospitality where you offer services but maintain status differences; and third, inclusion where you are someone's default family, where love precedes talk about what we believe and how we ought to live. This last one is prophetic. It expresses Jubilee. It is what happened in the early Jerusalem church, where people sold their goods to share, and "day by day the Lord added to their number those who were being saved."

❖

Prophetic communities are not idealistic, or they shouldn't be; they are realistic about the present age and see its corruption in the light of the age that is coming from God. They have a different understanding of the way time works from that of the world, which is still invested in competing for survival and approval in the present order that is passing away. Like Jesus, they are alive to the kingdom of God that is already breaking into history, convinced that God calls us to live now, whether it is legal or not, in the power and spirit of that kingdom where Jesus is Lord, and all peoples will live at peace with each other in a world of enough.

This vision is inherently communal. Old Testament prophets were usually spokespersons for "schools of prophets." John the Baptist and Jesus were both in this tradition with bands of disciples who lived the blessings and the persecutions of this time between the two ages (Matt. 5:1–12). The integrity of the prophet's message comes from living already by the rules of the age to come, a witness of both judgment and hope. Dorothy Day's public times of witness for peace and justice were credible because she shared her life and table with the homeless, who were crushed by a corrupt economic system.

Prophetic communities attract idealists, and it is not fair to dismiss their heroic impulses. Ideals are sometimes all that the young have for vision and motivation, lacking the experience of suffering, of trying many things some of which fail, and of finding renewal in God over a long-term struggle for justice. The problem with an ideal is that it is abstract, it is disembodied, it is left-brain, and in the biblical perspective, it tends to become an idol. Even good ideals that we sometimes call "values," like compassion, equality, justice, or inclusivity, which we might get from reading the Gospels, can become idols when we separate them from Jesus, who is a living spirit embodied in the concrete lives of humans who suffer.

The deeper and more enduring love we need is discovered as we faithfully practice Jesus's commandment, "Love one another as I have loved you," until it becomes our nature and Christ dwells in us. Apart from a renewing relationship with Jesus, these ideals tend to become our possessions, our projects, the standards by which we judge our sisters and brothers, and thus become destructive of the real community and real people that God has given us to love.

LIVING PROPHETICALLY WITH CHILDREN

One issue is sure to come up—let's call it the "concerned grandparent question": "How can you raise your family, our grandchildren, in a place that is so . . . not normal?" Several cheeky responses come to mind: "You got to raise us the way you thought was best. Now it's our turn." Or, "Given how we see the world, this is 'normal' for us." But those are conversation stoppers. A humbler response would acknowledge that every generation of parents has an awesome responsibility for which they are unprepared and in need of God's grace. And we want to engage grandparents, family, and friends in a deeper exploration of God's call on our lives.

"Normal" has two meanings—"average" or "according to the norm." God does not call us to be average by the world's standards. So where will we look for our "norm"? The biblical stories we read to children in the season of Advent rehearse the choice that Mary faced of welcoming God's Messiah into her life, come what may. We should not underestimate the capacity of children to respond with generosity to the needy, to sacrifice toward a common good, to be courageous for God. Our children's spirits are deeply nourished and fortified for a prophetic life by experiences of shared joy, forthright forgiveness, and unity celebrated with others. Alas, in our world, such a legacy is exceptional, not normal.

But we do need some practical wisdom concerning how we involve children in a radical discipleship lifestyle based on Scripture and other communities' experiences. Jesus's itinerant discipleship community probably did not include children, but the Jerusalem community undoubtedly did. The early church was noted for its adoption of abandoned babies into their community life, a life often under persecution. The church found homes for the children of martyrs. Tales of courageous witnesses, peacemakers, and martyrs should be storytime fare for our children, including the history of costly discipleship of persons they know.

Whatever our good intentions, there are sober lessons to learn. Reba Place Fellowship, for a decade in the 1970s, was so invested in outreach to needy people whom they welcomed into large ministering households that a peer group of children grew up feeling resentful that they did not get enough of their parents' love and attention. A season of repentance and correction followed, giving freedom for families with children to have their own apartments if they felt the need. From that time on, the community has been careful to not make children share living space with persons who have disruptive emotional issues. Like most other intentional communities, Reba has also made sure that its children are educationally prepared to support themselves in the contemporary economy; this enables them to remain in community out of personal calling rather than economic necessity. Nevertheless, Reba's conviction remains that one of the best gifts children can receive is the challenge of living for a purpose larger than themselves, larger than their nuclear family, a vision of the kingdom of God that will be a blessing to all people, especially the last and the least.

CHAPTER 27

Becoming Accountable—Visitations and Community Associations

We probably don't need to rehearse the tragedies of Jonestown, of David Koresh and his Waco, Texas, tribe, or of the Anabaptist debacle of Muenster in the sixteenth century to prove how in-group thinking and authoritarian leadership can become toxic, even fatal, to a community. Although such horrendous stories can be instructive, I don't expect a paranoid group to read this book, come under conviction, and repent of their ways. So who is this chapter on accountability for?

It is for anyone interested in growing communities to healthy maturity, and especially for communities thinking about long-haul sustainability who are looking for journey partners with a common calling and vision. Such groups expect that seasons of crisis will come, and they want someone else to know them well enough to show up and pitch in when they yell for help. They might already be connected with local churches and other intentional communities in their area, but there is not the close blood-type match that could allow for large transfusions of counsel and support when needed. These communities are past the adolescent stage of life when much of their energy comes from learning by making their own mistakes or by believing they are discovering things that no one else knows. They no longer have to prove to the "parents" inhabiting their minds that "we can do it ourselves."

COMMUNITY PEER REVIEWS

We have already discussed modest forms of accountability (see chapter 16) that include a mentor partnership with a more experienced community, having a board of directors, or belonging to an area community of communities. But as communities grow in maturity, they often seek to formalize their relationships of accountability. In this chapter we will look at visitations (periodic community reviews by peers from other communities) and community associations (or orders) that share a common rule of life with a commitment of mutual support.

Tim Otto tells how the Church of the Sojourners (SOJO) in San Francisco decided to join the Shalom Mission Communities (SMC) and how the community survived a season of trauma with the help of strategic visitations.

Tim Otto's Story

We got interested in SMC especially for the sake of accountability because we had watched what happened within the Church of the Servant King communities, where we had some connection. When a conflict grew up between the community in Gardena and the other groups, there was no person or set of persons that everyone was willing to trust and submit to as a mediator. In the end, it was clear that one person was going to decide and the conversation either had to end or accept that demand.

That was so frustrating for SOJO leader John Alexander. We looked around at other groups where we could be in a relationship of accountability. We read the pamphlet of Shared Commitments from Shalom Mission Communities and thought it was a great fit with us. So we attended an SMC camp meeting to get acquainted, and then joined the association. In 2001 we had a visitation group come to give us a community review, which, it turned out, was about six months before John Alexander died. Then a year later, our other senior leader, Jack Bernard, also died.

I recall how after Jack died we felt so incredibly discouraged that some persons left, and the rest of us wondered if this was the end of our community. It was so great to be able to call the same visitation team back, people who already knew our issues and whom everyone trusted. Sometimes visitation teams deal with community problems and conflicts, but after John's and Jack's deaths, we were mostly in need of listening and encouragement.

When the team came to be with us they said, "Given who John and Jack were, we understand why you are discouraged and feel like giving up." I think it was Allan Howe (from Reba) who then said, "But if we were starting a new church community and saw this group already gathered, we would be very encouraged and see a promising future." Such words were most heartening.

However, we were also dealing with a leadership vacuum. Dale and I needed to step up and join Laura in new roles. However, there were some persistent conflicts between us. So about four months later, when Dale and I could not resolve our struggles, we asked Allan Howe to come back and help us. He already had the background and knew us well. Together we sorted through the issues and Allan made some suggestions. It wasn't perfect, but it enabled us to move on.

The commitments our communities had to each other in SMC and the visitation groups have played an absolutely crucial role in our history. It is good to know that any covenanted member here can ask for a visit if she or he thinks something is going seriously wrong. So when something happens completely out of our control, others who know us well can come and hold out hope for us in whatever difficulty we are going through. We are huge fans of visitation groups, not just in times of crisis, but also as regular spiritual health checkups.

The Shared Commitments of SMC (shalommissioncommunities .org) express common values regarding stability, nonviolence, and self-giving love, leadership, possessions, vocations, decision-making, family, spirituality, and Good News. Concerning leadership, the statement concludes as follows: "We open our communities to the counsel and support of other Shalom Mission Communities in periodic visitations, to review our body life and our experience of leadership."

What is the inspiration for this idea of visitations? Surely, one comes from Henri Nouwen in *The Road to Daybreak*, as he discerns an early example in Mary's visit to her cousin Elizabeth, or rather, of the Holy Spirit's visitation in their meeting:

Two women are pregnant because of God's intervention. Elizabeth is the only one who can understand Mary and the faith that allowed her to say, "Let it happen to me." Neither Mary nor Elizabeth had to wait in isolation. They could wait together and thus deepen in each other their faith in God, for whom nothing is impossible. Thus, God's most radical intervention into history was listened to and received in community.

Nouwen's meditation on Mary and Elizabeth also happens to touch the heart of intercommunity visitations—the visitors share in the same divine calling and so have an inward understanding of the new life growing within the community they visit. Nouwen continues:

The story of the Visitation teaches me the meaning of friendship and community. How can I ever let God's grace fully work in my life unless I live in a community of people who can affirm it, deepen it, and strengthen it? We cannot live this new life alone. God does not want to isolate us by his grace. On the contrary, he wants us to form new friendships and a new community—holy places where his grace can grow to fullness and bear fruit.

So often new life appears in the Church because of an encounter. Dorothy Day never claimed *The Catholic Worker* as her own invention. She always spoke of it as the fruit of her encounter with Peter Maurin. Jean Vanier never claims that he started L'Arche on his own. He always points to his encounter with Pere Thomas Philippe as the true beginning of L'Arche. In such encounters two or more people are able to affirm each other in their gifts and encourage each other to "let it happen to me." In this way new hope is given to the world.

Communities are often born, and reborn, Nouwen suggests, in Spirit-inspired visitations where the dangerous and world-changing call from God is heard and affirmed, to let Jesus be born among us, come what may.

HOW A COMMUNITY VISITATION MIGHT UNFOLD

One mission of the Nurturing Communities Project is to acquaint other communities with this visitation tradition derived from monastic communities and from the more recent experience of Shalom Mission Communities.

A community visitation is set in motion when the host community contacts a few (usually three) persons whom they trust to conduct a community "checkup" and set a date two or three months in advance. This is accountability exercised by peers rather than by a hierarchy that stands over the community. Here is the way a visitation might typically unfold.

About two weeks before the visitation, the community members fill out a "satisfaction survey," a confidential questionnaire to indicate what is going well, what is not, how they experience leadership, how useful their covenant is, and what issues they hope might get attention in a community visit. The completed surveys are sent to the visitation team ahead of the visit.

The visitation might begin with a Friday afternoon meeting of the community leaders with the visitation team, to review plans for the weekend and to familiarize themselves with current community agenda.

On Friday evening the visitation team meets with the whole community, perhaps at a common meal, to get acquainted, to share hopes and expectations for the weekend, and for the visitors to sense the spirit of the community. It is important for all community members to arrange their schedules to be available, making the weekend something of a community retreat.

Saturday is given over to one-on-one meetings with the visitation team so that everyone who wants it has a chance to be heard. Small groups, or task teams in the community, might want to meet with the visitors as well.

Saturday evening is typically a social event, a talent show, a picnic, or an occasion for someone from the visiting team to give a teaching or lead a discussion on a topic the community has requested like "Updating and Renewing Our Covenant" or "Economic Sharing in Our Community."

Sunday may involve worshiping with the community, however that happens. Sunday afternoon is an occasion for the visitation team to huddle and prepare its report, which usually falls under the following headings: (a) observations summarizing what they have read and heard; (b) commendations on things that are going well, where the community is faithful to its calling; (c) concerns or suggestions addressing issues that might need attention and change; and (d) encouragement to remain faithful to the way of Jesus and the covenant that members have with each other. The evening then concludes with prayers of benediction. By the end of the visitation, the Holy Spirit often gives a heightened awareness of God's presence and of solidarity between the host community and the communities represented by the visitors—which is the real visitation.

Following the visitation, the host community will want to take several weeks to digest the report and to decide how to make it their own agenda.

SO HOW SHOULD THE COMMUNITY TAKE THIS REPORT? IS IT A WORD FROM GOD OR FROM HUMANS?

We get a fascinating glimpse into this question from the first three chapters of the book of Revelation, where we find "visitation reports" for seven churches in Asia Minor. It appears that the apostle John had a longstanding role of oversight for these seven church communities. But he did not need to visit them to know what was going on because he had an overpowering vision. "Someone like a son of man . . . his face was like the sun shining in all its brilliance" (Rev. 1:13 and 1:16) said to John, "Write on a scroll what you see and send it to the seven churches" (Rev. 1:11). In the divine revelation these churches are represented before God by seven golden lampstands and seven angels who are messengers continuously conveying to God "the spirit of the church" and ministering God's word to each of the churches.

Now this vision might seem way beyond strange to us, especially if we try to read it finding some literal connection for our circumstances. So, what can it mean that John is writing, not to the churches, but to the angel of each of the churches? Here's my idea. On visiting a community, very quickly we become aware of the spirit of the group—whether it is joyfully welcoming, weary and disheartened, living in the peace of reconciled relationships, or in tension with the leadership, for example. And those of us who live in community know that we are continually affected by and contribute to the spirit of the place, a spirit that is corporate, not just a collection of individuals with their private mood swings. In John's vision we see that God cares continuously about the spirit of a community, which is what a visitation should be discerning and addressing.

As we read the "visitation" reports of Revelation 2:2–7 we soon get a familiar feeling and recognize the format. The one "like a son of man" commands John to write, "To the angel of the church of Ephesus . . . 'I know your deeds, your hard works, and your perseverance. I know that you cannot tolerate wicked people, that you have tested those who claim to be apostles but are not, and have found them false. You have persevered and endured hardships for my name, and have not grown weary. Yet I hold this against you: you have forsaken the love you had at first. . . . Whoever has ears, let them hear what the Spirit says to the churches.'"

We see a familiar pattern in the letter to the churches: affirmations of faithful service; "But this I have against you"; and "Let anyone who has an ear listen. . . ."

So, is the visitation report a human word or a word from God? Yes, and yes.

Do these enigmatic words about ears and listening add anything to the summary? I remember that at the end of visitation reports we have often said something like this: "Our team feels immensely honored by your trust and honest sharing with us. We have given you our observations, commendations, and a few suggestions of possible changes. We are fallible humans trying to hear you all and listen to the Spirit. So don't take ours as the final word for what you should do. Take what we have said, discuss it, and sit with it before the Lord. See what your spirits and the Holy Spirit confirm. 'Whoever has ears, let them hear what the Spirit says to the churches.'"

About a month later, it is good for the visitation team leader to call back and ask how the community is doing with the agenda created by the report, and encourage them to keep listening to the Lord.

ASSOCIATIONS OF COMMUNITIES

A further development of mutual accountability emerges when individual communities band together or join existing associations of communities, what traditional monasticism has called "orders."

You are probably familiar, at least by name, with some of the monastic and missionary orders of the Catholic Church—Benedictines, the three orders of St. Francis, Dominicans, Jesuits, Christian Brothers, Sisters of Charity, Medical Mission Sisters, Maryknoll, and so on. Some orders are highly centralized in leadership like the Jesuits. Others like the Benedictines, I was surprised to learn, are not traditional hierarchies with a head in charge of all but are more organically organized in a federation of Congregations that resemble family trees, based upon the communities that gave birth to other communities over the centuries. Each Congregation, and the order as a whole, has named someone charged with visitations, keeping communications and relational connections strong between the communities.

What are the marks of these monastic and missionary orders, and how might these characteristics be instructive to the newest crop of lay Christian intentional communities? Here is a rough list of features that characterize an order:

Often there was a founder (like St. Francis) whose life modeled a certain charism, a gifted manner of service or ministry that has characterized the order.

An order has a rule of life (for example, Benedict's Rule) or a constitution that clarifies the expectations of a vowed life.

An order usually has a schedule of daily prayers and a prayer book with a set of Scripture readings, usually in a three-year cycle.

Orders provide an intensive formation period (as much as seven years), for educating and shaping the character of new members such that they are prepared to go anywhere in the order "knowing the ropes."

Orders have leadership consultations, a pattern of regional, national, and international conferences.

Orders offer a tradition of expertise (including lots of books) that comes from their common experiences in contemplative prayer and mission.

Orders form a family so that members know about the other communities in the order, pray for the same concerns, and keep in touch by visits, person exchanges, newsletters, and, now, the Internet.

Although lay communities who identify with the New Monasticism do not consider themselves an order, it is interesting to observe that they already have something like a rule of life (*School(s) for Conversion: 12 Marks of a New Monasticism*), a prayer book (*Common Prayer: A Liturgy for Ordinary Radicals*), periodic camp meetings (Papafest), leadership gatherings (the Family Reunion), and in some cases one-year apprentice programs that give rudimentary membership formation. As these communities grow, thrive, and connect, other features of "orders" are likely to emerge. Here are other lay examples of such tribes, all of them still growing.

The Hutterites of Anabaptist origins with pacifist convictions include more than two hundred farming colonies (fifty thousand members) in the northern US prairie states and central provinces of Canada.

The Bruderhof ("place of the brothers"), founded by Eberhard and Emmy Arnold following World War I in Germany, now has twenty-three communities with a few thousand members on four continents, primarily in the eastern United States and the United Kingdom. They were affiliated with the Hutterites until 1990.

Sword of the Spirit, with roots in the Charismatic movement, is an ecumenical association of thirty intentional communities in the United States and around the world with a celibate brotherhood (Servants of the Word) giving coherence and leadership to the larger association.

L'Arche began in 1964, in Trosly-Breuil, France, when Jean Vanier shared life with two men with mental disabilities and was transformed into a deeper understanding of Christ's love in communities of vulnerable weakness. L'Arche communities, built around core members with disabilities, now number about 150 groups in 40 countries affiliated with the International Federation of L'Arche.

The radical Catholic Worker communities, begun by Dorothy Day and Peter Maurin during the 1930s Great Depression era, now number more than two hundred communities or houses of hospitality, both urban and rural. Though the anarchist Catholic Workers would be allergic to any central organization, traditions of friendship, regional camp meetings, and intellectual solidarity support their charisms of community with the homeless and a witness for peace.

Shalom Mission Communities are the youngest of these associations, made up of five member communities with Anabaptist convictions, along with other "Shalom Connections" in the United States and El Salvador. SMC, although a generation older than most New Monastic communities, has chosen to engage strongly with this newer community movement in the Nurturing Communities Project.

None of these intentional Christian communities self-identify with the New Monasticism movement, and yet they share many of its values.

We could also add the Family Reunion to this list—an informal, occasional gathering of about a dozen communities sponsored by The Simple Way and its friends that has hosted PAPAfest camp meetings but has no ongoing structures. (Each of these community associations and others not mentioned here have their own websites if you want to learn more.) Finally, there are other, similar local or regional groupings of communities emerging in conversation with the Nurturing Communities Project. Shane Claiborne, Jonathan Wilson-Hartgrove, and other apostolic types, in their travels and speaking engagements on campuses and denominational youth conventions, keep spreading the word and making connections among groups that have taken the message to heart.

A WORD TO YOUNGER COMMUNITIES NOT YET AFFILIATED WITH AN ASSOCIATION OR ORDER

An association can feel like another layer of demands and relationships, a level of "insurance" that small communities do not have time, money, or attention to keep up with. These local communities are highly adapted to their neighborhoods and shaped by the unique personal journeys of those who have come together. They are not immediately attracted to the idea of coming under the umbrella of some preexisting "order." But as they visit each other, share ideas, people, conferences, books and other resources, and support intercommunity courtships (yes, they are happening), the idea of more intentional communities of communities keeps coming up.

Usually the communities who seek a more formal association have had some "wake up" experience like SOJO, where their need for committed relationships of accountability and mutual support was really impressed on them. Or like Koinonia Partners—when the community almost died, its vision for renewal has included getting other intentional communities on its board of directors, the functional equivalent of belonging to a community association.

Then there is the overhead cost. Shalom Mission Communities all contribute about $120 a year per member for the SMC budget to cover a part-time coordinator, a newsletter editor, and a contribution to the Nurturing Communities Project. Some groups who consider affiliation with SMC see this expense as a cost they could do without.

I hesitate to make a prediction based just on my own observations of intentional Christian communities over the years, but here goes anyway: I expect that a decade from now, the young communities that will still be standing are those who have affiliated with a wider association of communities or have formed new bonds of mutual support with other groups that serve the same function as the traditional monastic orders. Without such a network of wider care, an intentional community is not likely to outlive its present leaders. Where communities are made up of members in their twenties and thirties, this prospect seems beyond the horizon. But it is something they should pay attention to before their hair turns gray.

CHAPTER 28

Birthing and Nurturing New Communities from a Home Base

What metaphor is adequate for the way existing communities build, launch, plant, or birth new communities? Build like a carpenter? Launch like a boat maker? Plant like a gardener? Or birth like a pregnant mother?

Dorothee Soelle, in her memoir *Against the Wind: Memoir of a Radical Christian*, reflects on the pain of childbirth in her own experience and that of other women in her family. From this primal female experience, she gains insights into Romans 8:18–30, where the apostle Paul finds meaning in the sufferings of his church-birthing mission. "The whole creation has been groaning as in the pains of childbirth right up to the present time. Not only so, but we ourselves, who have the firstfruits of the Spirit, groan inwardly as we wait eagerly for our adoption to sonship, the redemption of our bodies."

Soelle writes, Paul "knew what illness, persecution, imprisonment, and torture meant. These cries and groans of a woman in labor do not signify doom and gloom; the image of birth evokes a new way of looking at struggle as transformation, a perspective understood by women in the pangs of hard labor."

No longer need we wrestle with the fruitless philosophical question of how a good and all-powerful God allows bad things to happen to good people. "A theology of pain," Soelle writes, "feminizes the question and relates our pain to the pain of God." The question then is not how to avoid pain, but rather, "How does our pain become the pain of God? How do we become part of the pain of Messianic liberation, part of the groaning of creation that is in travail? How do we come to suffer so that our suffering is the pain of birth?"

"We are capable of suffering because we are capable of love. Activities like loving, suffering, giving birth and dying are already a form of resistance against the imperatives of the economy under which we live. To bring children into the world and slowly to birth one's death, and to accept it rather than to get it over with, quickly and if possible without awareness of it—as our shabbiest fantasies would have it—are acts of participation in creation. . . . Just as a piece of bread can convince us of God, so this pain is a sacrament, a sign of God's presence. How could we ever have lost it?"

With the divine metaphor of childbirth in mind, the following tale is one of "conception and pregnancy," with the birth still to come. Josh and Candace McCallister are a young couple with two children, called to birth a new Christian intentional community. This is how Josh tells their story.

Josh McCallister's Story

We lived in Clovis, New Mexico, a small rural town where I was an associate minister in a Methodist congregation in charge of small group ministry and some mission projects. I talked with people in the church about forming small groups, about becoming spiritual family with one another. Most church members had no previous experience with this kind of community and had a hard time understanding the need for it. Candace, my wife, and I both felt frustrated with professional ministry. Our frustration had roots.

Previously, while still single, I had lived in community at Jesus People USA in Chicago. It had a transforming power on me for discipleship and spiritual maturity. This way of life struck me as a good and biblical thing to do.

Then Candace and I got married, and we went to Thailand with Word Made Flesh for a year, intimately sharing the pain and joys of people in a Bangkok slum in a ministry of presence. On the plane flight back from Bangkok, I remember reading in a music magazine (of all places) about Shane Claiborne and the New Monasticism movement. At some point we read his book *The Irresistible Revolution*, which further inspired us about living in Christian community, but it did not give us a lot of practical counsel. We read *School(s) for Conversion: 12 Marks of a New Monasticism* and attended a couple of Christian Community Development Association (CCDA) conferences, where we met Shane and Jonathan Wilson-Hartgrove.

In Clovis we were involved in some really good small groups, but we weren't clearly sharing our beliefs about discipleship, and we were very limited in acting out this life together with our participants. It was Candace who suggested that we might be called to start an intentional Christian community. You don't go to seminary to learn about that, so we started to research more experienced intentional communities where we might be instructed. By that time we had a child, so we had to proceed more deliberately and thoughtfully. We knew there were a lot of things about starting a community that we did not know. We wanted to do this with support, realizing that you don't model interdependence by acting independently.

I had read about Reba Place Fellowship's novice year in the *12 Marks* book, and this appealed to us as a way to learn about community. Our calling to start a community matched up with Reba's mission statement, which included "nurturing other . . . communities [of love and discipleship] as God gives us grace." Reba also had a history of sending people out to begin other communities, and they affirmed our own sense of leading.

We thought we might be with Reba only a year or two, but the first year we had another baby. The second year, we embarked on the novitiate to become covenant members. We thought, "You can't learn much about a room by standing in the doorway." This meant that our calling to start another community would be submitted to the community we joined. We asked ourselves, "Do we love and trust these people with our lives, money, our future?" Our hearts said yes. We figured that we'd learn most about Christian community by plunging fully into its life and responsibilities.

Candace was asked to serve on the central leadership team. If planting a community is God's will for us, we want the affirmation of our mentors, our small group, a community that knows us well and says we are ready. We wouldn't have it any other way.

While at Reba I discovered a whole lot of resources, both in readings and in conversations about birthing communities. Now I know whom to call when we have problems about household peacemaking, communal bookkeeping, relating to local churches, starting a business, or other practical matters. I have also discovered the online *Englewood Review of Books* and their excellent reading list for New Monastics. Candace and I talked a lot with other Reba parents about the kind of community we want to raise our family in and gained much from the experience and stories of older families here. There is not a lot written about raising children in community. Sara Wenger Shenk's book *Why Not Celebrate* is good, but out of print.

Looking ahead, the timing for our move is not yet clear. We want to commit to a place in the Southwest, probably New Mexico, and not leave for at least thirty years. We expect to study demographics, visit some poorer neighborhoods, walk the streets, and talk with people to see where a welcome might emerge. We don't want our neighbors to experience us as privileged white people moving into a Mexican barrio with an agenda for change.

We are open to planting a community that has the blessing of a local Methodist congregation, the denomination where we both have roots. We are grateful for the base we have received in salvation, Bible study, and prayer. But the limitations of those roots are also very real to us. We want to be involved in church renewal and contribute to a more rounded and committed communal view of the Christian life. We are encouraged that Dr. Elaine Heath at Perkins School of Theology is facilitating relationships between New Monastic kinds of communities and local United Methodist congregations. We have a lot of love for these churches and believe that there are people like us in the congregations who hunger for a more involved lifestyle conversion.

We have stayed in touch with about ten friends who are interested in intentional community with us. We have strong connections with Shalom Mission Communities and hope to spread the word in those circles and others when we are ready to move. We don't know how contemplative or activist the community will be. We expect to discern the Spirit's leading with our support base and with friends who join us as we go.

❖

What observations can others with a calling to be "midwives of community" draw from Josh and Candace's story? A great deal, I think.

We learn about community primarily by belonging and giving ourselves rather than by observing from the outside. This is an investment similar in time and effort to that of a pastor-in-training who goes to seminary or a monk's formation within an order. There is a profound difference in spiritual maturity between individuals starting a community on their own and persons sent by a community who have discerned the call together.

Communities open to the Spirit will realize that members are not their possession but are called together and sometimes sent out in a way that trusts God to care for both those who go and those who stay. There are labor pains and deep sacrifices involved in birthing a new community.

New communities are not constructed according to a blueprint of "best practices" or a franchise template. They are organically grown by the Holy Spirit from the unique gifts and availability of persons and communities in response to local needs. These contours are discerned by careful exploration, relationship building, and eyes of faith. But stories of community foundations are inspiring and carry a surplus of valuable lessons.

Christian communities with team leadership and experience-tested models of life together can be like hothouses for growing up new leaders. Where, then, do these young leaders go to enlarge their capacity? Giving birth to new communities with support from the home base is one good answer, for these are the new communities with the highest likelihood of surviving and thriving quickly.

Monastic orders have been planting new communities from a home base ever since the time of Benedict of Nursia, who in the sixth century founded twelve monasteries, each with an abbot and twelve monks. By contrast, the Hutterites have a more dramatic pattern of community multiplication that resembles the division of cells in a developing organism. When a colony has grown large enough that it should think about dividing, the overseer groups the families and single persons into two lists such that each one has a Servant of the Word (spiritual leader), a Secretary (farm manager), and other essential roles. The community buys land and sets aside funds for the new community buildings. On the fateful moving day, everyone packs up and gathers for prayer before lots are drawn to decide if it is group A or group B that will move. With hugs and tearful goodbyes, they load the vehicles and one group drives away while the other group unpacks their belongings and stays home. God has decided.

There are other formulas for how this works, as well. When Reba has started a new community or household, the folks interested in this venture will meet together as a weekly small group for a year or so. They test their callings, sort out who is committed, learn how to worship and function as a team, and write a covenant. Reba doesn't start with a building or a farm and look for people to fill it. The persons become a body first. There is a trust that once the people are called and committed, God will provide the physical arrangements at the right time, and so it happens. When Reba launched Plow Creek farm, both groups functioned out of one common treasury until the farm was producing and members had found local jobs.

Jean Vanier writes about the experience of founding new L'Arche communities with the help of seasoned Catholic priests or nuns who join the new communities to lend their experience and services.

There are more and more people today who belong to a community— frequently a religious community—and who feel called by God to join a newly founded community living closer to the poor. They belong then to two communities. This double belonging frequently works very well. The first community is like the mother community with which they keep deep bonds, while they flourish in the new one. It is as if they had needed the formation and growth in the mother community in order to be able to give their lives, and give life, in the new community. Their presence with all they have learnt in the mother community, is a great source of strength for the new one.

The Bruderhof family of communities has grown to about a dozen rural "hofs," each with two hundred to three hundred people, with dormitory-style residences and workshops, with a nursery, grade school, common kitchen, and dining hall. But in recent years they have begun to plant urban households under a different model. Charles Moore tells about those urban transplants and some lessons they have learned.

Charles Moore's Story

I grew up in California and went to college there. Later, I was part of a small inner-city community in Denver while teaching at Denver Seminary. Our efforts to connect with needy people in the city were a disaster on several fronts. We were too disconnected from the support we needed. We were in our thirties when my wife and I felt called to join the Bruderhof. That was about twenty years ago. Early on we were asked to live for a time in Harambe House (in Pasadena) with John and Vera Mae Perkins. We've been part of several Bruderhof communities, and I worked with the Plough publishing house much of that time. About six years ago my wife and I were asked to help start a new community in Albany, New York.

Many of our young people thought we should try community in the city, to engage with circles outside our own. We were aware of The Simple Way, Camden House, Shane Claiborne, and John Perkins of CCDA. We were led first to Camden, New Jersey, to connect there with the poor, which is a central value for us. But that was rather short-lived. We attempted something without fully counting the cost, without reckoning with the vast cultural differences between our way of life and a violent urban setting. But we still felt a need to try to live this life in a variety of contexts.

Instead of trying to find the most derelict part of the city, we have looked for places where we could connect more within the range of our own experience, but places that would also stretch us. We started houses in Albany, Harlem in New York City, overseas in London, and then some smaller towns. I think we have about a dozen newer groups now in different urban settings. We wanted to share what we were experiencing in community and also see how these contexts might reveal the blinders and boxes we've created for ourselves that need to be challenged. We wanted to grow in a two-way exchange.

These urban plantings are not mission communities; we expect each of them to be self-supporting. In Albany some of us hired out to work for others while some got a handcrafted sign business going. Some of our members were medical students—internists and residents who also brought home some income. Another community with a big house ran a daycare center. We picked up whatever work we could find consistent with our values, to sustain ourselves.

The birth and growth of these newer urban communities has taught us to not mistake the form for the essence of something. When you start a new endeavor, you need to hang onto the basics but let the local forms grow in an organic way. Attempts to impose what you have elsewhere are artificial and squeeze out the spirit of Christ.

When we send people out, they come from a really united place. We want to sustain that unity with many prayers, visits, and meaningful ways to encourage our sisters and brothers. We keep asking, "How is it going and what are you up against?" We send without severing.

Before we try to do anything for others, we first need to be who we are. A lot of people go into urban settings trying to respond to all the need they see. But we encourage people to go, first live out your commitment to be a community in Christ, and then be led and stretched from there. It might happen through people and groups you meet. It is easy to overload in a city context.

In the urban communities, we have found it pretty difficult to integrate children into public or private schools. The pressure on our children in the elementary and especially in the higher schools is really strenuous. When we moved to Albany, we had a child in a Catholic elementary school, but even there she got many mixed signals. We found it very difficult to connect with other parents in the school. Had we stayed longer, we'd have seriously considered homeschooling. Other families in the city have connected with homeschool networks. You don't want to isolate your children.

In smaller communities you end up wearing many leadership hats. We usually ask a mature couple to take the lead responsibility to care for our urban communities. But everyone works together as a family to figure out the needs and divvy up the responsibilities for maintenance, shopping, cooking, finances, and so on.

Our experience has taught us the paramount importance of commitment to sustain the witness that community in Christ is possible. If we have other ideals that are higher than community in Christ, our attachment becomes conditional. "This community is not simple enough for me, doesn't homeschool, isn't engaged enough with the poor, or does not fulfill my personal goals, so I will leave." But if our deepest desire is to live together as a witness to the kingdom of God, then we will find a common way.

As you can see, there are many practical, organic, Spirit-led ways that new communities are coming to life in our day. And if this is your calling, you are not alone. Many others are on the road, eager to share experiences and wisdom from the common journey. But it helps to discern our place in the much larger thing that God is doing.

In his day Jesus came proclaiming with judgment and hope, "The kingdom of God is at hand." The apostle Paul, through controversy and persecutions of all kinds, saw the birth of small Jewish-Gentile church communities as evidence of a new creation, God demonstrating before the powers that reconciliation for which all of history had been waiting.

Contemporary Christianity has struggled to find its place in this new thing that God is doing. Some Christians are eager to save souls for heaven, souls that remain deeply embedded in the status quo of the world, who do not expect heaven to transform this earth. Others labor to change the structures of injustice in our society to more closely resemble the kingdom of God, and yet their daily lives are often missing that love and experience of God's presence in the peace and justice of community.

Contemporary social movements are bringing together personal discipleship of Jesus, a witness for peace and justice, embodied in committed community. These movements are like the contractions of labor as Creation groans and shifts inwardly in preparation for the kingdom of God to be born anew. For this reason illness, suffering, persecution, instructive failures, and painful sacrifices for the sake of community all have meaning. May we all be caught up in the urgent push of God, in pain and labor for the birth of prophetic communities, signs of hope for a world renewed, whose face is Jesus.

CHAPTER 29

Exceptionally Gifted Persons and the Challenge of Submission

Some communities have the mixed blessing of an exceptionally gifted member who is "in demand" on a wider stage than the local fellowship. Such persons may be mightily used by God through writing, public speaking, or musical performance—which often takes them away from their home base. Stability of life in community relationships is where they are most likely to gain self-knowledge and humility, but this can be difficult for members who have gained a public persona. Furthermore, it is hard for gifted persons to submit when they lack peers who understand their calling and friends who can enter into their opportunities, and who are equipped to give good counsel. Communities themselves can be too impressed by a member's reputation or jealous of the same. For many reasons, "celebrities" can create unusual pastoral problems for Christian intentional communities.

Such people have included some of the most famous Christians of the twentieth century. In this chapter we will share stories and reflect on the lives of Teresa of Ávila, Dorothy Day, John Howard Yoder, Henri Nouwen, Thomas Merton, and others who became public, spiritual "celebrities" and faced the challenge of submission as well.

Teresa of Ávila was a gregarious member of the sixteenth-century Spanish Carmelite order who, by her own reckoning, lived a mediocre spiritual life for two decades before she became serious about her conversations with God. Teresa began to experience ecstatic visions, which caused grave concern to her superiors in the Spanish Inquisition. They ordered Teresa to write what she called *The Book of My Life* (often titled *Autobiography* by publishers) to test whether her visions were of the devil or not.

Teresa lamented, "Why do we run around crying, 'The devil! The devil!' when we can be saying 'God!' 'God!' and make the devils tremble?" Of these authorities she said, "Without a doubt, I fear those who fear the devil more than I fear the devil himself." The more Teresa tried to obey her superiors and suppress these supernatural experiences, the more they increased in frequency and intensity. Bad spiritual advice nearly drove her insane. Eventually, she found in John of the Cross (a monk a generation younger than herself) a spiritual advisor and confessor who shared her spiritual journey and in whom she could deeply confide.

Of these intimate experiences and conversations with God, Teresa wrote masterfully and prolifically—classics in Spanish literature and in mystical theology. But in her call to renew the lackadaisical Carmelite order, she met much opposition. Nevertheless, Teresa was energetic, charming, and quick to make friends who supported her cause. She never doubted the value of obedience, both to her vows and to the members of her order, but she was creative about how she practiced it. Going above her immediate supervisor, she won approval of her renewal mission and founded a dozen communities of sisters eager to suffer physical privations in a cloistered life of prayer and contemplation for the love of Jesus.

Anyone who reads Teresa of Ávila will connect with a vital, irrepressible, authentic spirit, but her ideas about submission to authority seem quaintly medieval. In our postmodern era, it is not so obvious why we should be submitted to spiritual guidance and to a local community in order to do God's will.

It seemed odd to many of Dorothy Day's friends that this feisty anarchist insisted on regularly going to a priest for confession, asked permission from the local bishop to start a Catholic Worker house, and repeated the claim that without Peter Maurin's ideas, she would not have found the purpose of her life. Despite her celebrity—and it was profound for the last forty years of her life—she refused to live like one. She went out of her way to explain to people that Peter Maurin's arrival on the scene, during the important years of formation for the Catholic Worker movement, was providential and that his writings gave her the visionary plan and assurance she needed to move forward.

Submission was key to sustaining a fruitful life for Day and the Catholic Worker. Her example shows that we are not really free to move forward in God's work with soul, mind, and strength unless someone is looking over our shoulder and speaking good counsel into our ear. The word of God can be clear to one person, but when it is confirmed by another, and then another—that is when God's work tends to be done. We need the family of faith around us speaking the truth in love. Those who are especially gifted, if they are also spiritually mature, will realize that their gifts do not make obedience optional, but even more necessary.

Alas, the church has often been crippled by leaders whose ambition and character have not been shaped or guided by a life of mutual submission in community. Allan Howe, member of Reba Place Fellowship, tells the story of a failed attempt to found a Christian intentional community involving his seminary professor John Howard Yoder:

Allan Howe's Story

Jerry Lind and I were students at the Associated Mennonite Biblical Seminaries in the late 1960s, primarily because we wanted to study under John Howard Yoder. Yoder was especially intrigued by our Howe family because we were members on leave from Reba Place Fellowship and because of his respect for John Miller, Reba's founder.

A friendship grew between the Lind, Howe, and Yoder families. The Linds and Howes decided to stick around another year after our graduations in order to explore intentional community with the Yoders. We began weekly meals and small group meetings. In 1968 Marcia and Jerry Lind, Jeanne and I, along with our babies, moved together into a house at 501 Cleveland in Elkhart, half a block from John and Annie Yoder with their family of five-going-on-six children. Annie Yoder welcomed us into their family zone and appreciated our support, especially in the many times when John was gone. The older girls, Becky and Martha, loved to hang out with Jeanne. Our families blended well.

John Howard Yoder was a rising star in the world of theology, and his Anabaptist vision of church as radical discipleship community undergirded a generation of neo-Anabaptists in their exploration of Christian community. In 1968 he was circulating among us early versions of the manuscript later published under the now famous title *The Politics of Jesus*. It was a heady time to explore community together as Jesus taught it and as John opened it for us.

Jeanne and I had had previous small group experience at Reba, so it felt strange to us to have community meetings where five adults sat in a circle of chairs while the sixth stood at his desk, shuffling papers, writing, reading, and occasionally making comments on group proceedings. Leadership was awkward. The obvious elder in the group was John, but his participation was idiosyncratic. We struggled with "How do we confront someone who has been our professor?"

Getting a leadership group together for the community proved almost impossible since John was traveling much of the time on speaking engagements around the world, or he was getting ready for the next trip. Within six months we all concluded that, for several reasons, it was not working. The Linds moved out, and teenagers Becky and Martha moved in with us to relieve stress on the Yoder household, which had just added a sixth child. The result is that we have a deep and lasting bond with the Yoder family despite the breakup of our attempted community.

John Howard Yoder felt deeply called to teaching, incessant writing, and theological dialog at the highest levels. Who were we to discern with him the best use of his gifts? I feel sad to think that John had no real peers to whom he could submit on questions of family, vocation, and character development.

How do you judge a career that produced a dozen books and six hundred articles? His powers of intellectual analysis were world class. He could be very gracious and skillful in ecumenical dialog. But interpersonal relations was Yoder's weakest area. Should he have reigned himself in to learn the disciplines and virtues of ordinary community relationships?

Yoder's resistance to counsel and to those near at hand came back to bite him years later when he was confronted by several women about his inappropriate sexual advances. He did eventually submit to church discipline on this matter, engaged in therapy, apologized to the women, and was restored to membership in the church a few months before his sudden death in 1997. John's own need for healing came against a negative view of psychologists and counselors generally. I think he would have helped himself and others if he had submitted to ordinary folks in his life and more fully embodied the vision of community that he taught and wrote about so prolifically.

❖

Henri Nouwen was likewise at the pinnacle of academic achievement. While a professor at Harvard Divinity School, he found himself emotionally exhausted and spiritually empty. He took a yearlong retreat with L'Arche communities at the invitation of their founder, Jean Vanier. At the end of that year he accepted a summons for what turned out to be the rest of his life, to live at Daybreak Community near Toronto.

Nouwen writes about that "twilight zone in our hearts that we ourselves cannot see. Even when we know quite a lot about ourselves—our gifts and weaknesses, our ambitions and aspirations, our motives and our drives—large parts of ourselves remain in the shadow of consciousness. This is a very good thing." It is a good thing, Nouwen argues, because we are completed by our friends and by our communities. Other people, especially those who love us, can see both our weaknesses and the significance of our lives in ways that we never can. "That's a grace, a grace that calls us not only to humility, but to a deep trust in those who love us. It is the twilight zones of our hearts where true friendships are born."

Such spiritual friendships are essential to self-knowledge, growth in maturity, and faithful service. Jesus sent his disciples out two by two.

The apostle Paul tended to travel with a few missionary companions. Jean Vanier travels on his many speaking engagements with one or two core members, persons with disabilities, to stay grounded in the ethos of his community. Jonathan Wilson-Hartgrove plans his travel itinerary with his community and limits his absences to one trip a month. With such guidelines it is easier to "live in the light," to stay grounded in relationships with sisters and brothers who look out for one's integrity.

Often, because of someone's fame, his knack for speaking well about our community, her artistic or intellectual virtuosity, or the community's dependence upon someone's fundraising ability, we become complicit in cutting such a person slack in their immaturities. We are motivated by admiration or envy of someone else's gifts, which isolates us from each other instead of breaking through, however poorly, with observations and questions that probe to the heart.

Exceptionally gifted people, it turns out, are also often lonely in unique ways. Most of us can find friends within our community—people who understand us well enough. Exceptionally gifted people have a need for peers, too, and often can find them only outside the community. Who can advise a creative songwriter about good stewardship of her gifts, a genius computer programmer, or a community organizer with exceptional drive? Usually a committed Christian with a similar gifting. The home community should care that each of its members has such connections somewhere.

Sometimes, after much soul-searching and conversation, a person will find that her community is not a fitting context for the exercise of her gifts and calling. However, no one should leave her or his community quickly over such an issue, but only after a careful process of discernment that should include the consent of one's covenant partners.

Allan Howe tells of a time when he and Virgil Vogt were summoned from Reba to Koinonia Partners in the early 1970s to advise three high-powered leaders—Ladon Sheets, Millard Fuller, and Don Mosley—on how to reconcile their differences. These tensions were not over interpersonal conflicts, but about different personal callings, and whether

Koinonia should become the kind of community that would actively support the callings of these exceptionally gifted individuals. In the end they were all blessed to go separate directions: Ladon Sheets went into war resistance activism affiliated with the Berrigan brothers and with Jonah House in Baltimore. Millard Fuller decamped to nearby Americus, Georgia, to begin Habitat for Humanity as a separate nonprofit corporation. And Don Mosley eventually moved with a few other Koinonia families to found Jubilee Partners, finding their charism in welcoming refugees and creatively protesting those injustices around the world that create refugees. In hindsight, it seems that all three of these men took what was good from Koinonia and planted it again in other settings to the glory of God. And Koinonia was blessed to carry on with its original charism of interracial partnerships and radical discipleship training in a rural setting.

Thomas Merton, in his autobiography, *The Seven Storey Mountain*, reveals a restless young man with extraordinary literary promise who explored and exploited his freedom in profligate living and moral dead ends until he came to an existential crisis. He realized that his life and his many gifts would be squandered unless he gave himself completely to Jesus in a disciplined community. With characteristic zeal and boundless energy, Merton looked for the most extreme example of monastic solitude and chose the Trappist Order as his spiritual home.

Basil Pennington's biography of Merton documents his restless petitions and appeals to his superiors, and finally to the pope himself, for "permission to leave Gethsemani to find a place of greater solitude in Latin America." When the answer from Rome came back as a final no, Merton was surprised to discover liberty in submission. "The decisions made have left me very free and empty. I can say they have enabled me to taste an utterly new kind of joy." In his journal he wrote, "I shall certainly have solitude. . . . Where? Here or there makes no difference. Somewhere. Nowhere. Beyond all where. Solitude outside geography or in it. No matter."

This restless search for greener monastic pastures occurred again and again for Merton, and usually the answer he got was no, although at some points he was granted exceptions to live a more hermetical life upon the monastery grounds. From his base of monastic solitude he entered into ecumenical dialog with visitors and correspondents in all directions, including Buddhism. A fellow monk once said of Merton, he "wrote very well about solitude, the little of it that he had."

On several occasions, Merton hosted retreats for creative writers, artists, and cutting-edge church leaders who came together in circles of friendship on the monastery grounds, providing for others what he needed for himself, a community of peers who could give each other counsels of fidelity within their different traditions.

As novice master in Gethsemani Abbey, Merton never believed that unthinking submission was a virtue. Rather, he urged his students to be alert to the deeper reasons for the practices that were to shape their lives in monastic community. Merton pushed the boundaries of submission in all directions, but not past the breaking point. When censored by his superiors from any publication in opposition to the Vietnam War, Merton fired off letters under pseudonyms such as "Benedict Monk" and "J. Marco Frisbee" to friends in the peace movement (Jim Forest, Dorothy Day, and Daniel Berrigan) who then passed them around widely, sometimes showing up as "letters to the editor" in *Catholic Worker* newspapers. But when a friend suggested that Merton defy the ban or leave the monastery, he replied, "This kind of response would create a scandal and just prove to them that they are right."

In *Contemplation in a World of Action*, Merton concludes his reflections on different kinds of freedom in this manner:

> It is necessary to accept restrictions, restraints, self-denial, sacrifice, and so forth. To people of our times so intent on human fulfillment, this can indeed seem scandalous. It takes a particular kind of insight to see what in so many respects is an unfulfillment is in truth a way to the highest kind of fulfillment. . . . Basically there is only one kind of freedom, which is the freedom of the Cross. It is the freedom that

comes for one who has completely given himself with Christ on the Cross, has risen with Christ, and has Christ's freedom—not simply in ordinary human spontaneity, but in the spontaneity of the Spirit of God.

This paradoxical word of submission for the sake of spontaneity in the Spirit of Christ is for us all. Exceptionally gifted people, it turns out, are not fundamentally different from the rest of us. Everyone in community is gifted. Although dealing with famous members is not a problem of most communities, we will recognize similar dynamics everywhere in varying degrees. We all are tempted to seek privilege because of our specialties. We all live with blind spots that are obvious enough to persons who share life with us on a daily basis. The variety of gifts we have been given by the Spirit complement each other in the body of Christ.

In this chapter we are invited to believe that Teresa, Dorothy Day, Henri Nouwen, Thomas Merton, and John Howard Yoder too by the end of their lives knew the reality of what they were talking about. This trust in the way of the cross transforms us especially when our dreams and reputations go on the altar, and, with sisters and brothers, we discern together what God wants. Sometimes our cross is the community itself and its leaders, where others don't see things our way, and we die with Jesus in order that God might do a new and resurrected thing with us all.

Embracing Renewal

On a bus ride in the mountains of El Salvador on a mission trip to our sister community, Valle Nuevo, a teenager sat down beside me and asked if I would be her mentor. Sarah Belser went on to explain that she had grown up in Reba Place Fellowship, taking it all for granted, but now, instead of going on to college, she believed God was asking her to stick around to study the history and theology of community as her inheritance. She had prayed about this decision for a long time and felt excitement about what God would do. Would I partner with her in this venture?

Sarah's request came like a gift of new wine from the Holy Spirit, an opportunity for renewal in her life and in mine. But neither of us realized that this conversation would mark the beginning of an extended season of renewal profoundly changing the whole Fellowship and inspiring many young people to follow after Sarah (actually, Jesus) in ways that continue to this day.

New wine calls for flexible, new wineskins, as Jesus taught (Matt. 9:17). Sarah and I needed a common project to give expression to the Spirit's impulse to pass on the excitement we felt. We proposed that Reba launch an intern program so that a few other young people could experience what Sarah wanted to learn.

We took a carload of folks to visit Vineyard Central in Cincinnati, where the Spirit had inspired a communal awakening with a lively internship we could learn from. We struck up a friendship with their leader, Kevin Raines, and heard from the younger tribe at Vineyard Central how their intensive experience of discipleship inspired them to join the community and enlarge its mission. We borrowed their manual, which Sarah adapted to our context. We organized an intern support committee and sent out brochures to young people near and far, offering a year at Reba focused on community, discipleship, and service.

Some Reba folks were skeptical that young people would really want to hang around. They knew that Reba had a history of courageous Spirit-led adventures years ago, but by now we had many gray hairs with almost no members in their twenties and thirties. However, in a timely visitation, Richard Hays, the Duke Divinity School professor, spoke a prophetic word to us from the stories of Sarah and Elizabeth who became miraculously pregnant in their old age. Someone suggested we invest our retirement fund in a new generation. Well, that was a joke since we had no retirement fund, but now we knew we were supposed to invest our last strength for God's future rather than our own.

The first year we made several mistakes, and the interns left early. But the second year some lively young people arrived, caught Sarah's enthusiasm, and had a great experience. Each year the exchange between interns and the community went better as we got over talking about "them" and learned to become a "we." In the third group of interns, Eric Lawrence actively recruited a band of friends from the University of Illinois in Bloomington to jump into the internship with him. It was a chaotic and exciting time of idealism, turbulent relationships, late night conversations, and a commitment to early morning prayers that quickly broke down. We had a glorious mess that looks much more like God's work in hindsight than it did in the moment.

At a community retreat Eric and company proposed a new business called the Recyclery that would repair and sell used bikes, teach kids how to care for them, and inspire the world to save fossil fuels. A community elder asked Eric the question on many of our minds, "And how long will you stick around to help this happen?"

"Hmmm, gotcha," Eric responded and pondered. "How about three years?"

Three years seemed like an eternity to Eric and his friends, but God works with such beginnings. The Recyclery is indeed a storefront business now, and Eric is married to Katie, parents of two lively children in our midst.

About that time Greg Clark, a Reba philosopher teaching at nearby North Park University, saw the vitality of Reba's Monday night potlucks and the internship orientation seminar that followed it. So he designed a course called "Intentional Christian Community" in which a vanload of North Park students would join our potluck and seminar for college credit. The first year only two students showed up, but word got around, and from then on it has been wildly popular, with a limit we had to set at fifteen.

Sarah Belser got married and moved on, and I continued to lead the intern program through various changes, always with a junior partner. A couple of years ago Celina Varela, my last junior partner, took over what we have renamed "the Reba apprenticeship." Many of these young people have stuck around to become members, so that our Fellowship meetings now have both old folks and a bulge of singles, newlyweds, and young families. Not only are the old folks pregnant as the prophecy foretold, but the young couples, too.

To socialize all these new people into a common life, we all— older and younger folks together—needed to meet more often. So our meeting schedule and our membership categories, our task teams and our demographics have all changed. A new generation of leadership is taking its place and changing the place. Because of this youth movement we have jumped into the renewal movement named the "New Monasticism" and helped host several PAPAfest events. Gardens are sprouting up and dumpster-diving has become institutionalized. New life with all its painful joys surrounds us daily. And it all began when a Reba youth alive to the Spirit started talking about others who might want to join the story and seek the kingdom of God with us.

According to the prophet Joel, whom the apostle Peter quotes in his Pentecost sermon (Acts 2:17–18), this is what times of renewal look like.

> In the last days, God says,
> I will pour out my Spirit on all people.
> Your sons and daughters will prophesy,
>> your young men will see visions,
>> your old men will dream dreams.
> Even on my servants, both men and women,
>> I will pour out my Spirit in those days,
>> and they will prophesy.

In our day this tends to look like hosting lots of visitors, conferences, and Schools for Conversion weekends, where the young people stay up late to share excitement with the guests while old folks go to bed early— so they can get up early to form committees and raise funds that will make it happen again.

One could multiply similar stories of Holy Spirit renewal in other intentional Christian communities around the country. For example, about eight years ago there was a "Hardcore Bible Study" in Minneapolis that drew together an improbable crowd of punks and misfits, issuing in a church called the Salvage Yard and a loose network of intentional community households that keep gathering the lost and reaching out to "such as we once were." They have kept in touch with other similar groups around the world through Steiger Ministries.

Meanwhile, Englewood Christian Church on Indianapolis's north side was a dying commuter congregation in a decaying urban setting until a new pastor, Mike Bowling, and a group of friends started meeting faithfully every Sunday night for years in prayer and earnest search of God's vision for the church and its neighborhood. Gradually unity was given to infiltrate their corner of the city with an intentional community that would turn the isolated church into a community center for its neighbors. The Holy Spirit has inspired a series of creative neighborhood development projects in housing, a preschool, common meals, a book publishing business, and a web of redemptive friendships that give hope to a neighborhood and to many individuals who were going down the drain. Since then, they have become strong participants of the interracial Christian Community Development Association, begun by John Perkins.

These stories, and countless others each community can tell, are cosmic expansions of that original big bang from the birth of the early church in Jerusalem. The Holy Spirit baptism called together a people from every language group around the Mediterranean, many of them pilgrims from the Jewish Diaspora gathered in Jerusalem for the Pentecost festival (Acts 2:5–13). The apostles reminded the excited new believers that this was the time foretold by all the prophets when history would turn—the age of the Messiah was at hand. Their repentance and baptism resulted in selling lands and houses wherever they had come from, in order to buy time to be together in a season of intense fellowship. They shared the love of Jesus, celebrated the joy of the Holy Spirit, used their possessions freely for the work of God, and rejoiced that they were found worthy of persecution like their Lord. For several years they experienced that same communal formation into a "one another" life as did the original disciples with Jesus.

A wave of persecution scattered the church, another phase of rapid inflation. Guided by the Holy Spirit, these early Christians gathered converts and planted the church throughout Judea and Samaria (Acts 8:1–8) and into urban centers like Phoenicia, Cyprus, and Antioch (Acts 11:19–30). A third phase followed when the arch-persecutor of the church, Saul, met the resurrected Jesus and was sent to share the Good News of reconciliation across the Gentile world.

What common themes can we discern in these stories of renewal?

The main actor is the Holy Spirit, who pours out the wine, while God's people scurry about devising wineskins to receive and share the bounty. It is crucial to make an investment of time, energy, and financial resources in the new thing that God is doing.

Renewal is often the result of a respectful tug-of-war between old-timers and newcomers in community. Newcomers have a need to remake community in order for it to become their own. The meaning of a practice must be fresh and authentic in order for them to give it a try. That is mostly a healthy impulse. But there are some things that can only be understood by practicing them until their meaning is revealed.

For example, I remember once when a college student joined a communal small group and felt impatient with a format where each person around the circle took turns to tell "thanksgivings and prayer concerns" from the week. The conversation seemed slow and awkwardly formal to him. But after a few weeks he had a sudden awakening, seeing for the first time the superficial character of the competitive student conversations he was used to on campus with their constant interruptions and marginalization of everyone but the most verbal. He realized that by doing what he did not at first understand, his mind and heart had been formed to see a new and beautiful reality.

But that does not make mindless repetition of meaningless acts a path to virtue either. Renewal for the small group might come by seeking ways to encourage spontaneity while assuring that everyone is listened to well.

Communities experiencing renewal are discerning the signs of the times in the spiritual movements and social crises around them and connecting with other groups where God is doing a new thing. But faux renewal also beckons, so faith communities need to be selective in the movements they will visit, invite in, and learn from. A generation ago most intentional Christian communities were strongly influenced by the charismatic renewal, which brought new gifts of the Spirit, ecstatic worship, inner healing, and a people hungry for community. But the movement also was infected with grandiose exercise of authority that wreaked havoc in many lives, resulting in fruit that did not last. (See Julia Duin, *Days of Fire and Glory: The Rise and Fall of a Charismatic Community*.)

Renewal will be a time of making mistakes and learning from them in deeper dialog. I have seen this take a lot of forms over the years, some profound and some superficial. "We've been accused of being judgmental—therefore we will hold in our thoughts and try to act more accepting to our guests." "Folks don't want to join our community because our expectations are too high, so let's lower them." No. True renewal will go beneath either-or dichotomies with long and patient conversations while listening to each one's truth and to the Lord.

Many sociologists have noted the life cycle of communities and institutions. They begin with charisma, high energy, inclusion of new people, creative institutional forms, and a vivid sense of purpose worthy of personal sacrifice in time and possessions. And they end in low energy, with the same old people doing the same old tasks for the sake of institutional self-preservation. But renewal will not come by tinkering with structures, either.

Jesus calls us to "bear fruit that lasts." I have observed in times of renewal that the Holy Spirit gives many gifts that, for a time, make the advance of the kingdom seem almost effortless. God is doing it, and we are carried along in the enthusiasm of signs and wonders. But Jesus was also dismayed by the fickleness of the spectacle-seeking crowds who melted away in hard times.

Instant maturity of character is not a gift of the Holy Spirit. Maturity is a *fruit* of the Spirit over time, the result of a life of discipleship that builds new habits of character and instills virtues through faithful service, suffering, and endurance. We should not be surprised that, between wonderful times in community, there are also times of hard slogging when our faithfulness depends on desperately honest prayers and daily infusions of God's grace in hidden service, times when there is nothing heroic to brag about. We get to know Jesus in the reality of his sufferings and crucifixion before there can be a Resurrection and a Pentecost.

The Spirit wants renewal for our communities even more than we do and is waiting with eager longing for the children of God to be revealed in our time. And just like individuals, communities can be born again, and again, and again. The pathway to renewal is not a list of three easy (or hard) steps some Christian guru has just discovered, but blessings that Jesus always has waiting for us.

Jim Forest, chair of the Orthodox Peace Fellowship and friend of Thomas Merton, digs up the original meaning of "blessed" in the Beatitudes. "In Classical Greek *makar* was associated with the immortal gods. *Kari* means 'fate' or 'death,' but with the negative prefix *ma* the word means 'being deathless, no longer subject to fate,' a condition both inaccessible and longed for by mortals. It was because of their immortality that the gods, the *hoi Makarioi*, were the blessed ones." In Christian usage, the *Makarioi*, the blessed ones, already participate in the life of God.

Blessed are the "poor in spirit," "those who mourn," "the meek," "those who hunger and thirst for righteousness," "the merciful," "the pure in heart," "the peacemakers," "those who are persecuted for righteousness' sake," for they already belong to God's life, which never ends. This blessing not only transforms our human existence from meaningless suffering into participation in the life of God, but in an astounding way, it also reveals to us the nature of God in the Crucified and Resurrected One.

Jesus teaches and invites us into a very different vision of history, not the one created by the "winners" of battles for supremacy, of empires that rise and all fall away. But history is made by people of the Beatitudes who, in suffering and faithfulness, in humility and hope, keep giving themselves for community, repairing and reconciling at the small scale what others have destroyed in their gross battles for dominion. These are the stories of death and resurrection that, by God's grace and mysterious power for those with "eyes to see," actually pass on life and renew history, making another generation possible.

We see this mysterious power for renewal in the apostles who, after Jesus's resurrection and gift of the Holy Spirit, gave their lives as persons no longer afraid of death, making disciples to the ends of the earth in careers of faithful witness punctuated in most cases by martyrdom. They have joined the circle-dance of Father, Son, and Holy Spirit, not just beyond time, but their victory with Jesus over death already changes everything before death. Living in the freedom of Christ characterized their lives in holy community already in the history of here and now.

As Dorothy Day often said in quoting Catherine of Siena, "All the way to heaven is heaven." And heaven on earth, we are assured, looks like the Beatitudes, looks like Jesus. The good news is that no one is excluded. Everyone is invited to lay down their weapons and join the circle-dance of the "Lamb who was slain from the creation of the world" (Rev. 13:8).

NOTES

A Preface the Author Hopes You Will Read First

The reference to Dietrich Bonhoeffer comes from *Life Together* (New York: HarperCollins, 1954), 26–27.

The quote from N. T. Wright is found in Shane Claiborne, Jonathan Wilson-Hartgrove, and Enuma Okoro, *Common Prayer: A Liturgy for Ordinary Radicals* (Grand Rapids: Zondervan, 2010), 72.

2. The Landscape of Disintegrating Community and Our Longing for It

The statistics about church closings and college students leaving the faith come from Tim Morely, *Embodying Our Faith: Becoming a Living, Sharing, Practicing Church* (Downers Grove, IL: InterVarsity Press, 2009), 26ff.

3. Contours of Resistance to Community

Catholics and Mennonites have traditions of instruction concerning a "seamless garment of life," opposing abortion, capital punishment, and war. That's not been the norm for most Protestants. The usual divide parallels political boundaries where evangelicals may have little to say in favor of peace but stand up for the unborn; and mainliners summon us to care for the poor but may not address the virtue of sexual restraint. But many in this younger generation are turned off by the culture wars and are coming round to the "seamless-garment" vision.

Here is the experience of Brandon Rhodes, who wrote chapter 3:

Intentional Christian community has been much of my life since 2003, years that surrounded me with people between 18 and 30 years old. I experienced it in the Chi Alpha Community in Eugene, Oregon, for three years; in organizing for creation care among Christian college students across the country; in writing for Jesus Radicals; and in helping found Springwater Church in Portland. For two years now I have also bumped into these generational lines through my work with the Parish Collective, a motley network of neighborhood-rooted intentional communities, churches, and Jesus-loving families. The distinctives of my generation stand out in contrast with others now as I have lived for four years in a more intergenerational community. We see this when older people are baffled at my generation's anxiety about commitment, for example. Sometimes bumping into these generational contours feels like a cross-cultural experience, and so has deepened our awareness of the need for patience and listening well to arrive at healthy community.

5. The Gospel Call to Discipleship in Community

The Wendell Berry quote comes from *Sex, Economy, Freedom and Community* (New York: Random House, 1993), chap. 8.

6. Searching for Your Community: Visits, Internships, and Mentors

The cultural phenomenon of delayed adulthood has been widely researched for a couple of decades, more recently under the rubric of "emerging adulthood," a phrase coined by psychologist Jeffrey Arnett in a 2000 article in the *American Psychologist*. According to the Wikipedia entry "Emerging Adulthood," it "applies to young adults in developed countries who do not have children, do not live in their own home, or have a substantial income to become fully independent in their early to late 20's." A standout resource on this subject is Christine Hassler, *20 Something Manifesto: Quarter-Lifers Speak Out About Who They Are, What They Want, and How to Get It* (Novato, CA: New World Library, 2008).

15. Taking on Work Schedules and the Seduction of Careers

Nouwen's reflections on the membership statements of persons joining the Daybreak community come from *The Road to Daybreak: A Spiritual Journey* (New York: Doubleday, 1988), 154.

17. Stop Going to Church and Become the Church

The quotations from John Alexander come from his manuscript *Stop Going to Church and Become the Church*, which is in the possession of Church of the Sojourners in San Francisco. The manuscript does not have page numbers. In the meantime, Jonathan Wilson-Hartgrove has edited and published this work on behalf of John Alexander in his book *Being Church: Reflections on How to Live as the People of God* (Eugene, OR: Cascade, 2012).

18. Covenant-Making in Story, Rule, and Liturgy of Commitment

The quote about the covenant character of all of Scripture comes from Richard Hays, *The Moral Vision of the New Testament: Community, Cross, and New Creation* (San Francisco: HarperSanFrancisco, 1996), 196–97.

Koinonia Partners' full covenant liturgy is available upon request through the community's website at Koinoniapartners.org.

19. On Why Your Community Might Need an Onion

The quote about members becoming responsible for their community as it is can be found in Jean Vanier, *Community and Growth* (Mahwah, NJ: Paulist Press, 1989), 131.

20. Creation Care, Food Justice, and a Common Table

Jonathan Wilson-Hartgrove's quote comes from *Conspire* 3, no. 4 (Fall 2011): 8.

Juliet Schor, in a video called "Plenitude: The New Economy of True Wealth," was found at http://front.moveon.org/the-secret-to-creating-jobs-that-wall-street-doesnt-want-you-to-know/ (accessed May 23, 2012). Shor is author of a book by the same name (New York: Penguin, 2010).

Sarah Miles's observation about our hunger to share bread extravagantly comes from *Conspire3*, no. 4 (Fall 2011): 14.

21. The Economy of God and the Community of Goods

Jodi Garbisson's essay "An Uncommon Purse" is reprinted with permission from the *Cherith Brook Catholic Worker*, Lent 2011, 4ff.

John Alexander's quote about the many kinds of common-purse communities comes from his unpublished manuscript, *Stop Going to Church and Become the Church*, in the possession of Church of the Sojourners in San Francisco. The manuscript does not have page numbers.

Gross National Product statistics for 2010 come from the World Bank website (worldbank.org).

Forbes magazine's website lists the world billionaires and their net worth, of which there were actually 1,146 in January 2012 (forbes.com).

22. A Spiritual Life for (and in Spite of) Community

Copies of "God Wants to Speak to You . . ." are available from the Reba Place Fellowship office at 737 Reba Place Basement, Evanston, IL 60202.

Henri Nouwen's quote "As soon as we are alone . . . chaos opens up in us," comes from *Making All Things New and other Classics* (London: HarperCollins, 2000) and from goodreads.com/author/quotes/4837.Henri_J_M_Nouwen.

The quote by Nouwen beginning "It is tragic to see how the religious sentiment of the West has become so individualized," comes from *Reaching Out: Three Movements of the Spiritual Life* (New York: Doubleday, 1975) and from goodreads.com/author/quotes/4837.Henri_J_M_Nouwen.

For more information on the new school building project in Sudan in the hometown of Church of the Sojourner friend Michael Ayuen de Kuany, see rebuildsudan.org.

Nouwen writes about the pain of "a second loneliness" within community in *The Road to Daybreak*, 224–25.

23. When People Leave

Jean Vanier gives counsel for circumstances in which a community member might be asked to leave in *Community and Growth*, 127.

24. Healing the Hurts That Prevent Community

For more about trauma and how to transform it, see Dr. Karl Lehman's book, *Outsmarting Yourself: Catching Your Past Invading the Present and What to Do about it* as well as the free media and resources at outsmartingyourself.org.

For more about the tasks involved in processing trauma see Dr Lehman's "Brain Science, Emotional Trauma, and the God Who Is with Us, Part II: The Processing Pathway for Painful Experiences and the Definition of Psychological Trauma," found at kclehman.com.

Learn more about Thrive conferences at thrivetoday.org.

For more explanation of calming exercises, deliberate appreciation, and attunement see *Outsmarting Yourself*, chaps. 18–20.

For groups interested in incorporating the Immanuel approach, training resources, free media, essays, and much more can be found at immanuelapproach .com. See especially the essays "Where/How Do I Get Training Regarding the Immanuel Approach" and "The Immanuel Approach (to Emotional Healing and to Life)." The basic elements of the Immanuel lifestyle such as recalling stories of God's faithfulness, inviting God's guidance, and voicing spontaneous thoughts that follow can be implemented immediately. To facilitate emotional healing sessions, it helps to see sessions modeled either on the Lehman *Live Ministry Series* videos or, ideally, in person. Perhaps the best way to learn is to work on your own healing journey with someone who is proficient in the approach.

25. Developing Common Work and Ministries

William Cavanaugh's quote about opening economic "spaces marked by the body of Christ" is found in his *Being Consumed: Economics and Christian Desire* (Grand Rapid: Eerdmans, 2008), viii.

27. Becoming Accountable—Visitations and Community Associations

Henri Nouwen's reflections on Mary's visit with her cousin Elizabeth, on Dorothy Day's transforming encounter with Peter Maurin, and Jean Vanier's inspiration for L'Arche communities, coming from Pere Thomas, are found in *The Road to Daybreak*, 101.

28. Birthing and Nurturing New Communities from a Home Base

Dorothee Soelle's comments on the fruitful nature of suffering and pain in childbirth and in social transformations can be found in *Against the Wind: Memoir of a Radical Christian* (Minneapolis: Fortress, 1995), 78–79.

Jean Vanier endorses the support that "religious" veterans from established communities have given to newly forming L'Arche groups in *Community and Growth*, 76.

29. Exceptionally Gifted Persons and the Challenge of Submission

Theresa of Ávila's comments on the devil and her anxious spiritual advisors come from *The Book of My Life*, trans. Mirabai Starr (Boston: New Seeds, 2007), chap. 25.

The fullest report of John Howard Yoder's misconduct and the Mennonite Church's discipline upon him is found in a series of articles written by Tom Price in *The Elkhart Truth*, July 12, 1992, and following. The American National Biography Online reports on this extended episode in Yoder's life: "During the 1990's allegations of sexual improprieties surface, and the Indiana-Michigan Conference of the Mennonite Church suspended Yoder's ministerial credentials in 1992. . . . Eight women in position of national leadership in the Mennonite Church brought misconduct charges against him. Yoder acknowledged that there was enough truth in accusations for him not to contest them. He faithfully submitted to the very long and arduous process of remediation, which included apologies to all the women involved as well as therapy. In 1997 he was reinstated in his service to the Mennonite Church." This happened only a few months before his death in December of that same year.

Henri Nouwen's comments concerning the importance of friends who can look into "the twilight zone of our hearts" and see in us what we cannot see ourselves come from *Bread for the Journey: A Daybook of Wisdom and Faith* (San Francisco: HarperSanFrancisco, 1997), March 14. Merton's expressions of freedom in submission come from Basil Pennington, *Thomas Merton, My Brother: The Quest for True Freedom* (Grand Rapids: Zondervan, 1990) and from Jim Forest, *Living with Wisdom: A Life of Thomas Merton* (Maryknoll, NY: Orbis, 1991).

Conclusion

Jim Forest's etymology of "blessed" in the Beatitudes comes from *The Ladder of the Beatitudes* (Maryknoll, NY: Orbis, 1999), 20.

The story of Englewood Christian Church's renewal as a Christian intentional community is told by C. Christopher Smith, *The Virtue of Dialogue: Conversation as a Hopeful Practice of Church Communities,* Kindle edition (Englewood, CO: Patheos Press, 2012).

SELECTED READING

Alexander, John. *The Secular Squeeze: Reclaiming Christian Depth in a Shallow World*. Downers Grove, IL: InterVarsity Press, 1993. The author, from the Church of the Sojourners in San Francisco, critiques the secular American culture as flat, boring, devoid of challenges worthy of a life. Jesus's story and call has the power to break through to relationships of depth and mystery.

———. *Stop Going to Church and Become the Church*. See chapter 21 above for a fuller description of this unpublished book in the hands of the Church of the Sojourners community, who can be contacted at churchofthesojourners .wordpress.com/.

Berry, Wendell. *Sex, Economy, Freedom and Community*. New York: Random House, 1993. A diverse collection of writings from America's master essayist on the deterioration of our natural environment, communities, and moral character, along with some insightful cures that arise from deep roots in biblical practice and reflection.

Bonhoeffer, Dietrich. *Life Together*. New York: HarperCollins, 1954. First published in German in 1939; first published in English in 1954. Various editions. Growing out of Bonhoeffer's communal experience in an "underground seminary" during the rise of Nazism, this is a classic, seminal book for anyone interested in the biblical basis for forming intentional community.

Bruggemann, Walter. *The Prophetic Imagination*. 2nd ed. Minneapolis: Fortress Press, 2001. Bruggemann surveys the prophetic tradition from Moses through Jesus, illustrating how prophets, both biblical and contemporary, expand our imagination to see oppression for what it is and to empower alternative communities of justice and creative resistance.

Cavanaugh, William. *Being Consumed: Economics and Christian Desire*. Grand Rapids: Eerdmans, 2008. The author provides a trenchant critique of the way the consumer economy consumes us. This is in contrast to the Christian story in which our desires are rightly ordered toward the kingdom of God as we partake of the Eucharist by which we, paradoxically and miraculously, become Christ, whom we have consumed. Gripping economics and theology!

Christian, Diana Leaf. *Creating a Life Together: Practical Tools to Grow Ecovillages and Intentional Communities*. Gabriola Island, BC: New Society Publishers,

2003. A nuts-and-bolts manual for building intentional community based upon secular examples. Christians will find a lot of technical usefulness in this book, although the purpose and motivations for community are fundamentally different.

Claiborne, Shane. *The Irresistible Revolution: Living as an Ordinary Radical.* Grand Rapids, MI: Zondervan, 2006. This book has inspired thousands of young people of all ages to question their status quo Christianity and swelled the ranks of a movement seeking to live the life of Jesus in Christian community among the poor, as modeled by the author and his community in North Philadelphia, The Simple Way.

Claiborne, Shane, Jonathan Wilson-Hartgrove, and Enuma Okoro. *Common Prayer: A Liturgy for Ordinary Radicals.* Grand Rapids: Zondervan, 2010. This book has been responsible for introducing a younger generation to faithful daily liturgical prayer as an undergirding for prophetic community life and witness. Reissued in 2012 as a condensed paperback pocket edition.

Claiborne, Shane, and Chris Haw. *Jesus for President.* Grand Rapids: Zondervan, 2008. Published during the 2008 election campaign, *Jesus for President* helps readers imagine how they can participate in Jesus's politics of radical love that transforms this world into the kingdom of God.

Duin, Julia. *Days of Fire and Glory: The Rise and Fall of a Charismatic Community.* Baltimore: Crossland Press, 2009. In the early 1970s the Church of the Redeemer in Houston, under the leadership of Graham Pulkingham, was the scene of Holy Spirit signs and wonders, miraculous healings, an outpouring of new songs and forms of worship, with many families relocating into the inner city for household ministry. But within a decade the rector was confronted with his sexual misconduct and most of the ministries had fallen apart. Julia Duin, both a journalist and a participant in the church, examines what happened.

Erlander, Daniel. *Manna and Mercy: A Brief History of God's Unfolding Promise to Mend the Entire Universe.* Minneapolis: Augsburg Fortress, 2007. Illustrated to look like a child's coloring book, this quirky biblical narrative engages children of all ages to reflect on how God inspires courageous food sharing and radical forgiveness, which calls together communities of resistance to the domination systems of our world.

Friesen, James, et al. *The Life Model: Living from the Heart Jesus Gave You.* Pasadena: Shepherd's House, 2000. Built on earlier versions of this book by James Wilder, this packed edition outlines practical steps to healing from life's traumas and growth to maturity in stages involving both personal and community collaboration.

Gandhi, Mohandas. *The Story of My Experiments with Truth.* Boston: Beacon Press, 1957. Many other editions as well. Originally written in serial form for Gandhi's newspaper, *Young India*, in the 1920s, this classic story of Gandhi's life tells of his personal and social experiments that developed many new strategies of nonviolent direct action for justice, social change, and reconciliation based on the ancient truths in most religions, but especially in Jesus's Sermon on the Mount.

Hays, Richard. *The Moral Vision of the New Testament: Community, Cross, and New Creation. A Contemporary Introduction to New Testament Ethics.* New York: HarperCollins, 1996. This master scholar demonstrates a unified vision of ethics in the New Testament under the themes of community, cross, and new creation. Reflecting Hays's formative experience in Christian intentional community, this book examines key twentieth-century ethicists according to the fruit of their writings in the church communities they inspired.

Jackson, Dave, and Neta Jackson. *Living Together in a World Falling Apart.* Carol Stream, IL: Creation House, 1974. This classic intentional community handbook features a dozen community visits from the movement a generation ago. The book was reissued in 2009 with further reflections by the authors.

Janzen, David. *Fire, Salt, and Peace: Intentional Christian Communities Alive in North America.* Evanston, IL: Shalom Mission Communities, 1996. Contains profiles of thirty intentional communities (some of which no longer exist) along with essays on the history of the movement.

Jeschke, Marlin. *Discipling in the Church: Recovering a Ministry of the Gospel.* Harrisonburg, VA: Herald Press, 1988. Advocating a return to church discipline, Marlin Jeschke goes to the classic text on the subject, Matthew 18:15–18, and demonstrates the value of this neglected practice for restoring lives and reconciling relationships in communities of integrity.

Lee, Dallas. *Cotton Patch Evidence: The Story of Clarence Jordan and the Koinonia Farm Experiment (1942–1970).* Americus, GA: Koinonia Partners, 1971. Dallas Lee tells the story of the first thirty years of this community of blacks and whites sharing common work and a common table in southern Georgia, despite violent attacks and a countywide boycott. The title refers to Clarence Jordan's "Cotton Patch Gospel" translation of the Greek into Southern vernacular, as the community itself was a translation of New Testament *koinonia* ("sharing") into the local context.

Lehman, Karl. *Outsmarting Yourself: Catching the Past Invading the Present and What to Do about It.* Libertyville, MO: This JOY! Books—A Division of Three Cord Ministries, 2011. Contains a wealth of stories from guided inner healing sessions with explanations of what is happening from brain science research, psychiatry, and broad experience of the Immanuel Healing Approach. The book contains references to further training opportunities for small group and community leaders.

Linn, Dennis, and Matthew Linn. *Healing of Memories: Prayer and Confession Steps to Inner Healing.* New York: Paulist Press, 1974. The Linn brothers have written a series of trustworthy Christ-centered books on healing of life's hurts. This small book outlines six steps of healing of painful memories through gratitude and forgiveness resulting in new and liberated behaviors.

Lohfink, Gerhard. *Does God Need the Church: Toward a Theology of the People of God.* Translated by Linda M. Maloney. Collegeville, MN: Liturgical Press, 1999. Late in life, this mature biblical scholar found and joined the intentional community called the Katholische Integrierte Gemeinde. He plumbs the reasons for the historic European church's collapse and concludes that the faith can only survive by a return to New Testament communal commitments, selling all to follow Jesus.

Longacre, Doris Janzen. *Living More with Less.* Harrisonburg, VA: Herald Press, 2010. Written in 1979, before the current wave of awareness that the world cannot afford the American Dream, this book is full of practical counsel about how Christians around the world live with more justice, simplicity, and joy, and with less of the stuff that clutters our spirits and our landfills. Buy the Thirtieth Anniversary reissue of this book with additional essays updating the relevance of this witness.

Merton, Thomas. *Contemplation in a World of Action.* Notre Dame: University of Notre Dame Press, 1999. Restored and corrected from the original 1971 edition. Merton maintained correspondence with many friends engaged in the civil rights and antiwar movement. In this series of essays he establishes the deep connection between sustained prophetic action and contemplation where we meet God and our true identity that cannot be shaken.

———. *The Seven Storey Mountain.* Boston: Harcourt Brace, 1948. An improbable bestselling autobiography of a young man who left behind a promising literary career and college teaching post to enter the Abbey of Gethsemani in rural Kentucky. *Time* magazine said it "redefined the image of monasticism and made the concept of saintliness accessible to moderns."

Miller, John. *The Way of Love.* Evanston, IL: Reba Place Fellowship, 1960. This pamphlet by a Reba founder outlines a few core practices (shared finances, living in proximity, reconciled relationships, etc.) that express and sustain a common life in the way of love as taught by Jesus. Reprinted edition (2000) available from rebaplacefellowship.org.

Mosley, Don. *Faith beyond Borders: Doing Justice in a Dangerous World.* Nashville: Abingdon, 2010. Mosley has written of his lifelong efforts to live the Sermon on the Mount in the context of Jubilee Partners community, Habitat for Humanity's beginnings, the Fuller Center for Housing, and other courageous partnerships, demonstrating the power of the gospel around the world to break through in reconciliation with folks whom the powers have made into our enemies.

Nouwen, Henri. *The Inner Voice of Love: A Journey through Anguish to Freedom.* New York: Doubleday, 1996. This is the unsparingly honest and painful journal of a widely respected spiritual counselor and priest as he struggled with his celibate commitment and need for love, a need that only God could fill.

———. *Making All Things New and Other Classics.* London: HarperCollins, 2000. This is a reprint of earlier works by Nouwen including *A Letter of Consolation* and *The Living Reminder.* In the lead essay, Nouwen awakens in the reader a hunger for God's presence through the practices of prayerful solitude in community.

———. *The Road to Daybreak: A Spiritual Journey.* New York: Doubleday, 1988. Nouwen's intimate diary of the journey of personal transformation from the pinnacle of academic achievement to a life shared in community with persons with mental disabilities who reveal Jesus to this masterful writer with a troubled soul.

———. *The Way of the Heart: Desert Spirituality and Contemporary Ministry.* New York: Ballantine, 1981. Drawing on the witness of the Desert Fathers, Nouwen introduces us to the role of silence, solitude, and prayer, centering us in God for effective ministry.

Pennington, Basil. *Thomas Merton, My Brother: The Quest for True Freedom.* Grand Rapids: Zondervan, 1990. Written by a spiritual master who shared Merton's monastic life, this book contains memories from fellow monks and analyses of Merton's engagement with monastic authorities, contemporary social issues, friends from around the world, and Merton's discovery of freedom through crucifixion of the false self.

Pollan, Michael. *Food Rules: An Eater's Manual.* New York: Penguin, 2009. A boiled-down version of the *Omnivore's Dilemma* arguments with easy-to-remember rules about what to eat such as "Eat food. Not too much. Mostly plants."

———. *The Omnivore's Dilemma: A Natural History of Four Meals.* New York: Penguin Press, 2006. This popular author and activist examines the nutritional value along with social and ecological consequences of four ways of sourcing food: the current industrial system, the big organic operations, the local self-sufficient farm, and the hunter-gatherer. Controversial, enlightening, and disturbing for people dependent on large-scale food production operations.

Rice, Chris. *Grace Matters: A True Story of Race, Friendship, and Faith in the Heart of the South.* San Francisco: Jossey-Bass, 2002. White author Chris Rice tells of his seventeen-year friendship with African-American Spencer Perkins (who died in 1998), in the interracial Antioch household affiliated with Voice of Calvary Ministries in Jackson, Mississippi. The struggles to sustain such a friendship and community reveal the painful shape of racism in our day and of the reconciliation possible by the grace of God.

Rutba House. *School(s) for Conversion: 12 Marks of a New Monasticism.* Eugene, OR: Cascade Books, 2005. Includes essays by participants in a 2004 conference hosted by Rutba House, at which time these twelve marks were discerned and announced as something of a manifesto of newer intentional Christian communities. The essays were written by younger communitarians, scholars, and veterans of older communities.

Scandrette, Mark A. *Practicing the Way of Jesus: Life Together in the Kingdom of Love.* Downers Grove, IL: InterVarsity Press, 2011. An inspiring array of stories, practices, and group experiments introducing people to more radical ways of following Jesus. See a brief review of this book in chapter 8 above.

Shenk, Sara Wenger. *Why Not Celebrate.* Intercourse, PA: Good Books, 1987. This excellent book about families and celebrations in community is, unfortunately, out of print.

Smith, C. Christopher. *The Virtue of Dialogue: Conversation as a Hopeful Practice of Church Communities.* Englewood, CO: Patheos. Kindle edition, 2011. It took several years of patient conversation in which people yelled, walked out, cried, and listened to the wounds of a broken and declining congregation till a core of folks at Englewood Christian Church bonded in a holy love for each other and began to invest in intentional community and many surprising ministries of community renewal. Chris Smith tells the ugly and tender story of Holy Spirit renewal in North Indianapolis.

Soelle, Dorothee. *Against the Wind: Memoir of a Radical Christian.* Minneapolis: Fortress, 1995. Activist and theologian Dorothee Soelle combines stories, passionate action, and top-notch scholarship about peacemaking, feminism, and hope for a more radical grassroots church.

Stringham, Jim. *God Wants to Speak to You. Are You Listening?* This pamphlet by a former China missionary and psychiatrist shares his experiences and counsel on how to "listen to the Lord" like Moses, Samuel, and Paul (with pen and journal in hand). Available from carepkg.org.

Teresa of Ávila. *The Book of My Life*. Translated by Mirabai Starr. Boston: New Seeds, 2007. See discussion of this book in chapter 29 above.

Vanier, Jean. *Community and Growth*. Mahwah, NJ: Paulist Press, 1989. This is the "Bible" of Christian intentional community resources, full of wise counsel from the founder of L'Arche communities centered on core members with mental disabilities, but applicable to all types of intentional communities. Be sure you get the second edition, which is much expanded over the first printing in 1979.

Wilson-Hartgrove, Jonathan. *The Wisdom of Stability: Rooting Faith in a Mobile Culture*. Brewster, MA: Paraclete Press, 2010. In the context of his community, Rutba House, and the black neighborhood of Walltown in Durham, North Carolina, Wilson-Hartgrove digs up the lessons of stability tested by monastic communities in all ages: by staying put rather than fleeing difficult relationships, we see God's power to transform ourselves and our neighborhoods as we learn patience, peacemaking, and forgiveness.

Wright, N. T. *After You Believe: Why Christian Character Matters*. San Francisco: HarperOne, 2010. Wright argues that the Christian life (between conversion and funeral) is neither about keeping rules nor about being spontaneous, but a process of practicing the Christian virtues until they become our second nature.

Yoder, John Howard. *Body Politics: Five Practices of the Christian Community before the Watching World*. Nashville: Discipleship Resources, 2001. This gem of a book, in only eighty pages, examines essential ecclesial practices described by the New Testament, and in so doing recovers the communal character of the "sacraments" as practiced by the early church, and largely ignored by contemporary Christianity.

———. *The Politics of Jesus*. Grand Rapids: Eerdmans, 1972. No one makes the case better for the radical, consistent nonviolence of the Gospels, the epistles, and Revelation than John Howard Yoder. This book may be the most influential contribution to theological ethics of the twentieth century.

Zwick, Mark, and Louise Zwick. *Mercy without Borders: The Catholic Worker and Immigration*. Mahwah, NJ: Paulist Press, 2010. Through the eyes and voices of refugees fleeing violence and destitution from south of the border, Mark and Louise Zwick tell the story of welcome that these waves of immigrants have found in the Houston Catholic Worker community, Casa Juan Diego. Seeing the face of Jesus in the poor cancels out any judgments we might have about their right to seek a better life among us.

ABOUT PARACLETE PRESS

WHO WE ARE

Paraclete Press is a publisher of books, recordings, and DVDs on Christian spirituality. Our publishing represents a full expression of Christian belief and practice—from Catholic to Evangelical, from Protestant to Orthodox.

We are the publishing arm of the Community of Jesus, an ecumenical monastic community in the Benedictine tradition. As such, we are uniquely positioned in the marketplace without connection to a large corporation and with informal relationships to many branches and denominations of faith.

WHAT WE ARE DOING

Books Paraclete publishes books that show the richness and depth of what it means to be Christian. Although Benedictine spirituality is at the heart of all that we do, we publish books that reflect the Christian experience across many cultures, time periods, and houses of worship. We publish books that nourish the vibrant life of the church and its people—books about spiritual practice, formation, history, ideas, and customs.

We have several different series, including the best-selling Paraclete Essentials and Paraclete Giants series of classic texts in contemporary English; A Voice from the Monastery—men and women monastics writing about living a spiritual life today; award-winning poetry; best-selling gift books for children on the occasions of baptism and first communion; and the Active Prayer Series that brings creativity and liveliness to any life of prayer.

Recordings From Gregorian chant to contemporary American choral works, our music recordings celebrate sacred choral music through the centuries. Paraclete distributes the recordings of the internationally acclaimed choir Gloriæ Dei Cantores, praised for their "rapt and fathomless spiritual intensity" by *American Record Guide*, and the Gloriæ Dei Cantores Schola, which specializes in the study and performance of Gregorian chant. Paraclete is also the exclusive North American distributor of the recordings of the Monastic Choir of St. Peter's Abbey in Solesmes, France, long considered to be a leading authority on Gregorian chant.

Videos Our videos offer spiritual help, healing, and biblical guidance for life issues: grief and loss, marriage, forgiveness, anger management, facing death, and spiritual formation.

Learn more about us at our website: www.paracletepress.com, or call us toll-free at 1-800-451-5006.

 SCAN TO READ MORE

You may also be interested in...

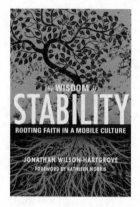

THE WISDOM OF STABILITY

We seem to know that rapid change and constant motion are hazards to our spiritual health. For the Christian tradition, the heart's true home is a life rooted in the love of God. *The Wisdom of Stability* speaks to each of us who seek an honest path of Christian transformation. A leader of the new monastic movement, Jonathan Wilson-Hartgrove shows how you can:

- Cultivate stability by rooting yourself more deliberately in the place where you live.
- Truly engage with the people you are with.
- Slow down and participate in simpler rhythms of life.
- Live in ways that speak to the deeper yearnings of the human heart.

ISBN: 978-1-55725-623-2
Paperback, $14.99

THE PARACLETE PSALTER

Early Christians commonly prayed the entire Book of Psalms in a month. This simple book offers you the opportunity to enter into this rewarding practice. The easy-to-follow organization, featuring the NIV text, will guide you through the entire Psalter every four weeks. You will come to know God as Friend, Shepherd, Defender, Father, Provider, Savior, and Lord, as you pray these words, allowing them to enter into your heart and life through faithful repetition and daily prayer.

ISBN: 978-1-55725-663-8
Bonded Leather. $29.99

Available from most booksellers or through Paraclete Press:
www.paracletepress.com; 1-800-451-5006. Try your local bookstore first.